Guide to
Mozambique

Philip Briggs

Bradt Publications, UK
The Globe Pequot Press Inc, USA

First published in 1997 by Bradt Publications,
41 Nortoft Road, Chalfont St Peter, Bucks SL9 0LA, England.
Published in the USA by The Globe Pequot Press Inc, 6 Business Park Road,
PO Box 833, Old Saybrook, Connecticut 06475-0833.

British Library Cataloguing in Publication Data
A catalogue record for this book is available from the British Library
ISBN 1 898323 45 3

Library of Congress Cataloging-in-Publication Data
Library of Congress Cataloging-in-Publication Data is available

Cover photographs
Front: Chris Johnston, Panos Pictures
Back: Ariadne van Zandbergen
Maps *Inside covers*: Steve Munns   *Others*: Hans van Well

Typeset from the author's disc by Patti Taylor, London NW10 1JR
Printed and bound in Great Britain by The Guernsey Press Co Ltd

Guide to Mozambique

Other Bradt Guides to Africa

Africa by Road   Bob Swain and Paula Snyder
Backpacker's Africa – Eastern and Southern   Hilary Bradt
Guide to Eritrea   Edward Paice
Guide to Ethiopia   Philip Briggs
Guide to Madagascar   Hilary Bradt
Madagascar Wildlife   Hilary Bradt, Derek Schuurman and Nick Garbutt
Guide to Malawi   Philip Briggs
Guide to Namibia & Botswana   Chris McIntyre and Simon Atkins
Guide to South Africa   Philip Briggs
Guide to Tanzania   Philip Briggs
Guide to Uganda   Philip Briggs
Guide to Zambia   Philip Briggs
Guide to Zanzibar   David Else
Guide to Zimbabwe & Botswana   David Else
Africa Handbooks: Ivory Coast, Senegal, Zaire

And then there's the rest of the world...

Send for a catalogue to:

Bradt Publications, 41 Nortoft Road, Chalfont St Peter, Bucks, SL9 0LA.
Tel/fax: 01494 873478

CONTENTS

ACKNOWLEDGEMENTS

This book has its roots in the earlier Bradt *Guide to Mozambique*, written and researched by Bernhard Skrodski during the civil war, when travel options in Mozambique were all but restricted to Maputo, the capital, Beira and a few offshore islands. Recent events have by and large made Bernhard's book a guide to another country, but I have chosen to retain his voice wherever possible. The excellent walking routes through Maputo are largely the work of Bernhard Skrodski, as are the sections on the economy, Bazaruto, Inhaca and Mount Binga.

I'm also tremendously appreciative of the travellers who wrote to Bernhard with update material: Jackie Nee, Julle Tulianen, BP Rawlins, the Co-ordinator of Projects at the Diocese of Lichinga and Iain Jackson. Worthy of a special mention is Andrew Chilton, whose densely packed and good natured 17-page missive did much to prepare me for my own trip to the north of Mozambique. I only hope the readers of this new guide see fit to keep me up to date on a country where things are bound to keep changing very quickly. Thanks as well to Jane Wilson Howarth, Hans van Well, Sally Crook, Vincent Parker and Bob de Lacy Smith, all of whom contributed to the text of this guide.

Thanks are due to Andre Kleynhans and Pedro Commissario of LAM for their outstandingly positive attitude to this project, to David Ankers of the Hotel Polana and John Elliot of the Hotel Cardosa in Maputo, and to Margie McDuff, Gilbert Bouic, Derek Schuurman, Mike Slater, Tracey Naughton and Don Beswick, all of whom made a significant contribution to my preparation of this book.

Last but never least, all my love and gratitude to Ariadne, for being a true companion both while we were on the road and when at home.

ABOUT THE AUTHOR

Philip Briggs is a travel writer and tour leader specialising in eastern and southern Africa. Born in Britain and raised in South Africa, Philip started travelling in East Africa in 1986 and has since spent the equivalent of four years exploring the highways and backroads of the subcontinent. His first book *Guide to South Africa* was published by Bradt in 1991. Since then, he has written Bradt's *Guide to Tanzania*, *Guide to Uganda*, *Guide to Ethiopia* and *Guide to Malawi*. He is also the author of the *Visitor's Guide to Kenya and East Africa* (Southern Books) and a frequent contributor to British and South African periodicals.

Ariadne van Zandbergen, who took the photographs for this book, is a freelance photographer and tour guide. Born and raised in Belgium, she travelled through Africa from Morocco to South Africa in 1994/5 and is now resident in Johannesburg. She has visited 19 African countries in total, and her photographs have appeared in several books, periodicals and pamphlets.

Introduction

Visit Mozambique today, and you'll probably find it difficult to imagine that only 20 years ago this now rather obscure country attracted a greater volume of tourists than South Africa and Rhodesia combined. It is, perhaps, even more difficult to imagine that a mere four years ago Mozambique was in the closing stages of a civil war which claimed the lives of 100,000 people and disrupted the countryside to the extent that roughly one-third of the population was forced to flee from rural areas to the relative safety of the cities or neighbouring countries.

Like many South Africans of my generation, I have only the haziest recollection of a time when Mozambique was celebrated for its convivial atmosphere, wonderful seafood and stunning coastline. I've spent most of my life living less than 500km from Maputo, the Mozambican capital, and I can barely remember a time when Mozambique wasn't at war. In the mind of many Westerners, I should imagine that Mozambique is little more than another name on that long list of feuding African nations which crawled briefly on to the lower rungs of the newsworthiness scale before being consigned back to media oblivion.

Mozambique today does not *feel* like a country recently emerged from war. True, many of the roads are lined with the bombed-out shells of buildings and pockmarked by vast potholes caused by mine explosions. But on the whole, the speed and success of civil reconstruction and social reconciliation since 1992 has been remarkable. There is, I think, a quite simple explanation for this. As a rule, civil wars elsewhere in Africa have been rooted in ethnic or ideological differences, exacerbated in many instances by the colonial experience, but with immediate causes that were essentially internal. By contrast, the causes of the Mozambican war were almost entirely external.

Renamo, the guerrilla army which initiated the war, was founded as a fifth column by white Rhodesians and renegade members of the Portuguese secret service. When Rhodesia became Zimbabwe, Renamo was retrained and supplied with weapons by white South Africans, allegedly with a degree of financial backing by secretive right-wing white American organisations which sought to promote a capitalist alternative to the socialist ruling party, Frelimo. Indeed, it would be easy enough to argue that Mozambique's war was not a civil war at all, but an extension of the apartheid struggle and Cold War fought out on the soil of an obsure African nation. Or perhaps it is just a coincidence that Renamo finally entered into negotations with Frelimo only months after the release of Nelson Mandela and barely a year after the fall of the Berlin Wall?

For whatever reason, Mozambique is no longer a country at war, nor is it one of those countries which you sense might return to war at the slightest provocation. This can be seen in work going on to rehabilitate the coastal resorts and game reserves that once made it one of Africa's most popular tourist destinations. This, inevitably, will be a slow process. South African and Zimbabwean holidaymakers are tentatively trickling back to the resorts that line the coast between Maputo and Beira, but word of Mozambique's revival as a tourist destination has yet to spread beyond its immediate neighbours. And, while you need only spend a few days at any backpackers' hostel in Malawi and Zimbabwe to realise that Mozambique has become the most talked about off-the-beaten-track destination in eastern and southern Africa, the fact is that very few backpackers are prepared do more than talk about visiting a country for which almost no reliable travel information is currently available.

So far as tourists are concerned, Mozambique might almost be two countries. Linked only by the solitary motor ferry that crosses the mighty Zambezi River at Caia, and divided by more than 1,000km of rutted road connecting Beira to Nampula, southern Mozambique and northern Mozambique offer entirely different experiences to visitors. The two parts of the country have in common the widespread use of Portuguese and a quite startlingly beautiful coastline. The difference is that the south coast of Mozambique is already establishing itself as a tourist destination, with rapidly improving facilities and a ready-made market in the form of its eastern neighbours. The north, by contrast, has few facilities for tourists – and it is unlikely to attract much tourism so long as flying there from South Africa is more expensive than flying to Europe.

The majority of people who buy this guide will probably confine their travels to southern Mozambique. Not only does this part of the country offer good roads, reasonable public transport, some exceptional restaurants, and any number of beach resorts suitable for all tastes and budgets, but it is within a day's drive of Johannesburg, the subcontinent's largest city and major international transport hub. The south coast of Mozambique is exceptionally beautiful – truly the archetype of palm-lined tropical beach nirvana – as well as boasting snorkelling, diving and game fishing to rank with the very best in the world. Add to this Maputo and Beira, two of Africa's most attractive cities, not to say the old-world gem that is

Inhambane town, and you are looking at a stretch of coast as varied and attractive as any in Africa. If southern Mozambique lacks one thing, it is a notable game reserve, but even this should be rectified within the next few years, following the announcement in late 1996 that Maputo Elephant Reserve is to be extended and restocked to form part of a unique upmarket sea-and-safari tourist development.

Any honest description of northern Mozambique is bound to repel visitors seeking comfort, predictability or packaged entertainment. Equally, it is likely to whet the appetite of travellers looking for an adventurous trip through one of southern Africa's least explored regions. The northeastern provinces of Zambézia, Niassa, Nampula and Cabo Delgado have a remote, isolated and self-contained feel – not surprising when you consider that they are collectively bordered by the unbridged Rovuma River and the undeveloped southeastern quarter of Tanzania to the north, and by the vast watery expanses of the Indian Ocean and Lago Niassa to the east and west.

Little visited even by backpackers, northern Mozambique offers the sort of challenging travel that recalls conditions in countries like Zambia, Tanzania and Uganda in the mid-1980s – but exacerbated by linguistic barriers, humidity levels that reach intolerable proportions in summer, relatively high costs, and a public transport system which in places defies rational comprehension. But, if travelling through much of northern Mozambique is more or less travel for its own sake (a great deal of bumpy motion with relatively few highlights), it cannot be denied that the area boasts two historical attractions of quite compelling singularity, namely the former Portuguese capital on Ilha do Moçambique and the ancient island town of Ibo. These, alone, are worth any number of days on the back of a dusty truck and nights in a smelly, sweaty pensão room.

Mozambique may not be the easiest country in which to travel; in the northeast it can be downright frustrating. But this will change, and even as things stand Mozambique is not a country without rewards. Looking to the future, I wish Mozambicans every bit of success in redeveloping their country and its tourist industry, and I hope very much that by writing this book I will encourage more people to visit them. For now, not the least of Mozambique's attractions is that it still offers ample scope for genuinely exploratory travel; it is that rare country which adventurous travellers can experience entirely for themselves, without the distorting medium of a developed tourist industry.

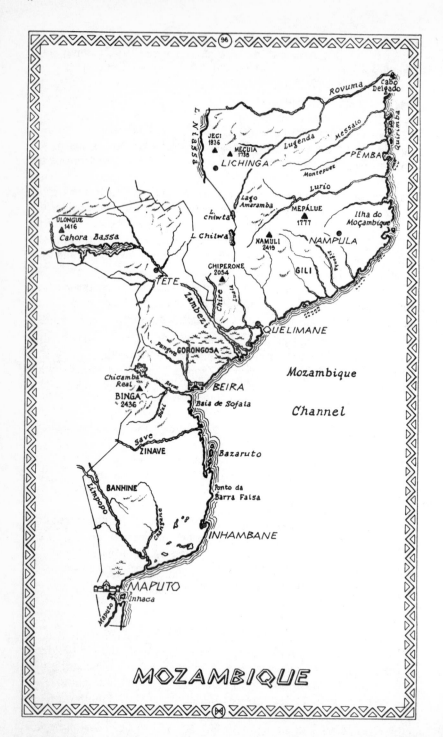

MOZAMBIQUE

Chapter One

Background

FACTS AND FIGURES

Location

Mozambique extends for 2,500km along the east coast of Africa, between latitudes 11° and 26° south and longitudes 30° and 40° east. It is bordered by the Indian Ocean to the east, and by South Africa to the south. The north of the country is bisected by Malawi, which forms the eastern border of Niassa and Zambézia provinces and the western border of Tete Province. The northern border east of Malawi is shared with Tanzania, while the northwestern border (west of Malawi) is shared by Zambia. The eastern border south of Malawi and Zambia is shared with Zimbabwe, South Africa and Swaziland.

Size

Mozambique covers an area of approximately 801,600 km², of which 17,500km² is water. It is the 16th largest country in Africa, roughly two-thirds the size of the neighbouring Republic of South Africa, about three times the size of Great Britain, and slightly larger than the state of Texas.

Principal cities

The capital city is Maputo, known in colonial times as Lourenço Marques. Maputo lies in the far south of the country, 430km east of Johannesburg by road. It has a population of roughly two million people. The next four largest cities in Mozambique, listed in order of estimated population, are: Beira (300,000), Nampula (150,000), Quelimane (135,000) and Chimoio (80,000).

Provinces

Mozambique is divided into ten provinces. Each province is divided into districts, further subdivided into administrative areas and civil parishes. Zambézia and Nampula provinces in the northern half of the country contain the richest agricultural land and 40% of the population, whereas the three southern provinces of Gaza, Inhambane and Maputo are mostly arid and previously served as labour reserves for Mozambique's industries and for mines and farms in South Africa.

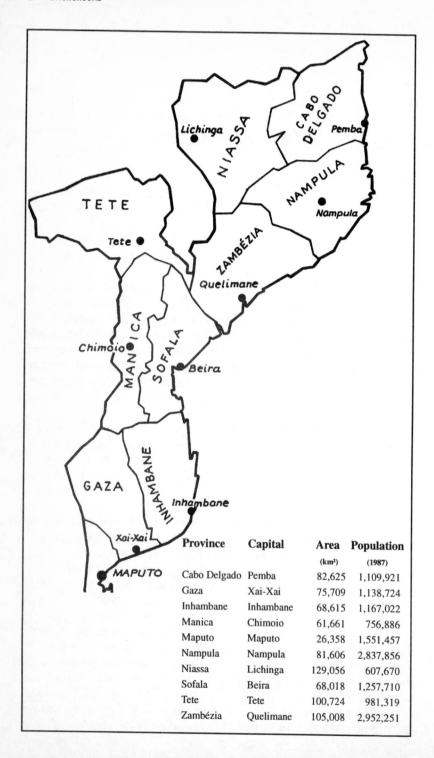

Province	Capital	Area (km²)	Population (1987)
Cabo Delgado	Pemba	82,625	1,109,921
Gaza	Xai-Xai	75,709	1,138,724
Inhambane	Inhambane	68,615	1,167,022
Manica	Chimoio	61,661	756,886
Maputo	Maputo	26,358	1,551,457
Nampula	Nampula	81,606	2,837,856
Niassa	Lichinga	129,056	607,670
Sofala	Beira	68,018	1,257,710
Tete	Tete	100,724	981,319
Zambézia	Quelimane	105,008	2,952,251

Time
Two hours ahead of GMT.

Flag
The national flag consists of three horizontal bands: from top, green, white-edged black and yellow. There is a red triangle on hoist side, centred around a yellow star bearing an open white book on which are depicted a crossed rifle and hoe in black.

Population
The population of Mozambique was estimated to be roughly 18 million in 1995, rising at around 3% per annum, and expected to exceed 20 million by the end of the century. The mortality rate of children under five (27.3%) is regarded to be the highest in the world, and the average life expectancy lies at between 45 and 50 years. Approximately 85% of the population live in rural areas, but there is an ongoing trend of gravitation to the cities.

Mozambique has one of the lowest population densities in southern and eastern Africa, currently standing at roughly 23 inhabitants per km². Excluding the desert countries of Namibia and Botswana, Zambia is the only country in the region more thinly populated than Mozambique. It has been suggested that the low population density is due to the protracted civil war. In fact, the interior of Mozambique has always been sparsely populated, and the population has grown by more than 50% in the twenty years since independence. The most densely populated provinces are Zambézia, Nampula and Maputo.

Minority population groups include Indians and Pakistanis, particularly around Nampula, and Portuguese, who are concentrated in the cities of Maputo and Beira.

Language
Portuguese is the official language of Mozambique, but it is generally only spoken by the 25% of the population who have been to school. This creates serious problems: the economic, business and legal language is Portuguese; tuition in high schools, colleges and universities is exclusively in Portuguese and thus debars the many who have had no chance to learn it at primary education stages; many of the younger people grew up in refugee camps and have had little formal education, let alone in what is essentially a foreign tongue; and three-quarters of the people are illiterate, despite considerable efforts (by themselves and by the government). The problems with education, both in languages and in general, have become so acute that some schools have started to work a shift system: children of one age group go to school every day for a few hours in the morning, children of another in the afternoon.

All of Mozambique's indigenous languages belong to the Bantu family. The root Bantu language is thought to have spread through east and southern

Africa during the first half of the first millennium AD, since when it has diversified into many linguistic subfamilies and several hundred distinct languages and closely related dialects. Roughly 60 distinct languages and dialects are spoken in Mozambique. The various dialects of Makua-Lomwe are spoken only north of the Zambezi, but they nevertheless account for the home language of around 40% of the total population of Mozambique. In the south, the majority of people speak dialects of Tsonga, a language that is also spoken in South Africa. Various Tonga and Shona dialects are spoken in central Mozambique.

In northern coastal regions, some people speak KiSwahili, a simplified Bantu language with some Arabic influences that became the *lingua franca* of coastal trading centres between Mogadishu and Sofala in mediaeval times.

Visitors who are unfamiliar with Portuguese and Bantu languages will find that most Mozambicans are extremely helpful and will do what they can to overcome your language barrier. The mixing of the people during the war has made them adept at getting along and making themselves understood in a variety of communication forms: a bit of gesturing and drawing in the dirt with a stick can overcome many barriers. Often, people will simply lead you to where you want to go.

Concern has recently been expressed in Lisbon that the end of Apartheid and the democratisation of South Africa will lead to the anglicisation of Mozambique. Since Portuguese is not an indigenous language and all of Mozambique's neighbours and SADCC partners (Angola excepted) use English as an official language, as do most donor countries, there would be a certain logic to displacing Portuguese with English as the main language of education and government. That said, I would place as high a priority on having KiSwahili (one of the simplest and most widely spoken Bantu languages) taught in schools throughout southern and eastern Africa, in order to help overcome the vast linguistic barriers to inter-regional trade and communication.

Religion

Roughly 50% of Mozambicans follow traditional African religions. These beliefs, along with traditional hierarchies and medicines, were suppressed during the communist era, being seen as backward and unscientific, but are now enjoying something of a resurgence, encouraged by the resumption of authority of many local chiefs in the absence of any other effective "management". Traditional healers are also enjoying a comeback as part of this cultural renaissance.

There are large Christian and Muslim minorities in Mozambique (25–30% and 20–25% respectively). Christianity is more common in urban areas while the Muslim faith is predominantly confined to the north. This has led to the incorporation of one or more elements of Christianity in most traditional beliefs. As in other African countries, the reverse is also true – there are often traditional elements in the way that Christianity is applied.

HISTORY

To AD1500

The interior

It is widely agreed that humanity evolved in East Africa. Mozambique itself has yielded few notable hominid fossils, but it is nevertheless reasonable to assume that it has supported human life for millions of years. Southeast Africa has incurred two major population influxes from West Africa in the last few millennia. The first occurred roughly 3,000 years ago, when the lightly built Batwa hunter-gathererers – similar in appearance and culture to the modern bushmen of Namibia – spread throughout the region. Roughly 1,000 years later, the Bantu-speakers who still occupy most of the region started to expand into eastern Africa, reaching the Indian Ocean coast in about AD400, an influx which broadly coincided with the spread of iron-age culture in the region. Although there is little concrete evidence of the mechanisms of this so-called Bantu migration, the records of early Portuguese adventurers leave us with a good idea of the main Bantu-speaking groupings of the southeast African interior at around AD1500.

The low-lying, relatively dry and disease-prone Mozambican lowveld was then, as it is now, relatively thinly populated, with the dominant ethno-linguistic groupings being the Makua north of the Zambezi River, the Tonga between the Zambezi and the Inhambane area, and the Nguni south of Inhambane into modern-day South Africa. The three main ethno-linguistic groups of the lowveld had discrete social and economic systems: the Makua had a matrilineal social structure as opposed to the patrilineal system favoured further south, while the Nguni had a cattle-based economy and the Tonga a mixed farming economy supplemented by revenue raised from the trade routes passing through their territory.

What the people of the lowveld had in common was a decentralised political structure, based around fragmented local chieftaincies. In direct contrast, the Karonga (or Shona) who occupied the highveld of what is now Zimbabwe had a highly centralised political structure with an ancient tradition of stone building that evidently dates to around AD1000. At the centre of this region stood the extensive and magnificent city of Great Zimbabwe, which is thought to have had a population of more than 10,000 at its peak. The economy of Karangaland was probably based around cattle-ownership, but its external relations were shaped by the coastal trade in gold, which has been mined in the Zimbabwean highlands since around AD900.

Karangaland appears to have gone through a major political upheaval in the second half of the 15th century. Great Zimbabwe was abandoned in roughly 1450, for reasons that remain a matter of speculation but are probably linked to local environmental degradation or a secession struggle. Whatever the cause, the abandonment of Great Zimbabwe coincided with a northerly reorientation of the highland kingdoms and a corresponding shift in the main trade routes. During the 15th century, the trade routes fanning from the Zambezi assumed greater importance, while the established route inland of Sofala along the Buzi River appears to have diminished in use. It is highly probable that the Karonga kingdoms known to the earliest Portuguese explorers were relatively new creations resulting from the upheavals of the late 15th century.

By 1500, the three main kingdoms of the highveld were Butua, in what is now the Bulawayo area of Zimbabwe; Monomotapa, in what is now central Zimbabwe; and Manica in the highlands of what is now the Zimbabwe–Mozambique border area. The upheavals also resulted in two Karanga chieftaincies being established in what had formerly been Tonga territory: Barue in the lowveld south of the Zambezi and west of Sena, and Kiteve in the lowveld between the Pungue and Buzi Rivers. Of these five main kingdoms, Butua was the only one to retain the stone-building tradition, while Monomotapa established itself as the paramount dynasty in the region.

The coast

The East African coast has long been a centre of international trade. Starting in around 2,500BC, the ancient Egyptians evidently entered into spasmodic trade with an East African port they knew as Punt. From about 600BC, the Phoenicians and Romans are known to have traded with an East African port called Rhapta. The location of Punt remains a matter of pure speculation, but detailed references to Rhapta in Ptolemy's 4th-century *Geography* and in an older Phoenician document *Periplus of the Ancient Sea* point to a location somewhere in present-day Tanzania, possibly near the mouth of the Pangani River.

The collapse of the Roman empire signalled a temporary end to maritime trade with the east African coast, and it presumably forced the closure of any contemporary trade routes into the African interior. Ptolemy claims that a Greek explorer called Diogenes saw two snow-capped mountains 25 days upriver from Rhapta and that he was told by other traders of vast lakes further inland, which indicates that 4th century trade routes must have penetrated the interior as far as Mount Kenya and Kilimanjaro, and possibly also Lakes Victoria and Tanganyika.

The rise of Islam in the 7th century AD revived the maritime trade with East Africa. The writings of Ali Masudi in AD947 make it clear that Arab mariners had by this time entered into regular trade with Madagascar and that they were aware that the main source of Africa's gold was Sofala, near the mouth of the Buzi River in what is now central Mozambique. The presence of 9th century Islamic ruins on Manda Island off the Kenya coast indicates that Arabic traders started settling in East Africa at a very early point in this era of trade. The 12th century geographer Al Idrisi refers to Sofala as an important source of iron, gold and animal skins, and he indicates that by this time China and India were both trading with East Africa. By the 13th century, the coast between Somalia and Central Mozambique was dotted with some 30 or 40 Swahili city-states, among the most important of which were Mogadishu, Malindi, Mombasa, Pangani, Zanzibar, Kilwa and Sofala.

Although many of these ancient Swahili cities have survived into the modern era, our best idea of what they must have looked like comes from the extensive ruins of those that haven't – notably Kilwa in southern Tanzania and Gedi in Kenya. The impressive rag coral architecture and overwhelming Muslim influence of such places has led many popular accounts to treat them as little more than Arabic implants. However, most modern historians are agreed that this is an outdated interpretation, and that there was a high level of integration between Arabic settlers and the indigenous peoples of the coast. It is true that the Islamic religion was adopted all along the coast, but then so was the Swahili language, which is self-evidently Bantu in origin, and which adopted elements of Arabic vocabulary only after the arrival of the Omani Arabs in the 18th century.

Several modern Mozambican ports have been built over medieval Swahili trade settlements – most notably Ilha do Mozambique, but also Angoche, Ibo and possibly Inhambane. However, the most important port south of Kilwa in mediaeval times, Sofala, is no longer in existence. The port of Sofala is thought to have been founded as a trading post in the 9th century, as a result of an Arabic ship being blown off course to hit land south of the Zambezi. Sofala is said to have had a population of around 10,000 by the 15th century. The absence of suitable building material meant that the mediaeval cities of Mozambique were never built as durably as those located further north, so little physical evidence of Sofala remains. Even if Sofala had been a stone city, it would now be submerged off the ever-mutating sandy shoreline south of the Buzi River.

Despite the absence of tangible ruins at Sofala, one should not underestimate its importance in mediaeval times, when it formed the pivotal link between the gold mines of Karangaland and Manica and the port of Kilwa. Sofala was best known to Arabs as the source of Kilwa's gold, but it was also an important trade centre in its own right, with direct maritime links to Madagascar and indirect links via Madagascar to India and Indonesia. Sofala's main exports, apart from gold, were worked iron, copper, ivory and cotton – the latter grown as far south as Inhambane by the 15th century.

There is strong evidence to suggest that Arab vessels explored the Zambezi as far inland as Cahora Bassa. It also seems highly probable that Muslim traders settled along the Zambezi long before the arrival of the Portuguese. Despite the oft-repeated assertion that Portugal founded the river ports at Sena and Tete in 1531, the greater probability is that Portuguese traders occupied existing Muslim settlements at these locations. Particularly compelling evidence of this comes from a 12th century Arab document which refers to a town called Seyouna located near the confluence of two large rivers and a large mountain – the similarity in name and the geographical details would point to Seyouna and Sena being one and the same place. It has also been suggested that a town referred to as Dendema in a 14th century document was in the same locality as present-day Tete.

Portuguese occupation of East Africa 1488–1530

The well established trade links that bonded East Africa to the Gulf and to Asia were to alter dramatically in the 16th century following the arrival of the Portuguese on the Indian Ocean. Throughout the 15th century, Portugal attempted to find a route around Africa, with the main impetus of establishing direct control over the eastern spice trade. After Portugal captured the Moroccan port of Ceuta in 1415, it also became conscious of the fact that somewhere in Africa lay the source of the gold traded in that city. Furthermore, the Portuguese Crown was eager to establish the whereabouts of the legendary kingdom of Prester John (the name by which they knew Ethiopia) and to forge links with this isolated Christian empire.

It took Portugal almost a century to circumnavigate Africa, quite simply because they underestimated the continent's size. Nevertheless, Portuguese explorers had sailed as far south as Senegal by 1444; they reached the Gambia River in 1446; Sierra Leone in 1460; and São Tomé in 1474. In 1485, under King João II, an expedition led by Cão sailed up the Congo River as far as it was navigable, then continued south as far as Cape Cross in present-day Namibia. Cão died near Cape Cross, but when the survivors of his journey returned to Portugal, King João ordered Bartholomew Diaz to continue where he left off. Diaz set sail in August 1487, and in early 1488 he unwittingly rounded the Cape of Good Hope into the Indian Ocean, eventually sailing to roughly 50km past where the city of Port Elizabeth stands today. At the same time as Diaz was exploring the route via West Africa, another Portuguese explorer, Pero da Covilham, made his way overland and along the east African coastline to Kilwa and Sofala. The two routes of exploration finally connected in 1498, when Vasco da Gama sailed around Africa, stopping at Mozambique Island before continuing as far north as Malindi and, with the help of a Swahili navigator, crossing the Indian Ocean to India.

In 1505, the Portuguese decided to occupy the East African coast. In July, Kilwa was captured and a friendly sheikh installed on its throne. Two months after that, a Portuguese boat landed at Sofala and was given permission by the local sheikh to erect a fort and trading factory – however the sheikh and his allies attacked the Portuguese stockade within a year of its foundation, resulting in the sheikh being killed and replaced by a Portuguese puppet. In 1507, a permanent Portuguese settlement was established on Mozambique Island, which so rapidly became the centre of Portuguese operations that Kilwa was abandoned by its colonisers in 1513.

Portugal also set about attacking rival Muslim centres of commerce: Oja, Bravo and Socatra on the north coast were sacked in 1507, and the islands of Mafia, Pemba and Zanzibar followed in 1509. Several Muslims from Mozambique Island and Sofala were forced to relocate to Angoche and Querimba Island, where they started a clandestine trade which was temporarily halted when Portugal razed Angoche in 1511 and Querimba in 1522. By 1530, practically the whole East African coast north of Sofala was under Portuguese control.

The East African coast 1530–1600

The boundaries of modern Mozambique were in many instances shaped by events during the first four centuries of the Portuguese occupation of the coast, but Mozambique as we know it is in essence a 20th century entity. The expansions and contractions of Portuguese influence between 1500 and 1890 don't really reflect a considered policy, but rather a haphazard sequence of largely unsuccessful attempts at formal expansion from a few coastal strongholds.

The Portuguese presence in East Africa was characterised by a high level of disunity. The interests of the Crown and the appointed Captain of Mozambique (who prior to 1670 ran the 'colony' as a private trade enterprise) were often in conflict, as were those of the many Portuguese deserters who fled from the few formal Portuguese settlements to intermarry with locals and form a distinct group of mixed-race *mazungos*. Contrary to popular perception, Mozambique prior to 1890 was not so much a Portuguese territory as it was a patchwork of endlessly mutating and fragmenting fiefdoms, some of which were under the nominal or real rule of the Portuguese Crown, but the greater number of which were lorded over by self-appointed despots, be they renegade *mazungos*, indigenous chiefs or Muslim sheikhs.

In the early years of the Portuguese occupation, the kingdom of Monomotapa (more accurately transcribed as Mwene Mutapa, that is, the state of the Mutapa dynasty) took on legendary proportions in the mind of its would-be conquerors. For centuries, it has been assumed that Monomotapa was a vast and all-powerful homogenous empire covering most of modern-day Zimbabwe as well as parts of Botswana and Mozambique. Modern academics, however, believe that the kingdom's size and importance was exaggerated by Portugal, and that the Mutapa dynasty ruled over what was merely one of many loosely defined Karanga kingdoms. Quite how Monomotapa's mythical status arose is an open question, but it is fairly certain that it would have suited Portuguese interests to perpetuate the myth that the whole interior was one vast centralised kingdom – especially after 1607, when Portugal signed a treaty with the Mutapa giving them full access to all gold, copper and silver mines in his kingdom.

The earliest sanctioned exploration of the Mozambican interior was made by Antonio Fernandes, who reported on the main gold trade routes over three journeys between 1511 and 1513, and who was probably the first Portuguese to visit the capital of Monomotapa in the Cahora Bassa Region. However, Fernandes's findings did not result in the official occupation of the interior – on the contrary, the Portuguese Crown appears to have been content to trade with local chiefs from its coastal fortresses. The disruption caused to the gold trade by the upheavals in Karangaland and the clandestine approach of the Muslim gold traders at places like Angoche forced the Portuguese to turn their attention to ivory, which by 1530 had replaced gold as the main item of export. The Portuguese fortresses on the coast also required large amounts of food, which created a secondary trade network between the representatives of the Crown and established chiefs. Despite initial tensions, the market for food and ivory eventually created a mutual dependency and stable relations.

Once Portugal realised that it would be unable to wrest control of the elusive gold trade from the Muslims by force, it attempted to take control of the routes to the interior by occupying the existing Muslim settlements at Tete, Sena and Quelimane in 1531.

The only concerted effort made by the Crown to conquer Monomotapa in the 16th century was an expedition of 1,000 men led by Francisco Barreto, which arrived at Sena in December 1571. Hundreds of Barreto's men had died of fever along the way and – ignorant of tsetse fly and mosquito-borne diseases – Barreto blamed his losses on the black magic of the Muslims at Sena. The Portuguese troops attacked Sena, killing most of its Muslim population and capturing the 19 men they identified as their leaders, who were then tortured to death at the rate of two a day. In July 1572, Barreto marched towards Tete with 650 men, but before he could reach his destination, his troops were attacked by a force of 16,000 Africans led by a Maravi king known as Mambo. Barreto's men were forced to turn back after killing some 4,000 of their attackers. Only 180 of the men who left Sena returned there alive, and Barreto himself died of fever on the way. Two years later, another group of soldiers marched 450km inland, defeating the Kiteve capital but achieving little else before they returned to the coast, with their numbers reduced by two thirds due to malaria.

The Portuguese occupation of Mozambique should not be seen as colonisation in the way we understand it today. Most of the infiltration of the interior and the coast away from the fortresses towns was the work of Afro-Portuguese half-castes (*mazungos*), many of whom were refugees from the Crown. Armed with muskets, many of these refugees married into local communities and assumed the role of surrogate chiefs, building up their own private armies and trade empires. During the 16th century, not only did various *mazungos* establish themselves at practically every port and island along the coast, but they also settled along the southern bank of the Zambezi as far as Tete, setting up what were in effect minor chieftaincies over the local Tonga people – basically, the forerunners of the *prazo* land grants of the 17th and 18th centuries.

Ironically, it could be argued that the most successful expansionists in 16th-century Mozambique were not of European but African origin. Probably as a result of a drought, cannibalistic Zimba warbands from the Maravi Kingdom of the Shire Highlands (in Malawi) swept into Mozambique in the late 1860s. The Zimba attacked Tete in the 1560s, they halted Baretto's progress in 1572, and they then continued northwards, razing Kilwa and Mombasa and eating many of their occupants. The Zimba were eventually defeated near Malindi in 1587, but the survivors returned southwards to settle in the area between the Rovuma and Zambezi Rivers, practically all of which was ruled over by one or other Maravi chieftaincy at the beginning of the 17th century.

Towards the end of the century, Portugal's dominance in the region was threatened by Turks, for which reason the fortifications of Mozambique Island and Mombasa were vastly improved and the coast was divided into two administrative regions with Cabo Delgado as the boundary. This border has remained significant ever since and now separates Tanzania from Mozambique.

The East African coast 1600–1800

In the early 17th century, Portugal experienced the first serious rivalry to its status as the dominant European power in the Indian Ocean. In 1602, barely a decade after the first Dutch and British ships had rounded the Cape of Good Hope, the Dutch East India Company (VOC) was formed with the intent of taking over Portugal's Indian Ocean trade. In 1607, the Dutch made a concerted effort to capture the Portuguese capital on Mozambique Island, a six-week siege which failed only because the invaders were unable to take the Portuguese fortress. After a second attempt at ousting Portugal in 1608, the Dutch fleets left Mozambique Island alone, but in alliance with English ships they captured several other Portuguese territories in the Indian Ocean. This period of instability ended in the late 1630s, when treaties were signed between the three countries.

The beginning of the 17th century also saw Karangaland fall into an extended period of instability following the death of the Monomotapa in 1597. The succeeding Monomotapa, Gatse Lucere, became dependent on the protection of the *mazungo* Diego Madeira's armies to retain control over his kingdom, which Madeira saw as more or less an invitation to take over Karangaland following the signing of a mineral rights treaty in 1607. Gatse Lucere died in 1623, to be succeeded by Inhamba, who in 1628 murdered the Portuguese envoy to his capital, prompting a full-scale war with Portugal. Inhamba was driven from his capital, and a baptised Mutapa was installed in his place. However, this puppet ruler had little support, and so in 1631 Inhamba led an uprising in which he recaptured the crown and killed several hundreds of Portuguese and their supporters. Meanwhile, the Maravi took advantage of the chaos in Monomotapa to capture Quelimane.

In 1632, Portugal had one of its few successful military forays in the Mozambican interior. Under the leadership of Sousa de Menesis, 2,000 troops landed at Quelimane, where they booted out the Maravi, then marched to Karangaland, destroyed Inhamba's army, and installed a vassal Monomotapa. So began a 60-year period in which Portugal was to have its only sustained control of Karangaland. During this time, major Portuguese settlements grew up around the various gold fairs of the interior, notably Dambarare (near modern-day Harare) and Masekesa (on the site of Manica town).

The Crown's tenuous supremacy in Karongaland ended in 1693, when a Changamire chief called Dombo attacked Dambarare and killed all its

Portuguese inhabitants. Other Portuguese settlements in Karangaland were evacuated and the Changamire proceeded to attack all the gold fairs in Manica. As things settled down, the Changamire took effective control of the highlands to found the Rozvi Kingdom, while the Portuguese kept control of the lowveld. This boundary is reflected in the modern one between Mozambique and Zimbabwe.

Events on the coast in the late 17th century reinforced what was eventually to become the northern border of modern Mozambique. In 1650, Muscat was captured by Omani Arabs and used as a base from which to launch an attack the East African coast. Omani ships attacked Zanzibar in 1652 and Mombasa in 1661. Ten years later, Mozambique Island was looted by Omani sailors, and once again it was only the fortress of São Sebastáo that prevented Portugal being ousted from their East African capital. The Omani never again attempted to attack Portuguese settlements in what is now Mozambique, but in 1698 they captured Mombasa. The coast north of Cabo Delgado was lost to Portugal forever.

The period between 1650 and 1800 saw the informal *mazungo* chieftaincies of the Zambezi Valley formalised into a network of *prazo* estates – large tracts of land granted to settlers and wealthy traders by the Portuguese Crown. The prazo leases were good for three generations, and they were inherited by females, presumably as a way of encouraging wealthy Portuguese to settle in the Zambezi Valley. In theory, no person was allowed to own more than one prazo, but in reality large blocks of prazos were linked by marriage. The holders of the leases, known as *prazeros*, ruled over their estates with absolute authority. In effect, the prazos were run as small feudal empires, and the prazeros derived most of their income by forcing tributes from people living on their estate rather than by developing the estate for agriculture.

Mozambique in the 19th century

The early part of the 19th century was a time of great hardship in southeastern Africa, as the region was gripped by severe droughts between 1794 and 1802 and again between 1817 and 1832. These droughts were to have far-reaching effects on Mozambique and many other parts of southeast Africa, most significantly amongst the Nguni people of southern Mozambique and the east coast of South Africa. During the first years of the drought, the Nguni became increasingly dependent on cattle raids to support themselves, which led to a high degree of militarisation and eventually to the centralisation of the Nguni into three main kingdoms: the Zulu, Swazi and Ndandwe. The Zulus, who emerged as the most powerful of these kingdoms under the leadership of Shaka, raided and looted surrounding territories, causing vast tracts of the South African highveld to become depopulated and forcing many people to migrate to other areas.

In 1819, the Zulus conquered the Ndandwe Kingdom, causing the survivors to emigrate from the area in a number of large warbands which grew in size as they raided and plundered the villages that they passed through. The warband which was to have the greatest effect on Mozambique was that led by Nxaba, who attacked Inhambane in 1824 and conquered many of the chieftaincies of Manica in 1827. In the early 1830s, with the drought at its peak, Nxaba was based around the Gorongosa area, and in 1836 he plundered Sofala. Following an Nguni leadership battle in 1837, Nxaba and his followers were forced to flee Mozambique, while the victor, Shoshangane, founded the Gaza Kingdom which covered most of Mozambique south of the Zambezi between 1840 and its conquest by Portugal in 1895.

Elsewhere, the Rozvi Empire of the Zimbabwean highlands was destroyed and the Changamire killed by an Nguni warband, and eastern Zimbabwe was eventually settled by the Matabele, another Nguni offshoot. Within Mozambique, an Nguni leader called Maseko established a kingdom north of Tete, while another called Gwangwara established himself along what is now the Tanzanian border. The Nguni invasion made travel in the interior unsafe, and Nguni warbands destroyed many of the gold fairs, practically forcing the closure of the trade.

Another significant feature of the first half of the 19th century, one that was not entirely unrelated to the drop in the gold trade, was a rapid increase in slave trading along the East African coast. Prior to the mid-18th century, slaves formed only a small part of the Indian Ocean trade network, but this started to change after the 1770s with the emergence of clandestine trade between the Muslims of Ibo and the French sugar plantations of the Indian Ocean Islands. In the 1770s, the number of slaves being exported from Mozambique was still relatively low – fewer than 2,000 annually – but as increasing restrictions were imposed on the trade out of West Africa, prices rose and so did the volume of slaves being exported from the ports of East Africa. Between 1825 and 1830, around 20,000 slaves were shipped out of Mozambique annually, to destinations as far afield as the USA and Brazil. It has been estimated that more than a million Africans were shipped out of the ports of Mozambique in the 19th century.

Britain persuaded Portugal to abolish the slave trade in 1836, in effect driving it underground – the number of slaves shipped out in the 1850s probably exceeded that in the 1830s. Public attention was drawn to this clandestine trade when the Scots missionary David Livingstone published reports of his Zambezi expedition of 1858–64. Following Livingstone's death in 1875, several Scots missions were established in the Shire Highlands (a part of modern-day Malawi that would otherwise almost certainly have been incorporated in Mozambique later in the century).

The great droughts undermined the agricultural base of the Zambezi Valley, forcing many prazeros to abandon their estates. By the mid-19th century, power in this important area had become consolidated under five large feudal fiefdoms ruled over by powerful *mazungo* families or other settlers. The Zambezi Valley became a lawless zone, characterised by interfamily feuds and mini-wars, starting in 1840 with a unsuccessful attack on the Pereira family by the Portuguese authorities, and reaching a peak in 1867–9 with four abortive and bloody attempts to capture the Da Cruz family stockade at Massangano. The Zambezi Valley was only fully brought under government control in 1887, when Massangano was captured by the governor of Manica.

An important feature of 19th century Mozambique was the strong British influence on the East African coast following its successful take-over of the Cape Colony in 1806 and Mauritius in 1810. In 1820, the British flag was raised on the southern part of Delagoa Bay, initiating a protracted period of disputes between Britain, Portugal and the Boer Republic of the Transvaal over the control of this strategic possession. This dispute was only resolved in 1875, when French arbitrators gave the whole bay to Mozambique. Meanwhile, as the so-called Scramble for Africa approached its climax, the Beira Corridor area became something of a battleground between the British imperialist and founder of Rhodesia, Cecil Rhodes, and his Portuguese counterpart Paiva de Andrada.

After a couple of years of haggling over boundaries and disputed territories, Britain and Portugal signed a treaty in May 1891 and Mozambique took its modern shape. The northern boundary with German East Africa (Tanzania) simply followed the border established centuries previously between the administrative regions of Mombasa and Mozambique Island. The northwestern borders were more keenly contested, but they were basically settled in favour of the power which had the higher presence in each area – hence northern Mozambique was bisected by the Scots-settled area that is now southern Malawi. The southwestern borders followed well-established divides: the border with Zimbabwe was similar to the one that separated the Rozvi and Portuguese spheres of influence between around 1700 and 1840; the western borders with the Transvaal followed the one agreed to in the Boer-Portuguese treaty of 1869; and the southern border with the British colony of Natal had been determined by French arbitration in 1875.

The colonial period 1890–1975

Mozambique is less arbitrarily delineated than many other countries in Africa. Nevertheless, it was anything but a cohesive entity at the time its boundaries were defined, and parts of the country remained entirely independent of Portugal as late as 1914. As an indication of the weakness of Portuguese colonial rule during the closing decade of the 19th century, it is interesting to note that Britain and Germany signed a secret treaty determining how Mozambique and Angola should be divided in the event of their being abandoned by Portugal.

Only four of Mozambique's ten modern-day provinces were directly administered by the colonial authorities. The area south of the Save River – basically the modern provinces of Maputo, Inhambane and Gaza – was given a reasonable degree of political coherence by the Gaza monarchy, who were conquered by Portugal between 1895 and 1897. The other part of the country that fell under direct colonial rule was the area around Mozambique Island (modern-day Nampula province), but the Portuguese presence in much of this area was rather tenuous until around the time of the outbreak of World War I. In 1904, the Portuguese in this area were attacked by a collection of Muslim and African chiefs, and they were forced to take refuge on Mozambique Island.

The rest of the country fell under indirect rule. The present-day provinces of Niassa and Cabo Delgado were leased to the Niassa Company between 1894 and 1929. The Niassa Company was almost totally ineffective until 1908, when it was taken over by a South African company and started to make its presence felt in the northern interior. The Yoa capital at Mwende was captured by the Niassa Company in 1912, but the Makonde Plateau remained independent until after World War I. Meanwhile, most of what are now Tete and Zambézia Provinces were controlled by prazeros, while the area now incorporated into the provinces of Sofala and Manica was leased to the Mozambique Company from 1891 to 1941.

A significant trend in the first decade of formal colonialism was the rising economic importance of southern Mozambique. This was directly due to the proximity of Lourenço Marques to the gold mines of the Witwatersrand in South Africa. Following the completion of the rail link to the Witwatersrand in 1894, the port at Lourenço Marques exported roughly a third of this wealthy area's minerals.

No less significant was the volume of migrant labour from southern Mozambique to the mines of Witwatersrand. The Witwatersrand Native Labour Association employed between 50,000 and 100,000 Mozambicans annually between the end of the Boer War and start of World War II. In some years, the tax contributed by the migrant workers of southern Mozambique amounted to more than half of the total revenue raised by the colonial government.

At around the turn of the century, Lourenço Marques was made the official capital of Mozambique, replacing the former capital of Mozambique Island after almost four centuries (strangely, every new source that I check to confirm the exact year when the capital was transferred has thrown up a different date, and I now have the choice of 1886, 1897, 1898, 1902 and 1907 – the year 1898 as quoted by the official Lourenço Marques city guide published in 1964 seems most plausible).

Migrant labour had been an important factor in the Mozambican economy even before 1890, but the volume of workers increased dramatically following the Colonial Labour Law of 1899. Not only did this decree divide Mozambicans into two classes, Indigenous and Non-indigenous, but it also required that all indigenous males and females aged between 14 and 60 had to work and had to pay hut tax. It can be argued that the Labour Law rescued Mozambique from the bleak economic future that many had predicted at the time of its formal colonisation, but it is equally true that by imposing the obligation to work on the indigenous population it allowed them to be exploited in a manner that was little better than slavery. Paradoxically, it was the people who lived in the prazos and company concessions who were most ruthlessly exploited – until the 1930s, people in these areas were regularly press-ganged into 'employment'. The migrant labour of southern Mozambique was socially disruptive, but it also meant better wages and a lower cost of living; so that even as late as 1967, roughly half a million Mozambicans (out of a total population of eight million) were working in South Africa or Rhodesia.

In 1926, Portugal's Republican Government was overthrown in a military coup, leading to the so-called 'New State', a dictatorship dominated by the figure of Antonio Salazar, Prime Minister of Portugal from 1932 to 1968. Salazar envisaged a future wherein Portugal and its colonies would form a self-sufficient closed economy with the mother country serving as the industrial core and the dependencies providing the agricultural produce and raw materials. Salazar outlawed the company concessions and prazos which had until then practically ruled two-thirds of Mozambique, and he was largely successful in his efforts to create a more unitary administration. Forced labour was replaced by forced agricultural schemes, leading to a tenfold increase in Mozambique's cotton and rice production between 1930 and 1950. As a result, Mozambique enjoyed something of an economic boom, particularly during World War II when Portugal's neutral stance allowed Mozambique to concentrate on food production and benefit from a 500% increase in the value of its exports during the years 1939–45. However, the war also meant a decrease in the activity of the mines of South Africa and Rhodesia, and the return of large numbers of migrant labourers, one result of which was the introduction of population control rulings that mimicked the South African Pass Laws.

The post-war period saw greater economic diversification in Mozambique, with the development of secondary industries, particularly in Lourenço Marques and Beira, and a boom in incoming tourism from South Africa and Rhodesia. The outcome of the war encouraged Salazar to drop his more fascist policies and to enter into NATO in 1949, one result of which was the admittedly rather semantic change in Mozambique's status from a colony to an Overseas Province.

After World War II, almost all of Europe's African colonies experienced a vociferous and sometimes violent campaign for independence. Generally, these calls for liberation were initiated by African soldiers who had fought for democracy in Europe and then returned home to find that they remained second-class citizens in the country of their birth. That no significant liberation movement existed in Mozambique prior to 1960 can probably be attributed to Portugal's neutrality during the war. Nevertheless, following a violent uprising in Angola in February 1961, the ever-astute Salazar decided to try to forestall the inevitable, firstly by allowing Portugal's

'Overseas Provinces' to be represented in the Lisbon government, and secondly by bestowing full citizenship on the indigenous population. In December of that year, Portugal's three colonial enclaves in Asia were reclaimed by India. Following this, Salazar decided that he would oppose similar calls from his African colonies with force.

Mozambique's first broad-based liberation movement was formed in exile in 1963, when President Nyerere of Tanzania persuaded a number of small-time liberation groups to amalgamate into an organisation called Frelimo, held together by the powerful leadership of Eduardo Mondlane, a Mozambican academic living in the USA. In 1964, Frelimo decided on a militant policy, and by the end of 1965 it had captured much of Cabo Delgado and Niassa Provinces. Portugal responded by arresting 1,500 Frelimo agents in southern Mozambique, effectively destroying the organisation in this part of the country. Meanwhile, Frelimo started to factionalise in the north, with the educated leadership on one side and the traditionalist chiefs on the other. In 1968, the Frelimo offices in Dar es Salaam were raided by traditionalists, and rioting in the Frelimo-run school in Dar es Salaam forced its closure. In February 1969, Mondlane was assassinated using a letter-bomb. The ensuing power struggle within the party forced out the traditionalists and saw the military commander, Samora Machel, take over the party presidency in May 1970.

Machel faced an immediate challenge in the form of 35,000 troops sent by the government to clear Frelimo out of northern Mozambique and to attack its bases in Tanzania. Instead of fighting, Frelimo evacuated the north, slipped through Malawi, and relocated its centre of internal operations to the area north of Tete. With the support of the local Chewa people, Frelimo attempted to destabilise the Tete and Beira Corridors and to disrupt the construction of the Cahora Bassa Dam, a policy which culminated in the derailing of trains to Beira in 1974.

The extent to which Frelimo's limited attacks influenced Mozambique's eventual independence is debatable. At least as significant were the concurrent political changes in Portugal. Upon entering the European Common Market in 1970, Portugal was forced to dismantle its rigid trade agreements with Mozambique. The result was an almost immediate realignment of the Mozambican economy towards South Africa – by 1974, South Africa had already become the main investor in Mozambique, as well as its principal trading partner. Even more critical to Mozambique's future was the left-wing coup that took place in Lisbon in April 1974. Within two months, the new government of Portugal had entered into negotiations with Frelimo. In September 1974, the two sides signed the Lusaka Accord: Mozambique would be granted independence after a mere nine months of interim government, and power would transfer to Frelimo without even the pretence of a referendum or election.

Independent Mozambique

Three factors were to prove critical in shaping Mozambique during the first two decades of independence: the mess left behind by the colonisers, the leadership of Frelimo, and the destabilising policies of South Africa's nationalist government.

It would be easy enough to see the first fifteen years of Frelimo government as typical of the sort of Marxist dictatorship that has characterised post-independence Africa. It would also be rather simplistic. Frelimo assumed a dictatorial role through circumstance as much as intent – there simply *was* no viable opposition in the decade following independence – and its progressive, humanitarian ideals were a far cry from the self-serving, repressive policies enacted by many of its peers. Frelimo's undeniable failures can be attributed partly to unfortunate circumstance, but most of all to its intellectual and interventionist policies – idealistic grand schemes which failed to take into account the importance of ethnicity, tradition and religion in rural African societies, and which ultimately alienated the peasantry.

Frelimo's most notable successes were on the social front. In the first few years of independence, primary school attendance doubled and enrolment at secondary schools increased sevenfold. The new government attempted to combat the quite appalling literacy rate of less than 5% at the time of independence by initiating an adult literacy scheme that benefited hundreds of thousands of Mozambicans, and it sought to undermine the problem of ethnicity by spreading the use of Portuguese as a common language. Despite there being fewer than 100 trained doctors in the country in 1975, Frelimo launched an ambitious programme of immunisations, praised by the World Health Organisation (WHO) as one of the most successful ever initiated in Africa. The scheme reached 90% of the population in the first five years of Frelimo rule, resulting in a 20% drop in infant mortality. Frelimo's emphasis on sexual equality was underscored by the fact that 28% of the people elected to popular assemblies in 1977 were women – a higher figure than almost anywhere else in the world.

Frelimo's critical failing was on the economic front, though it should be recognised that the post-independence collapse of Mozambique's economy was precipitated by several factors that were beyond Frelimo's control. Mozambique attained independence during the global depression that followed the 1973 Oil Crisis, which aside from having a direct effect on the economy also caused the South African gold mines to lay off two-thirds of their Mozambican workers in 1976, leading to an immense loss in Mozambique's foreign earnings. Worse still was the mass exodus of skilled Portuguese settlers and the related outflow of capital and asset-stripping which caused the collapse of many secondary industries within a year of independence. Frelimo attempted to abate this outflow by nationalising a number of industries, but at a pace that only caused the situation to spiral, and which gave many Portuguese settlers a pretext for destroying anything that they couldn't take out the country. Meanwhile, Frelimo's ambitious agricultural schemes were to some extent thwarted by climatic factors; disastrous floods hit the main agricultural areas in the summer of 1977/8, to be followed by four years of nation-wide drought.

Finally, Frelimo had to contend with South Africa's policy of 'destabilisation' and its support of Renamo, an guerrilla organisation which was founded by the Rhodesian Special Branch shortly after Mozambique's independence. Aided by several former members of the Portuguese Security Police, the Rhodesians conceived of Renamo as a fifth column to attack strategic bases in Mozambique, which at that time was allowing the Zimbabwean liberation movements to operate out of Manica. When Zimbabwe achieved independence in 1980, the South African Defence Force (SADF) took over Renamo and retrained its soldiers at Phalaborwa in the northern Transvaal. Renamo enjoyed considerable success with SADF backing – most notably by blowing up the Zambezi rail bridge in 1983 – and it boosted its ranks by kidnapping young boys in rural areas. With the assistance of various anti-Marxist American groups, South Africa managed to give its sponsored outlaws some sort of credibility by establishing Renamo offices in several capital cities, most of them manned by non-Africans.

On 16 March 1984, Mozambique and South Africa signed the Nkomati Accord, an agreement that neither country would support elements hostile to the other. Mozambique abided by the accord, but the SADF continued to give clandestine and possibly unofficial support to Renamo, helped by Malawi's President Banda, who allowed the organisation to operate out of his country. In September 1986, President Samora Machel of Mozambique, along with the presidents of Zimbabwe and Zambia, held a summit with Banda in Malawi and persuaded him to boot out Renamo. On the return flight to Maputo, Machel's plane was diverted by a South African radio signal and crashed in South African territory, killing everybody on board. Officially this 'accident' remains just that, but it will be interesting to see whether accidental causes remain a credible explanation by the time South Africa's ongoing Truth and Reconciliation Committee has packed up its briefcases.

In December 1986, Malawi signed a mutual security agreement with Mozambique's recently installed President Joaquim Chissano. Left with nowhere else to run, Renamo was forced to base itself permanently in Mozambique, where it took on a life of its own. Formerly, Renamo had limited its activities to occasional raids on strategic targets. From 1987 onwards, Renamo warbands roamed through the Mozambican countryside, supporting themselves with random raids on rural villages in what an official of the US State Department described as "one of the most brutal holocausts against ordinary human beings since World War II". By 1990, Frelimo's control barely extended beyond the main towns. It has been estimated that Renamo killed 100,000 Mozambicans during this period, and that as many as one-third of Mozambique's human population was displaced or forced into exile by the raiding warbands. The country's economic infrastructure, already crippled by the post-independence withdrawal of skills and funds, then by years of misplaced Marxist policies, was practically destroyed. Frelimo's social achievements were reduced to cinders along with roughly 2,500 primary schools and 800 clinics and hospitals. Teachers, doctors and educated administrative staff who hadn't managed to flee the country in time were systematically executed by Renamo.

In November 1990, pressured by overseas aid donors, Frelimo unveiled a new constitution denouncing its former Marxist policies and allowing for multi-party elections. However, the civil war continued into 1992, when the Rome Conference in October resulted in a cease-fire being signed by President Chissano and the Renamo leader Afonso Dhlakama. Mozambique has been at peace since then, and it remains under Frelimo rule following the first democratic election, held in October 1994, which achieved an 85% turn-out, with Chissano obtaining 53% of the presidential vote and Dhlakama 34%. Neither party achieved an absolute majority in the parliamentary elections, with Frelimo picking up 44% of the vote to Renamo's 38%. The strongest Renamo support came from the central provinces of Nampula, Zambézia, Sofala, Manica, and Tete, where it attained a majority of parliamentary seats, while the northern and southern provinces went to Frelimo. Renamo's relative success in the election came as a surprise to many, considering its history and the fact that it still has no real policies other than being anti-Frelimo. One would suspect that it is a result more of Frelimo's low-key campaigning and failure to connect with the populace at grassroots level than of any inherent virtues seen to be attached to Renamo.

ECONOMY AND INDUSTRY

Mozambique has achieved political stability, but it remains economically crippled, with a per capita GNP that halved between 1975 and 1992, by which time it had slid to the lowest in the world. The ongoing civil war has nullified most of Frelimo's social achievements, to the extent that Mozambique now has the highest infant mortality rate in the world.

Despite this, Mozambique is a country with tremendous economic potential. There is no shortage of arable land, water resources, or woodland. Extensive tracts of tropical hardwoods still exist in many places and, if managed responsibly, also offer possibilities. The country has considerable mineral reserves, and modern ports linked to a rail network constructed for the transportation of goods to and from the states of southern central Africa. The sea has plentiful supplies of fish, and the islands and coastline are ideally suited to tourism. This economic potential has never been developed to the full, neither in Portuguese colonial times nor since.

The country's economy is based on agriculture, which contributes almost 45% of the gross domestic product. The main export products are cashew nuts, sugar cane, cotton, sisal, coconuts and citrus fruits. At present, mainly as a result of the security situation as well as the lack of capital, only about 20% of the cultivable land is actually under production.

Identified by the government as being high-priority sectors for development are salt, sugar, copra, cotton and cashew nuts. To these are added processed fish and fruits. A number of items are given "medium priority" status, with further sectors to follow. It seems as though a lot of work is being carried out to structure the emergence of Mozambique as a successful producer and trader and signs are encouraging.

The second major contributor to the economy is industry, primarily food processing, textiles, edible oils, soaps and other consumer goods. During Portuguese times, Mozambique was the fourth industrial power in Africa, although, considering the relatively low rate of industrialisation of the continent, this is no great claim. In the first ten years after independence, the country's industrial sector came to an almost total standstill, primarily brought about because most whites had fled the country in fear of Frelimo and the uncertainty of their policies during the transitional phase to independence. Companies were deserted by their owners, machinery often destroyed.

The exodus of the settler population meant the loss of management expertise, skilled workers and capital. Both Frelimo's new economic policy, which concentrated solely on agriculture, particularly on the creation of large-scale mechanised State collective farms, and the civil war against Renamo contributed to the downfall of the country's industries. At the end of the 1980s, industry had ground to an almost complete halt. Despite the change of economic policies since then, the task of rebuilding the country's industrial base is not an easy one. There is too little private initiative and a lack of management skills for large-scale projects; trained workers are thin on the ground; and the foreign exchange needed for purchasing raw materials and parts is simply not available.

The north of the country has a craft industry, primarily in making wooden furniture of simple but handsome appearance. It doesn't seem to be organised and exporting items would be costly as they tend to be bulky and heavy. Other crafts include the well-known Makonde carvings. The Makonde are centred around Mueda in the northeast, and here you can get representative items of their work very cheaply. Other places where you might find selections are Nampula, Nacala and Pemba.

Foreign investment

Although the recent merger of markets into COMESA will help, it will be a long time before industry regains its previous dimensions. (COMESA is a co-operative trade and development arrangement intended to function at inter-African, continental, level.) Private foreign investment is again welcomed and the government is trying hard to improve conditions. A special foreign investment promotional office has been established:

GPIE, Caixa Postale 1101, Av 25 de Setembro 2049, Maputo. Tel: (258 1) 427938/492713; telex: 6 153 INCOOP

Private banks, both local and foreign, are now permitted to operate in the country and private farmland which was brought under state control during the revolutionary years is being returned to its Portuguese and South African owners. There are "industrial free zones" in Maputo, Beira, Mocuba and Nacala intended to encourage investors to come to the country. In these zones, certain taxes and duties are waived in favour of a small royalty on sales.

Certain businesses, previously state-owned, have been offered for sale by tender. In 1994, for instance, a short list of about a dozen enterprises covered a range of industries from plastics to pasta, from transport to tea – over US$60 million of sales turnover. However, fears have been expressed in the country of a sell-out of Mozambican resources to foreign countries. But without foreign investment Mozambique will have very little chance of ever getting back on its feet economically.

Without doubt, the most influential of all Mozambique's trading partners is South Africa, whose business people seem to be buying up everything – factories, mines, breweries, hotels, transport concerns and so on.

Foreign exchange

During Portuguese colonial times the main sources of foreign exchange were the export of agricultural produce; rail transport and provision of ports for South Africa, northern Rhodesia (Zambia), southern Rhodesia (Zimbabwe), Nyasaland (Malawi) and Swaziland; income from the supply of manpower to South African and Rhodesian mines and plantations; and tourism from South Africa and Rhodesia.

Except for agricultural exports, these sources of income have since more or less disappeared, although tourism is slowly beginning to re-emerge, particularly south of Beira. Rail transportation to neighbouring countries is now only possible on a small scale due to the effects of the civil war. After the government's severing of trade links with South Africa at the beginning of the 1980s, South Africa terminated the existing agreement on the employment of Mozambican workers by the South African mines. This agreement between Portugal and South Africa, dating from 1928, had been particularly lucrative for Mozambique since it meant that 60% of the salaries were paid at a fixed gold price.

Mineral resources

During colonial times there was almost no exploitation of the country's large mineral deposits. At this time very little in the way of geological exploration had been conducted in Mozambique: it is estimated that more geological investigations were conducted in Mozambique between 1977 and 1983 than during the entire colonial period. In the course of these investigations, rich deposits of coal, iron ore and phosphate, as well as gold, tantalum, chromium, copper, bauxite, nickel and many other minerals, were discovered. At present mining is still limited to coal, precious and semi-precious stones and gold.

FACIM Trade Fair

Mozambique's window on the world, economically speaking, is the FACIM. It is the most important, in fact the only real trade fair in Mozambique and attracts considerable international participation. It is held in Maputo annually towards the end of August. For further information, contact:

FACIM/Maputo Trade Fair, PO Box 1761, Av do Sarges. Tel: (258-1) 428991/423713/427151, telex: 6 411 FACIMMO

NATURAL HISTORY

Geography

The topography of eastern Mozambique is dominated by a low-lying coastal belt which widens from north to south to account for almost half of the country's surface area. The coastal plain rises gradually towards the west to meet a high plateau of 500 to 1,000m. Mozambique is generally characterised by relatively flat terrain, though much of the northwest is mountainous and several areas of the western plateaux are dotted with isolated granite inselbergs known in southern Africa as koppies.

In the areas bordering Malawi and Zimbabwe, there are a few mountains which rise to an altitude of above 1,800m. Mount Binga in the Chimanimani Range on the Zimbabwe border is Mozambique's highest peak at 2,436m (the *Time Out* map shows a 2,593m peak in the highlands west of the Chimoio–Tete road, but this is presumably a misplacement of Inyanga peak on the Zimbabwe side of the border). Other notable mountains include the massive inselberg of Gorongosa (1,862m) in Sofala Province; Mount Domue (2,095m) near Bragança in Tete Province; Mount Chiperone (2,052m) near Milange and Mount Namuli (2,419m) near Gurué in Zambézia; and Mount Txitonga (1,848m) and Mount Jeci (1,836m) on the Rift Valley escarpment north of Lichinga in Niassa Province.

Mozambique is traversed by several major river systems, all of which flow eastwards into the Indian Ocean. The mouths of these rivers have played a significant role in Mozambican history: many of the country's older towns are situated on large river mouths, and the rivers themselves often formed important trade routes into the interior. The Zambezi is Africa's fourth largest river and the Limpopo its tenth largest. The Zambezi basin, at 1,330,000km^2 is the third largest drainage system in Africa (after the Zaire and the Nile) and the 13th largest in the world. Of the 820km-long Mozambican section of the Zambezi, 460km are navigable.

Other main river systems are the Rovuma on the Tanzania border; the Lúrio on the border of Cabo Delgado and Nampula provinces; the Save on the border of Sofala and Inhambane Provinces; and the Lebombo in the south of the country.

Roughly 200km of the eastern shore of Africa's third-largest freshwater body, Lake Malawi, lies in Mozambique, where it is known as Lago Niassa. Further south, the lake formed by the Cahora Bassa Dam is one of the 15 largest in Africa, its exact ranking depending on the effects of rainy seasons and swamp flooding at three other lakes.

Climate

The climate in most of Mozambique is tropical and warm with a dry cooler season from April until September and a wet hot season with temperatures of around 28°C at the coast from October until April. In winter the weather at the coast is sunny and pleasantly warm (the average temperature in Maputo in June and July is 19°C). The dry and relatively cool winter months between April and September offer the most comfortable and easy travel conditions.

Temperatures and rainfall figures vary widely across the country. The hottest and most humid parts of the country are the coast and Zambezi Valley, while the coolest areas are those at higher altitudes, such as the highlands of Niassa and Nampula Provinces. Most of northeastern and central Mozambique has an annual average rainfall in excess of 1,000mm, with the wettest part of the country being the highlands east of Malawi, where several areas experience almost 2,000mm of rain annually. The south is generally much drier, with coastal regions south of Beira generally receiving around 900mm of rain and some parts of the interior of Gaza Province dropping to an average of below 500mm annually. The rainy season in the south runs from October to March, while north of the Zambezi it tends to start and end a month or two later.

		Temperature	Rainfall	Humidity
January	Maputo	21–30°C	130mm	73%
	Beira	24–32°C	270mm	75%
July	Maputo	13–25°C	15mm	73%
	Beira	16–25°C	30mm	79%

Vegetation

Most of Mozambique is covered in savannah, a rather loosely applied term that can be used to cover practically any wooded habitat that doesn't have a closed canopy. The main savannah type in Mozambique is brachystegia woodland (named after the most common tree), and characteristically this is much more densely wooded than are similar habitats in Zimbabwe and South Africa, and the trees are much taller. Brachystegia woodland is the dominant vegetation type throughout northern Mozambique, in the Zimbabwe and Zambia border areas, and along the coastal belt north of the Limpopo. In total, brachystegia woodland covers about 70% of the country, but it is replaced by mopane woodland in drier areas such as Tete Province south of the Zambezi and the interior of Gaza Province, and by acacia woodland in parts of the south and along the main watercourses of the north.

The beaches of the coast are typically coverered in dense, scrubby thickets and palm groves, the latter particularly impressive around Inhambane and Quelimane. The flood plains of major rivers such as the Limpopo, Zambezi and Pungue, and the area near Lake Chilwa on the Malawi border, are covered in alluvial grasslands and marshes. The largest alluvial plain in Mozambique is the Zambezi Delta, a vast marshy area of thick grassland and borassus palms that stretches for 120km along the coast and covers an area of roughly 8,000km².

Only a tiny portion of Mozambique is covered in true forest. Moist rain forests occur on the upper reaches of a few mountains, notably Mount Gorongosa in Sofala, the Chimanimani and Inyanga Highlands on the Zimbabwe border, and Mounts Murrumbala, Namuli and Chiperone in western Zambézia. Dry lowland forest occurs in patches in some coastal areas, notably in northern Cabo Delgado and around Dondo near Beira, while several rivers support thin belts of riparian forest.

Wildlife conservation

Mozambique's formerly abundant wildlife has been severely depleted by years of civil war and associated poaching – the elephant population, for instance, has dropped from 65,000 to no more than 15,000. Despite the fact that some 11% of the country's surface area has been gazetted as protected areas, there are at present no game reserves that are readily accessible to visitors.

Mozambique's four national parks are Gorongosa to the north of the Beira Corridor; Zinave on the southern bank of the Save River; Banhine in the centre of Gaza Province; and Bazaruto off the coast opposite Vilankulo and Inhassoro. Of these, only Bazaruto has tourist facilities, and it is strictly speaking a marine reserve as opposed to a conventional game reserve. The five game reserves are Rovuma on the Tanzanian border, Gile southeast of Nampula, Marromeu at the Zambezi Delta, Pomene on the coast between Inhambane and Vilankulo, and the Maputo Elephant Reserve on the coast to the south of the capital. None of these has any facilities for visitors, and only the Maputo Elephant Reserve is likely to be developed in the foreseeable future.

Without a large-scale programme of reintroducing animals, it is unlikely that any of Mozambique's reserves will replenish their wildlife stocks in the next decade to the extent that they become viable tourist attractions. In the Maputo Elephant Reserve, for instance, most large game species have been poached to extinction during the last decade, while the formerly prolific elephant population has been reduced to two breeding herds of around 30 head each.

The picture at Marromeu Game Reserve is only slightly better. The elephant population of the Zambezi Delta dropped from 1,500 to 300 animals between 1988 and 1990, and the buffalo population dropped from over 55,000 in the 1970s to 4,000 in 1990. Similarly, the populations of several other large mammals such as hippopotamus (5,000 animals in 1982), sable (3,500) and waterbuck (4,000) have seen an 80–90% drop in the last decade or so. Black rhinos, lions and leopards formerly occurred in this reserve in large numbers, but I have no information on their current status.

Gorongosa National Park, formerly regarded as one of southern Africa's finest reserves, is similarly depleted of animals, largely because it formed the focus of hostilities during periods of the civil war. On a more upbeat note, there are said still to be large herds of game in the far north of the country, especially away from the main roads in Cabo Delgado, Niassa and northern Tete.

With the civil war ended, turning conservation areas into earners of foreign revenue is a priority of the Mozambican government, with the support of the Endangered Wildlife Trust (EWT), the only conservation NGO currently registered in Mozambique. The EWT has played an important role in conserving the breeding turtle and crocodile populations of the Bazaruto Islands, and they are currently involved in rehabilitating the Maputo Elephant Reserve and in a bird atlassing project. Their Johannesburg headquarters can be contacted at Private Bag X11, Parkview, South Africa, 2122, tel (011) 486 1102, fax: (011) 486 1506. The Maputo Office is at Avenida 25 de Setembro 1514, tel: (01) 42 5365, fax: (01) 42 2434.

In 1996, the World Bank proposed a new project to link several of Mozambique's parks and reserves with those in neighbouring counties. Among the ideas mooted are to connect Maputo Elephant Reserve with several of the reserves in the KwaZulu-Natal Province of South Africa; to link Banhine National Park with the Kruger National Park in South Africa via an existing hunting concession by removing the international game fence that currently runs along the Kruger Park's eastern border and blocks the animals' traditional migration routes; and to create a Mozambican park adjacent to Chimanimani National Park in Eastern Zimbabwe. Before this proposal can go ahead, it will need the agreement of all three countries' conservation authorities.

Birds

Mozambique's excellent bird life has been little affected by the civil war, though, as elsewhere in Africa, forest-dwelling species are increasingly threatened by environmental encroachment, as are several species attached to wetland environments.

Mozambique is an important destination for Southern African birders. Of the 850-odd bird species that are resident in or regular migrants to Africa south of the Zambezi, roughly 30 have only been recorded in Mozambique or else have their main concentration there. Some of the birds fitting into one of these categories are the Madagascar squacco heron, eastern saw-wing swallow, Boehm's bee-eater, palmnut vulture, silvery-cheeked hornbill, green tinker barbet, little spotted woodpecker, green-headed oriole, slender bulbul, stripe-cheeked bulbul, white-breasted alethe, Swynnerton's robin, Gunning's robin, Chirinda apalis, black-headed apalis, moustached warbler, Robert's prinia, mashona hylotia, yellow-breasted hylotia, Vanga flycatcher, Woodward's batis, Mozambique batis, Livingstone's flycatcher, marsh tchagra, chestnut-fronted helmetshrike, red-headed quelea, cardinal quelea, olive-headed weaver, Nyasa seedcracker, East African swee and lemon-breasted canary.

Also of interest to South African birders are the few dozen species present in northern Mozambique that aren't on the southern Africa checklist or which have only been recorded in southern Africa as vagrants – see the box on *Birding in Mozambique* for more details.

BIRDING IN MOZAMBIQUE

Vincent Parker

Of all the bird species resident in Southern Africa, possibly the one which has been seen by fewest birdwatchers is the olive-headed weaver. A patch of tall brachystegia woodland just south of the town of Panda (60km inland of Inharrime in Inhambane Province) is the only locality in the region where the birder has a chance of seeing it. This may not be for long, as the continued presence of the species is threatened by extensive wood cutting in the area.

Other exciting birds to be seen in the brachystegia woodlands of the Mozambican interior south of the Save River include chestnut-fronted helmet shrike, racquet-tailed roller, mottled spinetail, Rudd's apalis, Livingstone's flycatcher, blue-throated sunbird, Neergard's sunbird and pink-throated twinspot.

Visitors to southern Mozambique seldom stray away from the coast. Exciting birds to be seen along the coast include crab plovers, which are seen regularly in and around the Bazaruto Archipelago in summer, and occasionally as far south as Inhaca Island near Maputo. One of the rarest birds in the world, Eleanora's falcon, has been seen at Vilankulo and Pomene. Vast flocks of migrant waders include bar-tailed godwit, terek sandpiper and great sandplover. The very rare gull-billed tern has recently been seen at freshwater lakes in three localities.

Indigenous woodland is very scarce along the coast, having been largely replaced by exotic coconut palms and cashew trees. However, the red-throated twinspot, Livingstone's loerie and brown robin can still be found near Xai-Xai.

In Central Mozambique, two localities of great interest to birders are Gorongosa Mountain (near Gorongosa National Park) and the forests north of Dondo. Species which cannot be seen elsewhere in Southern Africa include green-headed oriole and Gunning's akalat.

Northern Mozambique is particularly alluring to birders, since many areas have yet to be thoroughly explored and birdwatchers are likely to find species that are new to the Mozambique list – and possibly even new to science! Birders in northern Mozambique will certainly encounter species that are not included in southern African field guides, so they will need to refer to a second field guide (see the appendix *Further Reading*).

Some of the birds that are known to occur in northern Mozambique but not in Southern Africa are pale-billed hornbill; brown-breasted barbet; mountain, little, grey-olive, Fischer's and Canabis's greenbuls; Thyolo alethe; central bearded scrub robin; evergreen and red-capped forest warblers; Kretchmar's longbill; white-winged and long-billed apalises; white-tailed blue flycatcher, mountain babbler, red & blue and eastern double-collared sunbirds; Bertram's weaver; Zanzibar red bishop; African citril and stripe-breasted canary.

Vincent Parker is in charge of the Mozambique Bird Atlas Project, the first attempt to atlas the avifauna of this relatively unexplored country. All birders visiting Mozambique are invited to contribute their observations to the project. Contributors should keep a list of all species encountered at each locality they visit. Ideally, each locality should correspond with a Quarter Degree Square (15 minutes longitude by 15 minutes latitude). Contributors who are unfamiliar with a Quarter Degree Square should provide the latitude and longitude of each locality and include any species encountered within 5km of the central locality. Further information and field cards can be obtained from Vincent Parker of the Mozambique Bird Atlas Project at FNP, PO Box 4203 Maputo, fax: 42 2434; or c/o Endangered Wildlife Trust, Private Bag X11, Parkview 2122, South Africa, tel: (+2711) 486 1102.

Chapter Two

Planning and Preparation

TOURIST INFORMATION

The best source of current tourist information and advice is the Mozambique National Tourist Company (MNTC), based in Johannesburg, South Africa. The MNTC's office is Noswal Hall on the corner of Bertha and Stiemens Streets in Braamfontein, and the postal address is PO Box 31991 Braamfontein 2017, tel: (011) 339 7275, fax: (011) 339 7295. In addition to being one of the most efficient and reliable organisations of this type that I've encountered in Africa, the MNTC can make bookings for most upmarket hotels and beach resorts within the country, and they organise visas and coach bookings between Johannesburg and Maputo.

Those coming from Portugal might like to contact the Agéncia de Informaçao de Mozambique at Avenida Infante Santo 23, 4xP-1300, Lisbon.

WHEN TO VISIT

The coastal regions of Mozambique are best visited in the dry winter months of May through to October, when daytime temperatures are generally around 20–25°C. There is no major obstacle to visiting Mozambique during the summer months of November to April, but you'll find that climatic conditions are oppressively hot and humid at this time of year, especially along the north coast. Because most of the country's rain falls during the summer months, there is also an increased risk of contracting malaria and of dirt roads being washed out.

Unless you are a South African with children at school, it is emphatically worth avoiding the south coast of Mozambique during South African school holidays, when campsites as far north as Vilankulo tend to be very crowded and hotels are often fully booked. The exact dates of South African school holidays vary slightly on a provincial basis, but the main ones to avoid are those for Gauteng (the province that includes Johannesburg, South Africa's most populous city and only a day's drive from Maputo). To give a rough idea of the periods to avoid, there are four annual school holidays in Gauteng: a three-week holiday that starts in the last week of March and ends in the middle of April, a month-long holiday running from late June to late July, a two-week holiday starting in late September, and a six-week holiday from early December to mid-January. Any South African embassy will be able to supply the exact dates of school holidays for any given year. If you do visit southern Mozambique during school holidays, then you should make reservations well in advance for all the hotels and campsites at which you plan to stay.

School holidays in landlocked Zimbabwe see a substantial influx of Zimbabwean tourists into southern Mozambique, so that most resorts between Beira and Xai-Xai are more crowded than usual. Provided that you have a tent, you shouldn't get stuck during these periods.

Few South Africans or Zimbabweans currently venture north of the Beira Corridor, so school holidays have no notable effect on tourist patterns in northern Mozambique.

PAPERWORK

A valid passport is required to enter Mozambique. The date of expiry should be at least six months after you intend to end your travels; if it is likely to expire before that, get a new passport.

Visas

Visas are required by all visitors. They must be bought in advance at a Mozambican embassy, high commission or through the National Tourist Company in Johannesburg. You do occasionally hear of people managing to buy a visa at an overland border, but this is not normal procedure and the chances are that you'll simply be refused entry if you arrive at a border or at the airport without a visa. At the Mozambican Consulate in Johannesburg, a visa costs the rand equivalent of roughly US$25, and takes about a week to issue, though for a slightly higher fee you can arrange to have it issued within 24 hours. Of the various neighbouring countries, the cheapest place to get a visa is at Harare in Zimbabwe.

You must enter the country within one month of the date of issue stamped on your visa. Upon entry, your passport will be stamped for a stay of up to 30 days in the country without complication. If you intend to spend longer than 30 days in Mozambique, you will have to apply for an extension a day or two before your first 30 days are up. Extensions of up to 30 days can be granted for a small fee at any immigration office (there is one in each of the provincial capitals), provided that your total stay does not exceed three months.

If, in addition to other travels in Mozambique, you plan on using the Tete Corridor to get between Zimbabwe and Malawi, then you should apply for a multiple-entry visa.

There are Mozambican high commissions or embassies in the following countries:

Belgium Blvd Saint Michel 97, B-1040 Brussels. Tel: (2) 7362564/7360096/ 7322632. Telex: 65478 EMOBRU B.

France 82 Rue Laugier, F-75017 Paris. Tel: (1) 47649132. Telex: 641527 EMBMOXBF. Fax: (1) 42673828.

Germany Adenauerallee 46, D 53113 Bonn. Tel: (228) 224024. Telex: 2283631 EMBAMOC. Fax: (228) 213920; or Auaenstelle Berlin: Clara-Zetkin-Str 97/IV, D 10117 Berlin. Tel: 030 229 1751/229 1413. Telex: 115074 EUMM DD.

Italy Viale Shakespeare 57, Rome. Tel: (6) 5912554/5,5924354/5918736.

Malawi Commercial Bank Building, PO Box 30579, Lilongwe 3. Tel: (265) 784100/784696. Telex: 4793 EMBMOQ MI. Also on Kamuzu Highway, Blantyre (Limbe). (People requiring transit visas should get to the consulate before 08.30, so that their permit is ready to collect later on the same day. Other visas take three or more working days to issue.)

Portugal 7 Av Berna, P-1000 Lisbon. Tel: (1) 7971994/7971747/772734. Telex: 13641 EMBAMOC P.

Russia Ul Gilyarovskovo 20, Moscow. Tel: (095) 2844007/ 2843654/2844319. Telex: 413369 EMMOC SU.

Swaziland PO Box 1212, Mbabane. Tel: (268) 42904/42699. Tlx: 2248 WD.

Sweden Sturegatan 46, PO Box 5801, 10248 Stockholm. Tel: (8) 6660350.

Tanzania PO Box 15274, 25 Garden Av, Dar Es Salaam. Tel: (51) 67843/67494. Telex: 41214 EMBAMOC.

United Kingdom 21 Fitzroy Square, London W1P 5HJ. Tel: (0171) 383 3800.

United States 1990 M St, NW #570, Washington 20036-3404. Tel: (202) 2937146/ 8. Telex: 248530 EMOC UR. Fax: (202) 8350245.

Zambia PO Box 34877, Mulungushi Village, Villa 46, Lusaka. Tel: (1) 250468/ 253354. Telex: 42690/45900 EMBAMOC ZA.

Zimbabwe PO Box 4608, 156 Rhodes Av, Harare. Tel: (4) 790837/9; 793653/7. Telex: 4466.

A list of foreign embassies in Mozambique itself is given in the *Maputo* chapter.

Bringing a vehicle to Mozambique

The amount of paperwork involved in bringing a vehicle into Mozambique isn't overwhelmingly great, but you will have problems if your papers aren't in order, particularly if you're entering the country from South Africa. To take a vehicle out of South Africa, you must have the original registration papers to show at the customs office, and a letter of authorisation if the vehicle is not being driven by the registered owner.

At the Mozambican customs, you will need to show the temporary export permit given to you by South African customs, and to pay for third party insurance. We paid the rand equivalent of about US$20 at the Komatipoort border post, but the cost seems to vary slightly from one border to another.

Once you are through the two customs posts, you will have accumulated a ream of papers (temporary import permit, insurance chit etc), which you should retain at all times, since you'll be asked to show them at every roadblock, along with a valid driver's licence (an international driver's licence is a good idea, since most officials cannot read English).

Readers who are driving into Mozambique should carry the obvious spares (fan-belt, second spare tyre and rim) as they may be difficult to get hold of in the country. They should also carry a hazard triangle (the absence of one of these is a favoured pretext for extracting bribes from drivers) and ensure that seatbelts on the driver's and passengers' seats are working properly (see the section on *Driving in Mozambique* in *Chapter Four* for further advice).

MONEY MATTERS

Organising your finances

From the security point of view, it's advisable to bring the bulk of your money in the form of travellers cheques, as these can be refunded if they are lost or stolen. The most widely recognised currency countrywide is the US dollar, though South African rands are more popular south of Vilankulo, and Zimbabwe dollars are practically hard currency along the Beira and Tete corridors. Other internationally recognised currencies will be accepted in major cities, but they may cause some confusion at banks in smaller centres, and rands and Zimbabwe dollars are pretty useless north of Beira.

All visitors are advised to bring a small amount of money in cash (say around US$200), preferably in small denominations, in case there is a need to change money on the street when banks are closed. An argument for bringing a greater amount of cash is that it will fetch a much better exchange rate, up to 10% higher than travellers cheques. Personally, I think it somewhat foolhardy to bring the bulk of your money in a format that cannot be refunded if it is stolen, but the choice is yours. If you want to take advantage of the better rate for cash, you should be aware that only US dollars and (in the south) South African rands are widely accepted, and that US$100 bills and any bills issued before 1992 may be refused on the basis that they could be forgeries.

No matter how long you are travelling in Mozambique (or elsewhere in Africa except South Africa) make sure that you bring enough money with you so that you won't need to have any more transferred or drafted across. This is a notoriously tedious process and there is a real risk the money will never arrive. Even if it does arrive safely, you will battle to have it given to you in hard currency.

   Credit cards are accepted by some tourist class hotels and in many shops
and restaurants in the capital. You can also draw a limited amount of cash
against an internationally recognised credit card in the main branches of
banks in Maputo and Beira. Outside of major cities, credit cards are near to
useless.

Carrying money and valuables

It is advisable to carry all your hard currency as well as your passport and
other important documentation in a money belt. The ideal money belt for
Africa is one that can be hidden beneath your clothing. Externally worn
moneybelts may be fashionable, but wearing one in Africa is as good as
telling thieves that all your valuables are there for the taking. Use a money
belt made of cotton or another natural fabric; bear in mind that such fabrics
tend to soak up a lot of sweat, so you will need to wrap plastic around
everything inside the money belt.

Budgeting

Although Mozambique is not an expensive country by Western standards,
visitors should accept that their day-to-day expenses will be considerably
higher than they would be in most other countries in East or southern Africa.
By any standards, Mozambique offers poor value for money – what might
be described as African standards at Western prices. When I travelled in
countries like Malawi or Ethiopia, I had no objection to staying in a basic
African-style lodge for a couple of dollars and then occasionally paying
more for a better room. But in Mozambique I found it difficult not to feel
some resentment at regularly forking out up to US$15 for the sort of dirty,
basic room with smelly communal bucket showers and no lightbulb that
I'd pass over in Ethiopia for a tenth of that price. The same goes for eating
out: we regularly paid the sort of sum that would buy you a good steak or
two large pizzas in a South African restaurant for a plate of chicken or fish
and chips that could most kindly be described as ordinary.

   With Mozambique as elsewhere, any budget will depend greatly on how
and where you travel, but the following guidelines might be useful to people
trying to keep costs to a minimum. If you travel widely in Mozambique, it
will be difficult to keep your basic travel expenses (food, transport,
accommodation and drink) to much below US$20 per day for one person
or US$30 per day for a couple. Your main expense will probably be
accommodation: in many towns, you'll be lucky to get away with less than
US$15 for a double room, and there are plenty of places where even camping
costs around US$5 per person. A meal in a restaurant will typically cost
between US$4 and US$6 per head, though you can save considerably by
putting together your own food or eating at market stalls. Transport costs
will probably work out at around US$3–4 daily, assuming that you're on
the move every other day or thereabouts. Drinks are reasonably priced in

parts of the country south of the Zambezi, but they are very expensive in the four northeastern provinces – in somewhere like Pemba or Nampula, a can of soda often costs more than US$1 and a beer around US$1.50.

This said, budget travellers can travel more cheaply if they carry a tent, are selective about where they visit, and stay put in cheaper places for a few days. In the south, Vilankulo has good backpacker facilities that make it much cheaper than the other beach resorts – a full week at Vilankulo needn't work out at more than around US$50 per person.

Further currency information is given in *Chapter Four.*

WHAT TO TAKE

Luggage

If you intend using public transport or to hike, you will want to carry your luggage on your back. There are three ways of doing this: with a purpose-made backpack, with a suitcase that converts to a rucksack, or with a large daypack.

The choice between a convertible suitcase or a purpose-built backpack rests mainly on your style of travel. If you intend doing a lot of hiking, you're definitely best off with a proper backpack. If, on the other hand, you'll be doing things where it might be a good idea to shake off the sometimes negative image attached to backpackers, there are obvious advantages in being able to convert your backpack to a conventional suitcase. Otherwise, it doesn't really matter much which you use.

After having undertaken several backpacking trips in Africa, my own preference is for a large daypack. The advantages of keeping your luggage as light and compact as possible are manifold. For starters, you can rest it on your lap on buses, thus avoiding complications, such as extra charges for luggage, arguments about where your bag should be stored, and the slight but real risk of theft if your luggage ends up on the roof. A compact bag also makes for greater mobility, whether you're hiking or looking for a hotel in town.

The sacrifice you need to make in order to use a daypack is not to carry camping equipment and a sleeping bag. This will affect your budget, as camping can save you a fair amount of money over an extended stay in Mozambique, but there are few instances where you really *need* camping equipment. For non-camping purposes, a light sheet sleeping bag is almost as useful as the real thing (a sheet sleeping-bag still performs the important role of enclosing and insulating your body; it is only in really cold conditions that it will fail you – and there you can cover up with extra clothing). During my last few African trips, I've managed to fit everything I truly need as well as a few luxuries in a 35cl daypack weighing around 8kg. And, having made the conversion from a bulkier, heavier rucksack, I can only recommend it to other travellers.

Clothing

If you're carrying your luggage on your back, you'll want to restrict your clothes to the minimum. In my opinion, this is one or two pairs of trousers and/or skirts, and one pair of shorts; three shirts or T-shirts; at least one sweater (or similar) depending on when you are visiting the country and where you intend to go; enough socks and underwear to last five to seven days; and one or two pairs of shoes.

Trousers: Jeans are less than ideal for African travel. They are bulky and heavy to carry, hot to wear, and they take ages to dry. Far better to bring light cotton trousers. If you intend spending a while in montane regions, instead of bringing a second pair of trousers, you might prefer to carry tracksuit bottoms. These can serve as thermal underwear and as extra cover on chilly nights, and they can also be worn over shorts on chilly mornings.

Skirts: Like trousers, these are best made of a light natural fabric such as cotton. For reasons of protocol, it is advisable to wear skirts that go below the knee: short skirts will cause needless offence to many Mozambicans (especially Muslims) and, whether you like it or not, they may be perceived as provocative in some quarters.

Shirts: T-shirts may be better than button-up shirts, because they are lighter and less bulky. However, I've found that the top pocket of a shirt (particularly if the pocket buttons up) is a good place to carry my spending money in markets and bus stations, as it's easier to keep an eye on than trouser pockets.

Sweaters: Mozambique is generally warm at night, though at higher altitudes it can cool down in the evening. For general purposes, one warm sweater or sweatshirt should be adequate. In summer, a light waterproof jacket will be useful .

Socks and underwear: These *must* be made from natural fabrics, and bear in mind that re-using them when sweaty will encourage fungal infections such as athlete's foot, as well as prickly heat in the groin region. Socks and underpants are light and compact enough for it to be worth bringing a week's supply.

Shoes: Unless you're serious about off-road hiking, bulky hiking boots are probably over the top in Mozambique. They're also very heavy, whether they are on your feet or in your pack. A good pair of walking shoes, preferably made of leather and with some ankle support, is a good compromise. It's also useful to carry sandals, thongs or other light shoes.

Camping equipment

There is a strong case for carrying a tent to Mozambique, particularly if you are on a tight budget or have private transport. Campsites exist in most of Mozambique's more popular resorts. Travellers who intend doing a fair bit of off-the-beaten-track hiking or driving will find a tent a useful fallback where no other accommodation exists.

Backpackers who decide to carry camping equipment should look for the lightest available gear. It is now possible to buy a lightweight tent weighing little more than 2kg, but make sure that the one you buy is reasonably mosquito proof. Usable sleeping-bags weighing even less than 2kg can be bought, but, especially as many lightweight sleeping-bags are not particularly warm, my own preference is for a sheet sleeping-bag, supplemented by wearing heavy clothes in cold weather. Also essential is a roll-mat, which will serve as both insulation and padding.

Cooking utensils

In Mozambique, there is no real need for backpackers to carry a stove, since firewood is available at most campsites where meals cannot be bought. If you do carry a stove, it's worth knowing that Camping Gaz cylinders are not readily available, so bring a good supply of spare canisters. If you are camping in the rainy season, a box of firelighter blocks will help get a fire going in the most unpromising conditions. It would also be advisable to carry a pot, plate, cup and cutlery – lightweight cooking utensils are available at most camping shops in Western countries.

People who are driving into Mozambique are obviously in a position to carry far more equipment than people using public transport. Recommended cooking accessories are a grid and tongs for barbecues, a gas cooker and an adequate supply of canisters, a water container and pots, foil for baking potatoes and a selection of spices. A less obvious luxury which you'll probably be glad of is a device for squeezing citrus fruit; oranges and tangerines are available cheaply everywhere in Mozambique and fresh fruit juice is a welcome respite from fizzy drinks. If you don't like instant coffee, take some device for making fresh coffee (detaching the filter from a percolator is good enough) as well as a stock of ground coffee.

Photography

For photographs of people and scenery, an ordinary 50mm lens or – better for scenic shots – 28–70mm zoom should be adequate. If you expect to take photographs of animals or birds, a 70–300mm or similar zoom will be more appropriate. Low-speed 50 or 100 ASA films are ideal for most circumstances. You can buy 400 ASA print film in most large towns. If you want to use colour print film of other speeds, or any slide film or black-and-white print film, then bring all that you need with you.

I'm generally uncomfortable about taking photographs of people when I travel. Partly, this is because I've travelled so much in Muslim parts of

East Africa, and partly because I think flashing cameras in any social situation is rude and obtrusive. Another factor is that I get so fed up with being asked to take people's photos, I actually can't be bothered to carry a camera most of the time. However, nothing in our experience suggested that there is any cause to be edgy about taking photographs of people in Mozambique – on the contrary, the majority of Mozambicans go completely crazy in the nicest possible way when there's a camera around, and a flash can cause something close to mass hysteria. Nevertheless, some people definitely don't like to be photographed, and it would be very rude not to ask permission before you start snapping away, particularly in Muslim areas.

In markets and similar places, you may well find that people are initially reluctant to let you photograph them, but that as soon as one person agrees to be photographed then everybody else wants a bit of the action. Couples travelling together should take note that Mozambican women are less likely to object to being photographed by another woman than by a man.

Other useful items

Binoculars are essential for getting a good look at animals, especially birds. Compact binoculars have a crisper image than the traditional variety, they are much more backpack-friendly, and these days you can find adequate brands that are not significantly more expensive than traditional binoculars. The one drawback of compact binoculars is their restricted field of vision, which can make it difficult to pick up birds in thick bush. For most purposes, 7x35 traditional binoculars or 7x21 compact binoculars are fine, but bird-watchers will find a 10x magnification more useful.

If you are thinking of doing much snorkelling in Mozambique, it is certainly worth bringing your own equipment – not only because it will save you money in the long run, but also because snorkelling equipment is only available for hire at a handful of resorts.

If you stay in local hotels, it is best to carry your own padlock – many places don't supply them. You should also carry a towel, soap, shampoo, and any other toiletries you need.

People who wear contact lenses should be aware that the various fluids are not readily available in Mozambique. Bring enough to last the whole trip. Many people find the intense sun and dry climate in some African countries irritates their eyes, though this might not apply so much to Mozambique, which is generally moist and humid. Nevertheless, you could also think about reverting to glasses for the duration of your trip, if only because carrying contact lens fluids will add considerable weight and bulk to your luggage.

Toilet paper is widely available and cheap, but many communal toilets don't have any (including some in upper-range hotels). Always carry a spare roll with you.

Sanitary towels are available in most large towns, but it is advisable to carry some spares. Tampons are imported and available in cities only.

English-language reading material of any description is difficult to get hold of. Books are also very expensive, and there are few second-hand book stalls around. Bring a good stock with you – and, if you're remotely interested in what's happening in the world, you might also think about carrying a short-wave radio, as the only newspapers are Portuguese.

A torch is useful if you are camping or staying in towns where there is no electricity, and a travel alarm clock is absolutely essential for catching early morning buses.

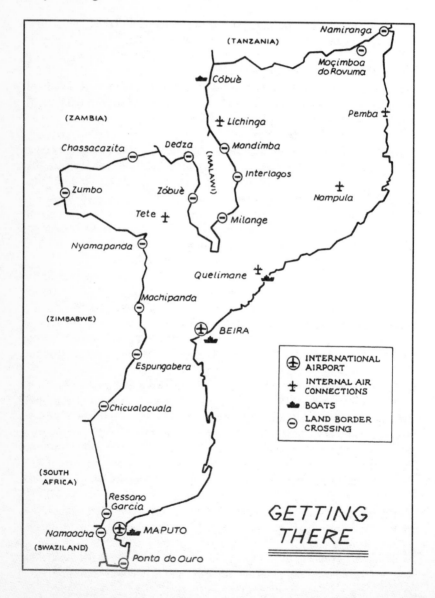

GETTING THERE

Chapter Three

Getting to Mozambique

This chapter discusses the various ways of getting to Mozambique, a subject that warrants its own chapter for a number of reasons. The first is quite simply that Mozambique's size and unusual shape mean there are an abnormally large number of different border crossings into the country. The second is that many of these crossings are rather difficult on public transport, and the section on the crossing from Tanzania in particular needs to include a fair amount of detail on that country. The third is to highlight the reality that northern and southern Mozambique are in some respects best treated as different countries. It may not be obvious from looking at a map, but crucial to planning any trip to Mozambique is the realisation that the provinces of Niassa, Cabo Delgado and Nampula form a discrete travel unit, one that is separated from the provinces Tete and Sofala by the poorly maintained 1,000km of road that connects Beira to Nampula via Zambézia Province and its capital city Quelimane.

BY AIR

Mozambique has two international airports, Maputo and Beira. The main international airport is the one in Maputo. Flights to Mozambique are operated by the Portuguese airline TAP from Lisbon via Madrid, and Mozambique's own airline LAM from Lisbon and Paris. LAM has daily flights from Johannesburg (except on Saturday) and several times a week from Manzini (Swaziland), Harare (Zimbabwe) and Lilongwe (Malawi). South African Airways (SAA) serves Maputo daily from Johannesburg, and the private charter flight company Metavia flies to Maputo twice a day from Johannesburg as well as from Nelspruit in the eastern Transvaal. Lesotho Airlines flies weekly from Maseru, Royal Swazi Airlines several times a week from Manzini. The Angolan airline connects Luanda to Maputo and the Brazilian airline VARIG serves the Rio route. Air Malawi has a service from Blantyre to Beira.

Maputo Mavalane airport (code MPM) is 8km from the city. There is no airport bus, but there are irregular city buses and few taxis. Beira airport (code BEW) is 13km outside the city. There is no airport bus and taxis only appear if they are bringing customers to the airport.

An airport tax of US$20 is payable in hard currency on flying out of the country. A tax of US$5 is charged for local flights – at some airports they will insist you pay this in hard currency, at others not.

Airlines

LAM (Linhas Areas de Mozambique)
Maputo: Av 25 de Setembro 1757. Tel: (258 1)46510/9 or 423355 (reservations). Telex: 6 386 MO, 6-331 MO. Fax: (258 1) 465568/465134.

Portugal: Rua Joaquim Antonio de Aguiar 69 r/c, 1000 Lisbon. Tel: 656118/9/659027. Telex: 16713 LAM LISBOA.

South Africa 1203 Kine Centre Building, Corner Commissioner & Kruis Sts. Tel: (011) 331 6082.

Swaziland Corner Tin & Walker Sts, Dhlan Obeka House, Mbabane. Tel: 45411.

SAA (South African Airways) Praça 25 de Junho. Tel: 420733.

TAP Avenida 25 de Setembro. Tel: 733714.

Metavia Maputo: Tel: 465074 ext 237; Nelspruit, Tel: 43141; South Africa:Telex: 335234SA; Air Lesotho, Swazi Royal Airways and VARIG can be booked through LAM.

In Europe, the best place to find cheap tickets to Africa is London. Due to the limited number of operators flying to Mozambique, you may well find that it's cheaper to fly to Johannesburg in South Africa or Harare in Zimbabwe, especially if you intend to visit Mozambique as part of an extended African trip. Two London travel agents specialise in Africa: African Travel Systems (6 North End Parade, North End Road, London W14 0SJ, tel: 0171 602 5091) and Africa Travel Centre (4 Medway Court, Leigh Street, London WC1H 9OX, tel: 0171 387 1211, fax: 0171 383 7512). Trailfinders (42–48 Earls Court Road, London W8 6EJ, tel: 0171 938 3366) and STA (117 Euston Road, London WC1, tel: 0171 465 0486, fax: 0171 388 0944) are both respected agents who do cheap flights world-wide, and particularly worth speaking to for round-the-world type tickets. There are STA branches in Bristol, Cambridge, Oxford and Manchester.

Provided that you have a valid passport and visa, and a return ticket, you should whiz through the entrance formalities at the airport with a minimum of fuss. The only reason why a fly-in visitor would be likely to arrive in Mozambique without a return ticket is because of an intention to travel more widely in Africa, an unlikely scenario given that it's far cheaper to fly to Nairobi, Harare or Johannesburg and start an extended African trip from one of these cities. Nevertheless, if for some reason you will be arriving with a one-way ticket, there is a small but real possibility that you will be given a rough time by immigration officials. Basically, what they will be concerned about is that you won't have enough funds to buy a flight out of the country. Obviously, the more money you have, the less likely they are to query your finances. And a credit card will almost certainly convince them to let you in. Assuming that you do intend to travel to neighbouring countries, you can underline this intention by arranging a visa or visitor's pass for the next country you plan to visit *before* you land in Mozambique.

The very worst that can happen if you arrive without a return ticket is that you will have to buy a ticket back to your home country before being allowed entry. Assuming you intend to leave overland, it is important you check with the relevant airline that this ticket will be refundable, and also that you select a departure date that will give you time to get to a country where you can organise the refund.

When you fly out of Mozambique, an airport tax of US$20 must be paid in hard currency (preferably US dollars or South African rands).

ARRIVING OVERLAND

Provided that you arrive at the border with a visa, you should have no problem entering Mozambique overland, nor is there a serious likelihood of being asked about onward tickets, funds or vaccination certificates. About the worst you can expect at customs is a cursory search of your luggage.

At most overland borders there is nowhere to change money legally, which means that you may have to do so with a private individual. Although this is not strictly legal, it is perfectly open at most borders and it appears to be tolerated by immigration and customs officials alike – though obviously it would be wise to be discreet in the presence of officialdom. Generally, the rates you get at borders are lower than they would be elsewhere. This is because the people who change money at borders are not generally in the business of trying to accumulate hard currency. They are simply providing a service to travellers, and they need to make a profit on transactions in both directions. At some borders, there's a lot of hustle attached to changing money privately, and especially along the Beira Corridor there is a real risk of being conned.

One way to get around all this would be to arrange in advance to be carrying money for the country you are entering – ask travellers coming in the opposite direction if they have any left-over cash to swap. If you can't do this, try to carry a small surplus of the currency from the country you are leaving (say around US$20) and to change this at the border rather than using up your hard currency. Whatever else you do, you should try to establish the rough exchange rate in advance and avoid changing significantly more money than you will need to get you through to the next town (or to the next banking day if you cross the border in the afternoon or over a weekend). It is a good idea to keep the money you intend to change separate from the rest of your hard currency and travellers cheques.

Overland routes into southern Mozambique

Southern and central Mozambique can be entered overland from five countries: South Africa, Swaziland, Zimbabwe, Zambia and Malawi. The majority of visitors who enter or leave Mozambique overland do so at the borders with South Africa, Zimbabwe or Malawi, but it is also straightforward to enter Mozambique from Swaziland. The border with Zambia is more remote and little used.

To/from South Africa

The most normal crossing is the Komatipoort/Ressano Garcia border post between Johannesburg and Maputo. It is also possible to enter Mozambique from Swaziland using the Namaacha border. People driving to Maputo from KwaZulu-Natal can enter Mozambique at Ponta do Ouro in the south, though they will need a 4WD if they intend to continue north to Maputo. Backpackers coming from KwaZulu-Natal can use the thrice-weekly bus service between Durban and Maputo via Swaziland.

Johannesburg to Maputo

Komatipoort lies 470km east of Johannesburg, a four to five hour drive along the well-maintained N12 and N4 through Nelspruit. If you want to spend the night in Komatipoort (not a bad idea if the alternative is arriving in Maputo in the late afternoon and absolutely a good idea if the alternative is driving part of the road to Maputo in the dark) there is a municipal campsite and a hotel in the town centre, and a more attractive resort on a dam about 3km out of town (signposted from the Nelspruit road) where you can camp for the rand equivalent of US$10/site or rent a bungalow for the equivalent of US$30/double. The border post lies about 5km out of Komatipoort – it's a simple crossing provided that all your papers are in order – after which it's a 108km drive along a good, recently resurfaced road through to Maputo.

If you are dependent on public transport, you have the choice of trains, buses and minibuses. A train service called the Komati Express runs three times a week between Johannesburg and Maputo, leaving Johannesburg at 17.45 on Tuesdays, Thursdays and Saturdays, and Maputo at 18.00 on Mondays, Wednesdays and Fridays. The journey takes about ten hours, a major advantage of which is that you will arrive at your destination in the morning, giving you plenty of time to find a room. Tickets cost the rand equivalent of about US$30 first class and US$20 second class. Bookings can be made in Johannesburg, tel: (011) 774 4505, fax: (011) 23 0271; in New York toll-free 1800 223 1880, or London, tel: 0171 287 1133.

A company called Panthera Azul runs a regular coach service between Johannesburg and Maputo. Tickets cost roughly US$35 and can be booked through the MNTC in Johannesburg (see Tourist Information) or by contacting Panthera Azul in Johannesburg, tel: (011) 331 7409, fax: (011) 337 7409, or Maputo tel: 49 4238, fax: 74 3315. Coaches leave Johannesburg from the corner of Kerk and Polly Streets at 07.30 Monday to Saturday and at 08.30 and 09.00 on Sunday. There is also an overnight bus on Saturdays leaving Johannesburg at 21.00. In the opposite direction, buses to Johannesburg leave Maputo from in front of the Panthera Azul office on Avenida Mao Tse Tung at 08.00 on Mondays to Fridays and at 09.00 on Saturdays and Sundays. On Sundays and Mondays, a second bus leaves from Maputo at 12.00. The journey takes around ten hours.

Minibuses are cheaper than buses and they leave on a fill-up-and-go basis from the Joubert Park minibus rank in Johannesburg and from the corner of Rua Albert Lithuli and Avenido 25 de Setembro in Maputo. Note that Joubert Park is one of the most risky parts of Johannesburg in terms of mugging and theft.

Hitching between Johannesburg and Maputo is feasible, though finding a lift out of Johannesburg itself is problematic and arguably rather dangerous – best to use public transport at least some of the way. On the Mozambican side of the border, there are minibuses through to Maputo. In the opposite direction, minibuses to the Ressano Garcia border leave Maputo from the same place as minibuses to Johannesburg. Once you're at the border, hitching on to Johannesburg should be easy enough.

Durban to Maputo
The other main crossing between South Africa and Mozambique is at Ponta do Ouro in the far south of Mozambique where it borders KwaZulu-Natal. This is the best border to use if you are coming from Durban and have a private 4WD vehicle. It's not of much use to backpackers, since there is no public transport and hitching would be slow. It is normally possible to get to Ponta do Ouro itself in a saloon car from Durban, but the road between there and Maputo requires a 4WD.

Panthera Azul runs a thrice-weekly bus service between Durban and Maputo. These buses leave Durban at 07.00 on Tuesdays, Fridays and Sundays, and Maputo at 07.30 on Mondays, Thursdays and Saturdays. The trip takes about 12 hours and costs US$45 one-way. Buses out of Durban leave from the main bus station in the city centre. Bookings can be made by ringing Durban 309 7798.

Pafuri
Maps show a road connecting South Africa and Mozambique, passing through Pafuri in the north of the Kruger National Park. It is illegal to use this road as there is no border post, and in any event the road is in horrendous condition.

To/from Swaziland
The Namaacha border post in Swaziland has no advantages over the Komatipoort border, unless you are already in Swaziland. The road from Mbabane (the capital of Swaziland) to Namaacha is in good condition, as

is the road to Maputo except for a potholed stretch of a few kilometres after Namaacha; it's navigable in any vehicle. There are buses from Mbabane to Manzini, from Manzini to Namaacha, and from Namaacha to Maputo. Each leg costs a little more than a dollar and takes up to two hours. Panthera Azul coaches between Durban and Maputo stop at Mbabane.

To/from Zimbabwe
Mutare to Chomoio
The most widely-used border post is the one on the Beira Corridor, 10km east of Mutare in Zimbabwe and about 20km west of Manica township. The 300km road between Mutare and Beira is surfaced and mostly in excellent condition; you should be able to drive it in less than five hours in any motorised vehicle. There are regular buses along this route, and hitching is a possibility. Trains between Mutare and Beira take about 12 to 15 hours and they run in either direction every other day, stopping at Manica and Chimoio. If you thinking of leaving Mutare by road late in the day, bear in mind that there is no accommodation in Manica, though there is a campsite and chalet complex about 20km further towards Beira at the Chicamba Real Dam (see page 152), as well as accommodation in Chimoio another 50km towards Beira.

In a private 4WD, a scenic alternative to the Nyamapanda crossing is the Selinda/Espungabera border post south of the Chimanimani Mountains. So far as I'm aware, there is no public transport along this route, and hitching is unlikely to be a realistic option.

Harare to Tete
It's difficult to see why anybody would want to use the Nyamapanda border post between Harare and Tete unless they were crossing directly to Malawi via the Tete Corridor. If you decide to go this way, it's straightforward enough: any bus between Harare and Blantyre can drop you at Tete, from where there are daily buses to Maputo and Beira via Chimoio.

Chicualacuala
I recently met somebody who had driven between Zimbabwe and Mozambique via the Chicualacuala border post and Zimbabwe's Gonarezhou National Park. I understand that there is no official border post here, and that at present the road is only fit for 4WD vehicles, though there is some talk of upgrading it in the near future. For now, it may be best to avoid it.

To/from Zambia
In practice, it's probably only possible to cross between Zambia and Mozambique if you have private transport, using the Chassacazita border post 290km north of Tete and 53km south of the main Lusaka–Chipata Road. I've never met a traveller who has used this route, but the last time I

was in Zambia (1995) I did talk to a local who had cycled to Petauke from Tete and who claimed there is nothing in the way of public transport along this road. You could, presumably, get through in a 4WD (or on a bicycle!). If you're mad enough to try hitching, any bus heading between Lusaka and Chipata can drop you at Petauke or Katete townships, both of which have basic local lodgings for around US$4/room. I'd be interested to hear from anybody who uses this route.

The other possibility is the border post at Zumbo on the confluence of the Luangwa and Zambezi Rivers. This could be an interesting route, since both Zumbo and the village on the Zambian side of the river were formerly important Portuguese towns, but it would also be rather challenging. There is no vehicle ferry here, as far as I'm aware, and although backpackers could certainly find a boat to take them across the river, there is little transport out of Zumbo. Again, it would be good to hear from anybody daring enough to give it a try.

To/from Malawi

Assuming that you are confining your Mozambican travels to Tete, Beira and points further south, then the best place to cross into Mozambique from Malawi is the Zóbuè border post between Blantyre and Tete. The road from Blantyre and Tete is surfaced and well-maintained. In a private vehicle, you should get through in three to four hours, depending on delays at the border. If you're driving yourself, it's worth bearing in mind that the border becomes completely chaotic during the hour after after the first Blantyre to Harare bus pulls in. Plan your trip so that you arrive at the border before 07.30 or after 09.30.

The easiest way to get from Blantyre to Tete is to use one of the buses which cross daily between Blantyre and Harare via the Tete Corridor. Several such buses leave Blantyre at around 06.00 every morning, arriving in Tete before midday. The only problem with using the buses to Harare is that they aren't licensed to drop off passengers in Mozambique – they'll drop you in Tete, no problem, but they will have to charge you the full fare of roughly US$15 to Harare. The alternative to using a Harare-bound bus is to catch a local bus from Blantyre to the border town of Mwanza, and then to cross into Mozambique on foot. At Zóbuè, the town on the Mozambican side of the border, there are at least two hotels within 100m of the border post. From Zóbuè you could either try to hitch or else board one of the regular passenger trucks to Tete. There are a few resthouses in Mwanza if for some reason you want to spend the night there before crossing into Mozambique.

An alternative route to Zóbuè, more direct if you're driving from Lilongwe as opposed to Blantyre, is via the Dedza border post. The road from Dedza to the Tete Corridor is in fair condition, and any vehicle should make it through except perhaps after heavy rain. There is no public transport along this route, and hitching could be very slow.

Overland routes to northern Mozambique

Northern Mozambique can be approached from two countries: Malawi and Tanzania. It can also be approached from southern Mozambique, along the 1,000km road between Beira and Nampula. The latter trip will take two to three days in a private vehicle. If you are backpacking, it will take at least four days, and you will probably be dependent on getting lifts with trucks (for further details see *Chapter Eleven*), so there is a good case for flying from Beira to one of the towns in the north. There are no international flights into northern Mozambique.

To/from Malawi

There are at least four ways of crossing between Malawi and northern Mozambique: by rail from Liwonde to Cuamba; by road from Mangochi to Mandimba; by road from Mulanje to Milange; or by boat from Likoma Island to Cóbuè. The best route to use depends largely on which parts of Mozambique you intend to visit, bearing in mind that getting around Malawi is much easier and cheaper than getting around Mozambique.

Mangochi to Mandimba

This is the best crossing for motorists, who should be able to manage it in any vehicle with reasonable clearance, except after rain. It is also the most straightforward route in most other circumstances, and even though it is less well-known to backpackers than the rail crossing further south (I've yet to hear of another traveller using it), it is undoubtedly more efficient. To give some idea, we were able to travel the 405km between Lichinga and Blantyre via Mandimba in roughly ten hours using public transport – excellent time anywhere in Africa, and particularly for a trip punctuated by a border crossing and several changes of vehicle. Using this route, you could reasonably expect to get between Cuamba or Lichinga and most parts of southern Malawi between Cape Maclear and Blantyre in a day.

The first step in getting to Mozambique via Mandimba is to get to Mangochi, a medium-sized town on the Shire River roughly 250km north of Blantyre and 70km south of Monkey Bay. Any bus heading between Monkey Bay and Blantyre can drop you at Mangochi. There are also regular minibuses between Blantyre and Mangochi, leaving Blantyre from Limbe bus station and taking about three hours. There are several resthouses to choose from in Mangochi if you want to spend the night there.

Transport to the border leaves Mangochi from the bus station a few hundred metres from the PTC supermarket. If you can't find a vehicle heading all the way, then hop on the next vehicle heading to Namwera, a sizeable town with several resthouses where you can easily pick up another vehicle covering the last 10km to the border post. The road between Mangochi and Namwera is very scenic, crossing a couple of densely wooded hills and with some great views back to Lake Malombe.

After exiting Malawi, it's a good 7km or so to the Mozambican border post at Mandimba. You may be lucky and catch a lift, but more likely you'll have to arrange a bicycle-taxi. The bikes are very uncomfortable and the road is hilly enough that it would speed things up to organise separate bikes to carry yourself and your pack. Once you've crossed into Mozambique, you're no more than 100m from the main Lichinga–Cuamba road, and provided you arrive before around 14.00 you should be able to find transport out of Mandimba in either direction. Alternatively, there's a pleasant little resthouse with double rooms for US$5 and an acceptable restaurant just behind the filling station on the main road through the town.

Liwonde to Cuamba

The most popular crossing with backpackers is the series of train services connecting Liwonde to Cuamba and eventually Nampula. This route involves three different train journeys: one from Liwonde to the Nayuchi border post; another from the border to Cuamba (where you have the option of going north by road or rail to Lichinga); and then the recently opened passenger service from Cuamba to Nampula.

Liwonde, the starting point for this trip, is a small town with several resthouses lying about 1km off the main road between Blantyre and Monkey Bay. Any bus covering this route can drop you at the turn-off. Trains to the Nayuchi border leave Liwonde at 08.00 on Monday and Thursday, and arrive at the border about three hours later. From the Malawian border post, it's about 20 minutes' walk to its Mozambican counterpart – just follow the crowd. It's easy to change excess kwachas into meticais with people coming in the opposite direction, and you'll get a much better rate than you will from professional money-changers.

On the Mozambican side of the border, there is a basic restaurant and a small pensão in the small town of Interlagos (positioned exactly halfway between Lakes Chilwa and Chiuta). However, if all goes to plan, you should be able to pick up a train to Cuamba on the day you arrive – the services are scheduled to connect with each other. The train journey from Interlagos to Cuamba should take around four hours, though on a bad day it might take as long as eight hours. Coming in the opposite direction, trains from Cuamba to Interlagos also leave on Mondays and Thursdays, in theory connecting with the return train from Nayuchi to Liwonde on the same days. From Cuamba, there is a daily passenger train to Nampula, and a daily bus north to Lichinga (see *Chapter Twelve*).

Likoma to Cóbuè

Currently a rather obscure option, the crossing between Likoma Island and Cóbuè on the shores of Lake Malawi (Niassa) may well become increasingly popular if plans to introduce a visa service at Cobúe materialise.

Likoma Island is a part of Malawi entirely enclosed by Mozambican waters. Lake ferries run between most major ports on the Malawian side of the lake and Likoma, and there are several places to stay on the island.

From Likoma, fishing dhows operate as a ferry service to Cóbuè, taking roughly one hour to cover the 10km stretch of water. At Cóbuè, the Australian run Hotel Santo Miguel has clean rooms for US$10 and facilities for camping.

At present, anybody can visit Cóbuè as an overnight trip from Likoma. No visa is required for a stay of 24 hours or less, but you do need a visa for a longer stay, or if you plan to travel further into Mozambique. It's worth noting that the immigration officer at Lichinga has tentatively agreed with the owner of the Hotel Santa Miguel to allow visas to be issued at Cóbuè. That said, I would strongly suggest that you get independent confirmation of this before rushing all the way to Cóbuè without a visa – if this plan doesn't go ahead, it would mean retracing your steps to Lilongwe or Blantyre to get a visa.

From Cóbuè, it's possible to get to Metangula by truck or by boat. From Metangula there is regular transport through to Lichinga, the provincial capital of Niassa.

Mulanje to Mocuba

This is the most southerly border crossing between Malawi and northern Mozambique, and it is only worth thinking about if you're determined to visit Quelimane. The Muloza/Milange border post connects Blantyre and Mulanje in Malawi to Mocuba and Quelimane in Mozambique. A fair 120km tar road connects Blantyre to Mulanje town and the border post. The 190km road from the border to Mocuba is rocky and sandy in stretches, but provided that you drive carefully and it hasn't rained recently even an ordinary saloon car should make it through. The road from Mocuba south to Quelimane is better – pristine tar for 46km to Malei, then firm dirt for 33km to Namacurra, and finally 66km of potholed tar to Quelimane. If you are travelling in the opposite direction, note that the turn off to Milange at Mocuba isn't signposted.

If you're doing the same route on public transport, there are plenty of buses from Blantyre to Mulanje town, about 20km before the border. The trip takes three to four hours, depending on whether you catch an express bus or a stopping bus. Some buses to Mulanje continue on to the border, but if you arrive in Mulanje late in the day, you're advised to stay put for the night and to continue travelling on the following day. The Council Rest House opposite Mulanje market has clean rooms for less than US$2 and the Mulanje View Hotel on the main road to Blantyre has motel-style rooms for around US$5. At Milange town, immediately after crossing into Mozambique, the Pensão Esplanada is relatively poor value, as it charges US$7 for an indifferent single.

Getting between Milange and Mocuba may prove problematic. Until recently there was no public transport along this road, and hitching was unpredictable – a correspondent writing in 1995 waited at Mocuba for three days hoping to find a lift to Milange. However, in late 1996 I met a traveller who had found a *chapa* (a truck customised to carry passengers) heading from Milange and Mocuba, so it would appear that the situation has improved of late. What you most certainly don't want to do is take a lift unless it's going the whole way to Mocuba, as there is no accommodation along the way. Once at Mocuba, there are two pensãos and regular trucks heading towards Quelimane or Nampula.

To/from Tanzania

The overland trip from Dar es Salaam, the Tanzanian capital, to northern Mozambique is one of the most interesting and exhausting in this part of Africa. The town you want to head for is Mtwara, which lies about 30km north of the Rovuma River on the border with Mozambique, and there are three ways of getting there: by boat from Dar es Salaam, by road from Dar es Salaam, or by road from Mbeya. More extensive coverage of this area is included in my *Guide to Tanzania* (Bradt Publications, second edition 1996), from which the following brief notes are drawn.

Getting to Mtwara

The easiest way to travel between Dar es Salaam and Mtwara is by boat. The vessel which covers this route most regularly is the *Canadian Spirit*, which runs to a rather whimsical schedule. In late 1992, it did the trip every other Thursday, stopping only at Mafia. Between 1992 and 1996, I heard all manner of odd rumours about its activities (the owners had gone bankrupt, the boat itself was no longer seaworthy, it was plying between Dar es Salaam, Kenya and Somalia). In 1996, it was back doing the Mtwara run every Wednesday, stopping at Mafia and Lindi on route. The only advice I can give is to ask around at the jetty in Dar es Salaam or Mtwara to ascertain what the current situation is – the one certainty is that the schedule will change from time to time.

Assuming that the *Canadian Spirit* is running, the trip takes roughly 24 hours. It is a well maintained boat with an immaculate first class lounge (though as the lounge is placed at the back of the boat and the weather can get very rough, second class may prove to be more comfortable). First class to Mtwara costs around US$15 and second class US$10, in addition to which you must pay the usual US$5 port tax in hard currency. The only other passenger boat which runs between Dar es Salaam and Mtwara is the *Mnependazi*, which is cheaper and I'm told more pleasant, but only does the trip once a month.

The best reason for bussing between Dar es Salaam and Mtwara is simply that it will allow you to explore what is undoubtedly the highlight of Tanzania's southern coast, the ruined city of Kilwa Kisiwani. Lying on an island about 2km offshore, Kilwa was the focus of the Swahili Coast's gold trade prior to the arrival of the Portuguese in 1500, and the ruined city includes some beautiful mosques, a house with a swimming pool and sunken audience court, as well as a fort dating to the Portuguese area.

Except during the rainy season, when the roads along the south coast are often impassable, buses run every day between Kariakoo Market in Dar es Salaam and Kilwa Masoko, the mainland settlement opposite the island – a rough trip taking about 12 to 15 hours. You could also catch a bus heading to Lindi or Mtwara (these leave Dar es Salaam from the more central Morogoro Road bus station) and ask to be deposited at the junction town of Nangurukuru, from where there are regular pick-up trucks to Kilwa Masoko, taking about 20 minutes. Once in Kilwa Masoko, there are at least three inexpensive local guest houses to choose from (Mjaka Enterprises is probably the best, with single rooms with a net and fan for around US$3), and it's easy to organise a fishing dhow to take you across to Kilwa Kisiwani for the day. Also worth a look is Kilwa Kivinje, a fascinating small town which served as the terminus of the Lake Malawi slave caravan route for much of the 19th century. Pick-up trucks run back and forth between Kilwa Masoko and Kilwa Kivinje throughout the day, taking about half an hour in either direction.

When you're ready to head south from Kilwa Masoko, catch an early morning pick-up truck to Nangurukuru to wait for transport coming from Dar es Salaam. The next main town is Lindi, an agreeable if rather run-down place situated on a beautiful bay. If you want to overnight in Lindi, I can recommend the Town and South Honour Guest Houses, though if you arrive early enough in the day, you could head directly to Mtwara – the two towns are connected by a good tar road, and buses take no longer than three hours.

The other road route to Mtwara is from Mbeya near the Zambian border. This is a really rough trip, which can take several days. There are regular buses along a good tar road from Mtwara to Njombe and from Njombe to Songea, with each leg taking around five hours. In Njombe, the Lutheran Centre Hostel has clean and inexpensive dormitory accommodation, and the Milimani Hotel has comfortable self-contained doubles, with nets and hot showers, for well under US$10. In Songea, the OK Hotel has reasonably priced self-contained doubles and a good restaurant, and there are several cheaper guest houses, of which the Deluxe and New Star stand out. There are no buses along the appalling 370km road that connects Songea to Masasi. A lift on a truck costs US$12 and a lift in a 4WD costs US$20. The journey normally takes two days, with an overnight stop at Tunduru where you can find a basic room for US$6. Once at Masasi, the principal town on the Makonde Plateau, there are regular buses on a good tar road to Mtwara. If you need to spend the night in Masasi, there are several guest houses on the road between the bus station and the Masasi Hotel. The Masasi Hotel itself used to be very good value (a large self-contained room with nets and fans cost less than US$4 in 1993) but I've heard no recent reports.

Mtwara itself is something of a let-down – a rather bland, sprawling port built to service a post-war Groundnut Scheme which never got off the ground. There are quite a few basic lodgings dotted around town – the

Kisutu Guest House next to the market and bus station is as good as any and reasonably priced at US$3 for a single with net and fans. On the beach, about half an hour's walk from the town centre, the CATA club offers a higher standard of accommodation at affordable prices. More interesting than Mtwara is Mikindani, sprawled along the main road 10km back towards Lindi, which is where Livingstone started his final journey into the African interior.

Mtwara to Palma

When you are ready to leave Tanzania, you have three options: to cross directly overland via Mwambo, to catch an ocean-going dhow between Msimbati and Palma, or to use the very obscure Moçimboa do Rovumu border between Masasi and Mueda.

If you want to use the direct overland route, the first thing you must do is catch a Landrover to Mwambo and visit the immigration office to get an exit stamp. From Mwambo, you'll probably have to walk the 5km to a village on the north bank of the Rovumu River where you can pick up a dugout canoe into Mozambique. Once across the river, it's about 2km to the immigration office at Namiranga, from where you may be lucky and get a lift through to Palma, the next town, but far more likely you'll have to walk. The problem with this is that it's roughly 50km to Palma, perhaps 10km less if you can find somebody who'll show you the shortcut.

The best of the three options is to catch a fishing dhow from Tanzania directly to Palma or Moçimboa da Praia. The important thing to know if you are doing this is that the dhows don't leave from Mtwara itself, but from a nearby village called Msimbati. There are buses between Mtwara and Msimbati, and there is an immigration office once you're there. The dhows are private fishing boats: they leave when the weather and tides are right, and fares are negotiable (around US$6–7 per person feels about right). It's worth asking the immigration officer if he can help you find a dhow heading south. The trip shouldn't take more than ten hours, depending on the weather and where the boat is heading to. Bear in mind that the dhow will probably be heading to where the sailors live; if you are lucky, you'll be dropped right at Palma or Moçimboa da Praia, but you may also be dropped at a village on a beach about three hours walk from Palma – a tricky route, for which you'll need to adopt a local as a guide. You can complete your entry formalities at Palma. If you are heading in the opposite direction, things are much simpler, insofar as you can pick up a dhow at either Palma or Moçimboa da Praia, and you'll almost certainly be dropped at Msimbati.

The route between Masasi and Mueda is definitely for the adventurous only, with the compensation that this must be among the most remote roads anywhere in East Africa, and it passes through some wildly beautiful scenery. The easiest bit of this trip is to get to Newala, a small Makonde town that lies 40km from the border. Buses run to Newala daily, both from

Masasi and from Mtwara, and there are a couple of adequate resthouses when you arrive. From Newala, expect to walk the 40km to the border post (the road is impassable other than on foot or bicycle), where a dugout canoe will take you across the river to Moçimboa do Rovumu. There's not a great deal of transport along the 90km road between Moçimboa do Rovuma and Mueda – I have a secondhand report of volunteer who claimed, quite plausibly, to be the first European to cross this way in more than two years, and who waited two days for a tractor ride.

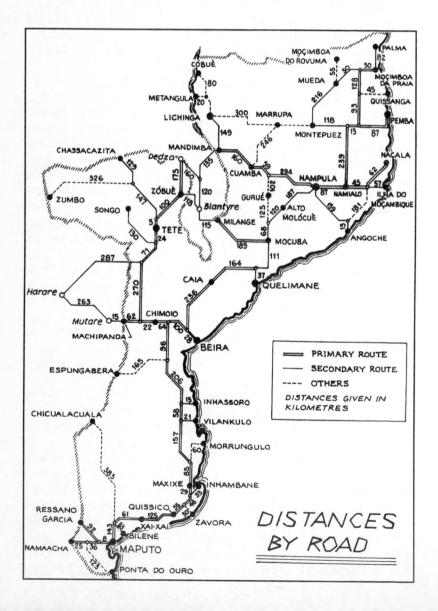

DISTANCES BY ROAD

Chapter Four

Travelling in Mozambique

GETTING AROUND

Driving in Mozambique

Many of Mozambique's major roads were heavily mined during the civil war. Roads throughout the country are gradually being upgraded, and it seems probable that the entire main road from north to south will be surfaced within the next few years. As things stand, the only roads that are easily navigable in any saloon car are those connecting Komatipoort to Maputo, Maputo to Inhassoro, Beira to Chimoio and the Zimbabwe border, Chimoio to Tete, Tete to the Malawi and Zimbabwe borders, and Nampula to Nacala and Pemba.

The road between Inhassoro and Beira is passable in a saloon car provided that you go very slowly, your vehicle has good clearance, and it hasn't rained for a while. Elsewhere in the country, a 4WD is practically essential. Bear in mind even where roads are in good condition, you will generally need to use rougher roads to get to them (for instance, you could drive from Pemba to Nampula in a saloon car, but neither town is linked to anywhere else by a surfaced road) .

The main hazard to your vehicle on Mozambican roads comes from potholes. You are advised to keep your eyes glued to the road ahead and to slow down for oncoming traffic, since a vehicle passing in the opposite direction will impede your ability to manoeuvre around an unexpected pothole. If you are driving in a vehicle with an unprotected sump, it is probably worth carrying a spare one. It's also a sensible precaution to carry an extra spare tyre and rim (you can pick up spares like this cheaply at a scrapyard in South Africa). Livestock and pedestrians frequently wander into the middle of the road, and motorists tend to be more reckless than in Europe, so drive more defensively than you would at home. Driving at night is inadvisable, partly for security reasons, but also because the general chaos on the road is exacerbated by vehicles lacking headlights.

Frequent roadblocks are part and parcel of driving in Mozambique. You can expect to be stopped at most roadblocks, and to be asked to produce your driving licence, vehicle registration and temporary import papers.

You may also be required to show that you have traffic triangles stashed away somewhere in the vehicle, and you could be in for a heated discussion if you're not wearing a seatbelt. Otherwise, contrary to all the horror stories about officiousness that we heard in advance, we were never detained for longer than a couple of minutes at a roadblock, and we were never treated with anything less than courtesy or asked to pay a fine or bribe, even on the two occasions when we were stopped for a genuine offence (driving in a one-way street and not wearing a seatbelt).

Good maps are hard to come by and those generated from aerial photographs can be downright misleading – a lot of the old Portuguese routes and structures are no longer used, but still show up as stripes on these pictures rather better than do the more organic African tracks and settlements. Also, the massive movements of people during and since the war have led to places marked on maps being not much more than memories and settlements of a few thousand people not being recorded at all. Particularly in off-the-beaten-track areas, believe the roads you can see and believe the tyre tracks, navigate with your eyes looking through the windscreen and not with your head buried in some chart!

Land mines still pose a threat to anybody who wants to indulge in some off-road driving, so stick to the track. For ecological reasons, drivers are strongly urged against driving along dunes and beaches.

Petrol costs roughly the same in Mozambique as it does in South Africa, around US$0.50 per litre.

Public transport
Rail
There are a number of rail services in Mozambique, most of which are only infrequently used by travellers. In the south, the service between Maputo and Johannesburg in South Africa is efficient and well-maintained, whereas the one-class service between Beira and Mutare in Zimbabwe is slow and the train is very scruffy. In the north, there is now a daily service connecting Nampula to Cuamba, and a twice-weekly service connecting Cuamba to Liwonde in Malawi.

Road
Reasonably reliable bus services connect Maputo, Beira, Chimoio, Tete and points in between. The recommended lines for long-hauls between these towns are Oliveira's's and Virginia, but there are also several local bus companies which connect the various towns between Maputo and Beira. The Mozambican word for bus is *machimbombo*.

Just about anywhere in Mozambique can be reached on a chapa. This term is the Mozambican equivalent of the East African *matatu*, and it is evidently applied to just about any vehicle apart from a bus that will carry passengers, be it an open truck or pick-up truck or minibus. The most common type of chapa is a large truck with caged sides, a canvas or plastic

MAPUTO

Above: *City centre with the cathedral in the foreground*

Below: *Close up of Samora Machel from a street mural near the airport*

Makonde face mask, Nampula

Makua girl with white face mask, Pemba

CRAFTSMEN AT WORK

Above: *Makonde carver, Nampula*

Below: *A young tailor operates his sewing machine.*

'roof', and inward-facing benches around the sides. In the south, the only instance where you regularly need to use chapas is along the short roads connecting places like Bilene and Inhambane to the EN1 between Maputo and Beira.

Chapas are a more important form of transport in the northeastern provinces of Zambézia, Nampula, Niassa and Cabo Delgado, where there are fewer buses. The main bus company in this region, Transnorte, covers the roads connecting Pemba, Nacala and Nampula, as well as the road between Cuamba and Lichinga. There is also a bus service between Nampula and Quelimane. Elsewhere, you'll be dependent on chapas and trucks.

On most routes through the north, the bulk of public transport leaves at 05.00. Travellers coming from elsewhere in Africa will be used to being told that buses leave at 05.00, only to arrive at the bus station and find that they have to sit around for an hour or two before anything actually leaves. Things work differently in Mozambique: when people tell you that buses or chapas leave at 05.00, there's every chance that they'll all have gone if you aren't in position a good 10 to 15 minutes earlier.

Getting around Mozambique is complicated by the fact that few places have central bus or chapa stations. Instead, there is an informally agreed departure point for vehicles going in any given direction, frequently along the road a good 20 minute walk from the town centre. What this means is that you generally need to be out of your hotel room at least half an hour before the time you're told that transport leaves. If you're not a morning person, you can alleviate this somewhat stressful scenario by locating the right spot to wait for transport on the afternoon before you travel.

Hitching is a viable option south of Vilankulo, where there is a fair amount of private transport, and on the roads between Tete, Chimoio and Beira. It is generally slower in northern Mozambique. Bear in mind that the line between hitching and public transport is rather blurred in Mozambique as elsewhere in Africa: most truck drivers will informally carry passengers for the same fee as charged by buses and chapas, and so you should expect to pay for any lift offered to you by a Mozambican.

Boat

There are regular ferries between Maputo and Catembe, and Maputo and Inhaca Island. Boats must also be used to get to the island of Ibo, and to get between Vilankulo or Inhassoro and the Bazaruto Islands. In the north, private fishing dhows connect most ports north of Angoche, where they are an option to travelling by road.

Air

LAM run regular internal flights between the major centres such as Maputo, Beira, Quelimane, Tete, Nampula, Lichinga and Pemba. Flights are relatively expensive – for instance, around US$100 one-way between Quelimane and Beira – but they are certainly worth thinking about as an alternative to

road transport between the north and south (the overland trip between Beira
and Nampula can take up to a week on the back of trucks, during which time
you'd probably spend almost as much money as you would if you flew).

MONEY

The unit of currency is the Metical (MT), plural Meticais. In late 1996, the
rate of exchange was between US$1 = 11,000 MT and US$1 = 12,500 MT,
depending on where changed and whether cash or travellers cheques.
Meticais come in bills of various denominations, ranging from 500 MT to
100,000 MT.

Foreign exchange

Foreign currency can be changed into meticais at most banks as well as at
private Bureaux de Change (cambrios) in cities. The two main commercial
banks to be found in the country are the Banco Commercial do Mozambique
(BCM) and Standard Bank. There are BCM branches in most towns of
reasonable size, and branches of the Standard Bank can be found in Maputo,
Beira, Tete, Nampula and Pemba. Private cambrios exist in Maputo, Beira
and Nampula. Banking hours are from 08.00 to 11.00, while cambrios
generally keep normal shopping hours.

Assuming that you're taking a mixture of travellers cheques and cash,
it's worth giving some advance thought to where and how you will change
your money. Generally speaking you'll get the best rate for cash at private
cambrios (at the time of writing somewhere around US$1 = 11,600 is the
typical rate). The only cambrios I'm aware of that accept travellers cheques
are the one in Nampula and the one at the Polana Hotel in Maputo. The
former is exceptionally good value, as it charges less than 1% commission
on travellers cheques, and the one in the Polana is also good value with a
commission of 2%. The banks give a slightly lower rate on travellers cheques
and they charge a hefty commisson – a full 5% of the total amount you
change at all branches of the BCM and a straight fee of US$7 at any Standard
Bank. This means that the effective bank rate for travellers cheques is
currently likely to work out at below US$1 = 11,000 MT, and that you are
better changing sums of above US$140 at Standard Banks but smaller
amounts at the BCM. Couples who change travellers cheques at the Standard
Bank should bear in mind that they will effectively pay half the commission
if all the cheques changed are in one of their names.

There is a fairly open black market for cash in Mozambique, one that
you will be practically forced to use if you arrive in the country overland
outside of banking hours. US dollars get the best rate – anything from
around 11,600 to 12,000 MT in most parts of the country, and as much as
12,500 MT in Lichinga. South African rands cash are as good as US dollars
in and around Maputo, while Zimbabwe dollars can easily be exchanged in
Chimoio, Beira or Tete, and Malawi kwacha or Zimbabwe dollars in Niassa

and Tete. I would avoid changing money on the street, since there are several con artists about – far better to ask at a hotel, shop or restaurant.

Change

In many African countries, getting change for a large banknote can be a tedious process. In Mozambique, trying to do so can be enough to turn the most phlegmatic soul into a fist-gnashing wreck. At times we felt as if nobody ever has change for anything; we often had difficulty getting, say, 10,000 MT change on a purchase of 40,000 MT paid with a 50,000 MT note. Worse still, even at upmarket restaurants the general spirit in Mozambique seems to be that if no change is available then you don't get any change. Memorably, in Tete, we had to wait an hour to get 40,000 MT change for a 5,000 MT bottle of cola paid for with a 50,000 MT note, and eventually had to buy a second cola (which we gave to a few kids rather than let the guy who served get away with it) to make up the 5,000 MT difference. Obviously, the thing to do is always try to have a good selection of bills at your disposal. If you don't have the right money, check before you pay whether change is available, and if it isn't then suggest that somebody actually finds some before you hand over any money.

More information on foreign exchange is given in the *Maputo* chapter.

Prices

With few exceptions, everything in Mozambique can be paid for in local currency. When you travel in southern Mozambique, you'll find that many hotels and restaurants quote prices in South African rands or US dollars, but that few places insist on being paid in the specified currency. The main exceptions to this are the upmarket hotels in Maputo and on the Bazaruto and Inhaca Islands.

Due to the instability of African currencies in general and the metical in particular, all prices in this book are quoted in US dollars, using the rough conversion rate of 10,000 to one. This means that a hotel room costing 75,000 MT will be quoted as costing US$7.50. In fact, depending on how and where you changed your money, a price of 75,000 MT could work out at anywhere between US$5 and US$6.50. Given the variability of exchange rates and inevitability of inflation, using a rough but round figure as a divisor makes more sense than attempting to be more precise.

The prices quoted in this book were collected between August and December of 1996. They may well be subject to inflation during the lifespan of this edition.

Overcharging and bargaining

Tourists to Africa may sometimes need to bargain over prices, but this need is often exaggerated by guide books and travellers. Hotels, restaurants, supermarkets and buses generally charge fixed prices and cases of overcharging in such places are too unusual for it to be worth challenging a price unless it is blatantly ridiculous.

You're bound to be overcharged at some point in Mozambique, but it is important to keep this in perspective. Some travellers, after a couple of bad experiences, start to haggle with everyone from hotel owners to old women selling fruit by the side of the road, often accompanying their negotiations with aggressive accusations of dishonesty. It's possible that the whole thing has become something of a vicious circle: if every second tourist you deal with accuses you of overcharging them, the obvious response is to ask an inflated price which you can then drop when the haggling starts. Aggressive posturing may be the easiest way to find out whether you are being overcharged, but it is very unfair on the vast majority of people who are forthright and honest in their dealings with tourists. There are better ways of dealing with the problem.

The main instance where bargaining is essential is when buying curios. What should be understood, however, is that the fact a curio seller is open to negotiation does not mean that you were initially being overcharged or ripped off. Curio sellers will generally quote a price knowing full well that you are going to bargain it down – they'd probably be startled if you didn't – and it is not necessary to respond aggressively or in an accusatory manner. It is impossible to say by how much you should bargain the initial price down (some people say that you should offer half the asking price and be prepared to settle at around two-thirds, but my experience is that curio sellers are far more whimsical than such advice allows for). The sensible approach, if you want to get a feel for prices, is to ask the price of similar items at a few different stalls before you actually contemplate buying anything.

In fruit and vegetable markets and stalls, bargaining is often the norm, even between locals, and the most healthy approach to this sort of haggling is to view it as an enjoyable part of the African experience. There will normally be an accepted price-band for any particular commodity. To find out what it is, listen to what other people pay (it helps if you know the local tongue) and try a few stalls – a ludicrously inflated price will drop the moment you walk away. When buying fruit and vegetables, a good way to feel out the situation is to ask for a bulk discount or a few extra items thrown in. And bear in mind that the reason why somebody is reluctant to bargain may be that they asked a fair price in the first place.

Above all, don't lose your sense of proportion. No matter how poor you may feel, it is your choice to travel on a tight budget. Most Mozambicans are much poorer than you will ever be, and they do not have the luxury of choosing to travel. If you find yourself quibbling with an old lady selling a few piles of fruit by the roadside, stand back and look at the bigger picture. There is nothing wrong with occasionally erring on the side of generosity.

ACCOMMODATION

Maputo and Beira have hotels suited to most tastes and budgets, but in other towns hotel standards are low and prices high by comparison with many neighbouring countries. Hotels in Mozambique are generally former colonial hotels in various states of renovation or disrepair; it is unusual to come across the sort of cheap local lodgings that are common in countries like Malawi or Tanzania. There are few places in Mozambique where you'll pay significantly less than US$10 for a room in the cheapest pensão.

Organised campsites are mainly restricted to the beaches along the coast south of Beira, and prices tend to be quite high by African standards. Many campsites are part of beach resorts which also have chalet or banda accommodation at hotel prices. There are backpacker-oriented resorts or hostels in Vilankulo and Maputo, and at Barra Beach near Inhambane.

Further details of accommodation are included in the regional chapters.

EATING AND DRINKING

The strong Portuguese influence and the ubiquitous presence of fresh seafood makes eating out in Mozambique a more pleasurable experience than it is in many other African counties, though outside of the major cities most menus lack variety, and restaurants are generally expensive when compared with elsewhere in Africa.

Our experience was that, with the exception of the capital and Beira, meal prices in any given town in Mozambique tend to vary far less than do standards – a first-rate meal in the best restaurant may only cost 20% more than the equivalent dish in a dump. It seems as if the going rate for, say, chicken and chips in Tete is US$4–5, regardless of quantity, quality or ambience, and we felt that it made more sense to eat where we wanted to, as opposed to trying to save a dollar here and there by going for a cheaper looking place.

To ask for the menu in a restaurant, ask for the *ementa* or *cardapio* – the term *menu* implies a set menu. Most menus are in Portuguese, and although some places also have English translations on the menu, you'll get by more easily if you familiarise yourself with the terms and practices that follow.

In coastal areas, most restaurants concentrate on seafood. The most common dish, and the cheapest, is normally fish (*peixe*), which typically costs around US$3–5 and is served fried with chips as accompaniment. Fried or grilled calamari (*lulas)* is also served in most restaurants, and is generally about the same price as fish. Also quite cheap where it is served is crab (*caranguejo*).

Mozambique is deservedly famous for its excellent lobster (*lagosta*) and prawns (*camarão*), though you should be aware that these dishes are no cheaper in Mozambican restaurants than they are in South Africa – typically around US$10–15 for a plate of prawns. That said, if you're not too hungry, a plate of prawns is often adequate to feed two, which makes it rather more affordable.

Inland, the staple restaurant fare is chicken (*galinha* or *frango*), often dosed in delicious but very hot peri-peri sauce. Many restaurants quote a price for a whole chicken: often this is specified (*galinha enteiros*) but where it isn't the price should serve as a reliable guide as to whether it's a whole or half chicken (anything above US$6 at the time of writing will almost certainly be a whole chicken). Normally you can ask for a half chicken, even if a whole chicken is indicated on the menu. It's a question of taste, but we preferred to ask for our chicken grilled (*grelhado*) rather than fried (*fritas*). Prices for a half chicken range from US$3–5.

Particularly in towns near the Zimbabwe border, for instance Tete and Chimoio, many restaurants also serve meat dishes (*bife* or *carne*). Bearing in mind that the term *bife* refers to any meat (*bife do porco* is pork and *bife do lambado* is lamb), nine times out of ten the only meat served *will* be beef as we know it. The traditional Mozambican way of serving steak is to dose it in vinegar and/or lemon juice and (apparently) boil or fry it before covering it with a fried egg – an acquired taste, though better restaurants in the main towns will serve grilled steak if you ask for it.

Whatever you order, it will almost certainly come either with rice (*arroz*) or with chips (*batata fritas*). Rice in Mozambique is of a poor quality, and it's often cooked to a lumpy mush, which means that chips are almost always the better option, even if you're fed up with greasy food.

Many restaurants serve snacks (*petiscoes*) as well as full meals, and in some towns there are reasonably good delicatessens (*pastalerias*). Sandwiches (*sandes*) are almost invariably served in fresh, tasty rolls (*pao*), and can be good value for money, with the most common fillings being eggs (*ovo*), cheese (*queijo*) and spicy sausage (*chouriço*). Many places also serve steak rolls (*prego no pao*) and hamburgers (spelt in a variety of reasonably recognisable ways, for instance *amburque*). Otherwise, snacks are typically just a small portion of a familar dish – *galinha petiscoes*, for instance, might be a quarter chicken with a roll or a few chips.

For cheaper meals, you could head to the markets where you can usually get a plate of fish or chicken stew with rice or *posho* (maize porridge) for around US$2. The other option is to put together your own meals. A fair variety of fishes, vegetables, fruits, grains and pulses, spices and fresh bread can be bought in markets in most towns. In larger towns, there are usually well-stocked supermarkets selling everything from margarine and biscuits to imported fruit juices and beers.

Drinks

The usual brand-name soft drinks are widely available in Mozambique. In parts of Mozambique south of the Zambezi, locally bottled soft drinks are cheap by international standards – around US$0.40 for a 340ml bottle. In some restaurants you may have to specify that you want the local drink (by asking for, say, Coca Cola *nacionale*), otherwise waiters may make the rather cute assumption that you'd much prefer to spend twice as much on an imported can of the identical liquid. In the north, only imported sodas are available and these are relatively expensive at around US$1 per 240ml can.

If the fizzy stuff doesn't appeal, you can buy imported South African fruit juice at supermarkets in large towns throughout the country, at the rather inflated price of about US$2–3 per one-litre carton. Tap water is generally unsafe to drink, but bottled mineral water is widely available, again at rather inflated prices. You can save about 50% of the cost of fruit juice and mineral water by buying off the shelf and asking your hotel to put it in their fridge.

The most widespread alcoholic drink is beer. In the south, locally brewed beer, *cerveja nacionale,* is markedly cheaper than imported beers. The local brands are 2M (pronounced *dozyem*) and Manica, and both come in 500ml bottles (*garaffa*) and have recently been introduced in 450ml cans (*lata*). The local brands are reasonably palatable, with my preference being for 2M, since Manica often has a slighly sweet taste, especially the canned variety. Imported South African beers such as Castle, Lion and Carling Black Label are widely available. These generally come in 450ml cans and are of a higher standard than local beers. In the south, we mostly drank local brands, since they're a lot cheaper and pleasant enough, but in the north the price difference is negligible and we mostly drank imported beer. In parts of Niassa Province, imported Malawi Carlsberg 'Green' and 'Brown' (named after the colour of the label) is widely available, surprisingly inexpensive, and to my taste the 'Green' variety is more pleasant than any Mozambican or South African beer. In Maputo, imported beers are cheapest bought on the street, where they cost around US$1 per can. They are a bit more expensive in local bars and supermarkets, and can cost up to US$3 in tourist bars and hotels.

Portuguese wines and a variety of spirits are available in most tourist-class hotels and bars, as well as in some supermarkets.

BAGS OF WATER

The oddest custom we encountered in Mozambique was that of dangling several plastic bags filled with water from the awnings above open-air restaurants. Careful inspection showed that the bags were invariably hanging from the supports and not from the awnings, which eliminates the obvious explanation that they are weights to prevent the awning from blowing away. My linguistically-impeded enquiries elicited two equally improbable explanations: that the bags were filled with water to keep the air moist (on the hot, humid Indian Ocean?); and that they were there to keep away moths. Well I can't think of a more plausible explanation... I think this falls into the category of "answers on a postcard, please".

COMMUNICATIONS

Tourist information and services
There are tourist offices in Maputo and Beira, though neither is a particularly useful source of information. For independent travellers, the Last Resort in Vilankulo and Fatima's in Maputo are the best places to pick up current travel information.

Newspapers
The main daily newspapers are the *Noticias* (Maputo), which supports the government, and the *Diario* (Beira). The main weeklies are the *Savana*, the *Domingo* (coming out on Sundays) and the magazine *Tempo*.

English language publications include *Mozambique Opportunities*, for business people, and *Mozambique File*, a monthly news service. South African newspapers are also available in Maputo, normally a day or two old and at a very high price.

Telephone
Mozambique's telephone system is reasonably efficient. From overseas, it's one of the easiest African countries to get through to first time. The international code is +258, and area codes are as follows:

Beira	03
Chimoio	051
Chókwè	021
Maputo	01
Nacala	06
Nampula	06
Quelimane	04
Songo	052
Tete	052
Xai-Xai	022

The ringing tone is a single short tone followed by a longer pause, and the engaged tone equal lengths on and off. For international calls, dial 00 to get the operator. For directory enquiries dial 13.

Post
Post from Mozambique is cheap and reasonably reliable, but it is often very slow. Poste Restante letters can be collected in most large towns, and they should be addressed as in the following example:

Philip Briggs
Poste Restante
Maputo
Mozambique

Electricity

Electricity is 220V AC at 50 cycles. Two-pin plugs are in use. Stabilisers are required for sensitive devices and adaptors for appliances using 110V. Batteries are useful during power cuts.

Radio and television

Radio Mozambique broadcasts on three channels in Portuguese as well as several local languages. Since 1981 there has been experimental television, *TV Mozambique*, which broadcasts imported Portuguese and Brazilian programmes alongside Mozambican programmes. There is also an independent station, *RTK Television,* with an English language bias. Many upmarket hotels pick up the South African channel *M-net* and other international satellite channels.

Maps

The best map of Mozambique is without doubt Ravenstein Verlag's 1:2,000,000 *Mozambique Road Map*, which is reasonably accurate so far as roads are concerned and shows most towns of importance. This map should be available in any good travel book shop, but if you have difficulty getting hold of a copy you can contact the publishers directly at Auf der Krautweide 24, 65812 Bad Soden.

The recently published *Time Out* map of Mozambique is more readily available than the Ravenstein Verlag one, at least in South Africa, but it really is a waste of money – riddled with errors and omitting many important towns.

PUBLIC HOLIDAYS

In addition to the following fixed public holidays, Good Friday and Easter Monday are recognised as public holidays in Mozambique.

New Year's Day	1 January
Heroes' Day	3 February
Women's Day	7 April
Labour Day	1 May
National Day (Independence Day)	25 June
Victory Day	7 September
Armed Forces Day	25 September
Family Day	25 December

There are also marked commemorative days:

Day of African Unity	25 May
International Children's Day	1 June
Resistance Day	16 June
Assumption of Power by Transitional Government	20 September

In addition, Maputo has a public holiday on November 10.

Chapter Five

Health and Safety

Written in collaboration with Dr Jane Wilson Howarth

Mozambique boasts an array of tropical diseases but, although most travellers who spend a while in the country will become ill at some point in their trip, the cause is most likely to be straightforward Travellers' Diarrhoea or a cold. Provided that you receive the necessary immunisations before you travel to Mozambique, the only major cause for concern once you are in the country is malaria, which can be combated to a large extent by taking sensible precautions (a subject which is covered more fully below).

PREPARATIONS

Travel insurance

Don't think about visiting Mozambique without a comprehensive medical travel insurance, one that will fly you home in an emergency. The ISIS policy, available in Britain through STA (Tel: 0171 388 2266), is inexpensive and has a good reputation.

Pack a good insect repellent, at least one long-sleeved cotton shirt and one pair of long trousers, a hat and sunscreen; these are important insurance measures.

Immunisations

British readers are advised to visit one of the 36 British Airways Travel Clinics (Tel: 0171 831 5333 for the nearest location) before they visit Mozambique. These clinics are amongst many which now have daily-updated computer links with centres for tropical medicine. It is thus easy to ascertain what you risk in a particular season and region. It is advisable to make such enquiries several weeks before you depart, as some immunisations involve more than one shot over a course of a two or three weeks. The clinics also stock a range of products useful to travellers, including bed-nets, repellents etc.

You will need a yellow fever immunisation, and may be required to show an international immunisation certificate as proof of this. It is wise to be immunised against meningitis, polio and tetanus. Hepatitis A immunisation with the Havrix vaccine, launched in the UK in 1992, is also recommended. The immunisation, which can be given by your GP or any travel clinic, is more expensive than most (£40). Don't let this dissuade you from having it. Havrix gives you ten years' protection against a disease which could effectively end your travels and leave you ill for several months. If you intend travelling far from medical facilities, consider typhoid and rabies immunisation. Rabies shots are cheapest when arranged through a travel clinic since one ampoule can be used for eight patients; your GP is unlikely to have that number of applicants unless you are travelling as a group.

Medical kit

Take a small medical kit with you. This should contain malaria tablets and a thermometer, soluble aspirin or paracetamol (good for gargling when you have a sore throat and for reducing fever and pains), plasters (band-aids), potassium permanganate crystals or another favoured antiseptic, iodine for sterilising water and cleaning wounds, sunblock, and condoms or femidoms. Some travel clinics in Britain will try to persuade you to buy a variety of antibiotics as a precaution. This is not necessary: most antibiotics are widely available in Mozambique, and you should be hesitant about taking them without medical advice. Depending on your travel plans, it is a good idea to carry a course of tablets as a cure for malaria – the combination of Fansidar and quinine is currently recommended. As restaurant meals in Mozambique tend to be based around meat and carbohydrate, some people may like to carry vitamin pills.

Further reading

Dr Jane Wilson Howarth, *Healthy Travel: bites, bugs and bowels* (Cadogan, 1995).

HOW TO MAKE ORAL REHYDRATION FLUID

People with diarrhoea or who are vomiting regularly need to take in more fluids or they will become dehydrated. When the intestine is upset absorption of fluids is less efficient. All solids, especially if they are greasy, are poorly tolerated and may cause colic. The ideal solution is a mixture of two heaped teaspoons of glucose and a three-finger pinch (less than a quarter of a teaspoon) of salt in a glass of cooled boiled water. Drink a glass of this at least every time your bowels open; more often if you want. If you feel nauseous or are actually vomiting, sip the drink very slowly. If glucose is unavailable, sugar, palm syrup or honey are good substitutes. If none of these, or boiled water, are available, put a pinch of salt in any flattened sweet soda drink such as Coke (which is available just about anywhere in Mozambique).

Any clear solution is OK to drink; sweet black tea and herbal infusions, drinks made from Marmite and Bovril and clear thin soups. The secret is to drink a combination of salt and sugar, so add a little salt to sweet drinks or sugar to salty drinks. The solution should taste no more salty than tears. Quantity is more important than constituents.

MEDICAL FACILITIES

There are private clinics, hospitals and pharmacies in most large towns, but unless you speak Portuguese you may have difficulty communicating your needs beyond relatively straightforward requests such as a malaria test – try to find somebody bilingual to visit the hospital with you. Consultation fees and laboratory tests are remarkably inexpensive when compared to those in the West, so if you do fall sick it would be absurd to let financial considerations dissuade you from seeking medical help.

You should be able to buy such commonly required medicines as broad spectrum antibiotics and Flagyl at any sizeable town. If you are wandering off the beaten track, it might be worth carrying the obvious with you. As for malaria cures and prophylactics, Chloroquine, Fansidar and to a lesser extent quinine tablets can be bought in just about any town, but it is not always so easy to get hold of Paludrine and Larium. That said, it's far better that you carry all malaria related tablets on you.

If you are on any medication prior to departure, or you have specific needs relating to a known medical condition (for instance if you are allergic to bee stings or you are prone to attacks of asthma), then you are strongly advised to bring any related drugs and devices with you.

DISEASES

Diarrhoea and related illnesses

Diarrhoea affects at least half of those who travel in the tropics. The best solution is to rest up for a day, and to stop eating heavy, greasy foods, avoid alcohol, and take only clear fluids. Stick to a very light, plain diet – lots of fluids plus dry biscuits or boiled potatoes or rice. The bacteria which are responsible for most diarrhoea and related symptoms (such as the abdominal pains caused by the stomach trying to expel bad food) will normally die within 36 hours if they are deprived of food.

Blockers such as Imodium, Lomotil and Codeine Phosphate should only be taken if you have no access to sanitation, for instance if you *have* to travel by bus. Blockers keep the poisons in your system, and so make you feel bad for longer. They are sometimes useful if bowel cramps persist for more than 48 hours, as can be the case with salmonella poisoning. On the other hand, it is dangerous to take blockers with dysentery (evidenced by blood, slime or fever with the diarrhoea). Really, if diarrhoea or related symptoms persist much beyond 36 hours, the sensible thing to do is consult a doctor or pharmacist. The chances are you have nothing serious, but you may have something treatable.

When you have diarrhoea, it is important to drink a lot. Paediatric rehydration fluids such as *Dioralyte* and *Rehidrat* are excellent, or you can make your own salt and sugar rehydration fluid (see box). If you are vomiting you can still absorb sipped fluids, and Dioralyte better than most. Sip the drink slowly and avoid anything that is very hot or cold. Try to drink a glass of rehydration fluid every time your bowels open. If you are not eating, you need to drink around three litres of fluid daily in a temperate climate, more if it is hot, you are at a high altitude, or you have fever or diarrhoea. If you are vomiting, do not worry about the quantity you produce – it is never as much as it looks. Dehydration is the only serious complication of diarrhoea and vomiting; provided you keep sipping slowly you will replace sufficient lost fluids, even if you have cholera.

Stomach problems associated with severe flatulence, abdominal distension, stomach cramps and sulphurous belching may well be caused by giardia. This is not a serious illness, but it is unpleasant enough that you will want treatment as quickly as possible. Giardia is cured with a course of Flagyl (Metronidozale), 2g daily for three days, and this is readily available in Mozambique. You shouldn't touch alcohol while taking treatment for giardia.

If you have diarrhoea with blood or you have a fever, see a doctor for a stool test. Provided that you are taking plenty of fluids, you need not be in a great rush about this, but nor is there any point in delaying: chronic diarrhoea will make it practically impossible to travel anywhere, and if nothing else seeing a doctor will ease your mind.

How to avoid diarrhoea and other food- and water-borne diseases

There are a great many myths about how diarrhoea is acquired, but most travellers become sick from contaminated food. Salads, especially lettuce, are always a likely source of diarrhoea. Food which is freshly cooked or thoroughly reheated should be safe, and sizzling hot street foods are invariably safer than those served at buffets at expensive hotels. Ice-cream is an ideal medium for bacterial cultures and it is often not kept adequately frozen due to power cuts. Ice may be made with unboiled water, and it could have been deposited by the roadside on its journey from the ice factory.

In any third-world country, you'll hear all sorts of contradictory information about the safety of drinking tap water. In Mozambique, my impression is that you should avoid drinking tap water wherever possible. The best way to purify water is by boiling it: simply bringing it to the boil kills 99% of bugs, and keeping it on the boil for a further two minutes kills everything at altitudes of below 4,500m (which is everywhere in Mozambique). Boiling water is more effective than using iodine, which is in turn more effective than any chlorine-based water purification tablet.

Malaria

Malaria kills about a million Africans every year. Of the travellers who return to Britain with malaria, 92% have caught it in Africa. The disease is present throughout tropical Africa at altitudes of below 1,800m, and the *Anopheles* mosquito which transmits the malaria parasite is most abundant near the marshes and still water in which it breeds.

For all practical purposes, malaria should be considered to be present throughout Mozambique throughout the year. The only areas from where it is entirely absent are mountainous regions above an altitude of 1,800m, and since the few such places that exist in Mozambique can only be visited by passing through malarial areas, precautions should be taken wherever you plan to travel. That said, the risk of catching malaria is much higher along the coast or on the shore of Lake Niassa than it is at higher altitudes, the prevalence increases the further north you travel along the coast, and the disease is far more likely to be caught if you visit Mozambique during the wet summer months than if you visit between May and August.

The first step in preventing malaria is to take prophylactic drugs. You can ignore any stories you hear on the travellers' grapevine about it being better to acquire resistance than to take tablets. It is not possible to build up an effective resistance to malaria, and travellers risk death by not taking precautions. It is foolhardy not to take malaria tablets.

The drug currently recommended for visitors spending less than three months in tropical Africa is Larium (Mefloquine). Larium is generally effective in preventing malaria, and surveys on returning travellers have shown fewer side-effects than with the combination of Chloroquine and Paludrine (the other option). However, side effects from Larium can be more dramatic when they do occur. Many people who use Larium experience sleeplessness or disturbing nightmares, and in extreme cases (generally only in curative doses) the drug can lead to serious psychological problems. Larium should definitely not be taken by someone with a history of psychological problems or severe depression. If you don't fall into this category, and you are a non-pregnant adult, Larium is the recommended drug. You can exclude side effects by taking it for two to three weeks prior to departure; if it starts affecting your moods or sleep patterns, you might want to switch to the Chloroquine and Paludrine combination. If you are spending more than a year in the region or planning a pregnancy (when you should take special advice), you should probably take Chloroquine (two weekly) and Paludrine (two daily) from the start, as Larium is a new drug and doctors are uncertain about how long it is safe to take it for.

Malaria resistance patterns change, resulting in changes to the effectiveness of any given drug. Your GP may not be aware of new developments, or have specialist knowledge regarding potential side-effects and contra-indications; you are advised to consult a travel clinic for current advice, or to phone 0171 636 7921 for recorded information.

Just as important as taking malaria pills is making every reasonable effort not to be bitten by mosquitoes between dusk and dawn. Many travellers assume that simply taking pills gives then full protection against malaria. It doesn't. It stuns me how many travellers wander around at night in shorts and flip-flops in parts of Africa where malaria is prolific. Resistance to prophylactics is widespread in Africa, and the most certain way not to catch malaria is to not be bitten by mosquitoes. This doesn't mean that avoiding bites is an alternative to taking pills – nobody will be able to prevent every potential bite. You should try to do both.

Even if you take your malaria tablets meticulously and take care to avoid being bitten, you might still contract a resistant strain. Headaches and pains, a general sense of disorientation or flu-like aches and pains, may mean malaria. It is vital that you seek medical advice immediately. Local doctors see malaria all the time; they will know it in all its guises and know the best treatment for local resistance patterns. Untreated malaria is likely to be fatal, but even prophylactic-resistant strains normally respond well to treatment, provided that you do not leave it too late.

If you are unable to reach a doctor, you may well be forced to diagnose and treat yourself. For this reason, it is advisable to carry a cure in your medical kit. Expert opinion is that most safe and effective cure available at present is the combination of Fansidar and quinine. This cure needs to be used in conjunction with a thermometer, so carry one of these as well. The correct procedure is to take two quinine tablets every eight hours until the fever subsides, for a maximum of three days. When the fever subsides, or if it hasn't subsided after three days, take a single dose of three Fansidar tablets. Provided you follow this procedure before the symptoms have become chronic, it is practically 100% effective. Be warned, however, that you must try to drink a lot of water after you take Fansidar.

The quinine/Fansidar combination is a slow cure, for which reason some people will advise you to skip the quinine altogether and to take the Fansidar straight away. There is certainly an argument for going straight on to Fansidar (I've spoken to several people who have been up and walking within 24 hours of taking it), but the problem with this approach is that, on its own, it is not always completely effective. It could easily be that the best cure for malaria changes during the life-span of this edition, so seek current advice from a travel clinic or another reliable source before you leave for Mozambique.

Malaria typically takes one to two weeks to incubate but it can take as long as a year. This means that you may only display symptoms after you leave Mozambique, for which reason you are advised to continue with prophylactics for at least four weeks after returning home. It is all too easy to forget your pills once you are in the everyday routine of life at home, but you should make every effort to remember. If you display symptoms which could possibly be malarial, even if this happens a year after you return home, get to a doctor and, in order that they don't overlook the possibility, ensure that they are aware you have been exposed to malaria.

Finally, if you have a fever and the malaria test is negative (though this does not exclude malaria), you may have typhoid, which should also receive immediate treatment. Where typhoid-testing is unavailable, a routine blood test can give a strong indication of this disease.

BILHARZIA OR SCHISTOSOMIASIS

Dr Jane Wilson Howarth

Bilharzia or schistosomiasis is a common debilitating disease afflicting perhaps 200 million people worldwide, but those most affected are the rural poor of the tropics who repeatedly acquire more and more of these nasty little worm-lodgers. Fortunately travellers and expatriates generally suffer fewer problems if they acquire bilharzia because they pick up relatively few parasites and so their burden of worms is less; they are also likely to realise they have bilharzia early and get it treated promptly.

When someone with bilharzia excretes into freshwater, bilharzia eggs hatch and swim off to find a suitable freshwater snail to infest. Once inside the snail, they develop, change and emerge as torpedo-shaped cercariae; these are only just visible to the naked eye, and can digest their way through human or animal skin. This is the stage that attacks people as they wade, bathe or even shower in infested water, and unfortunately many lakes, including Lake Niassa, and also rivers and irrigation canals in Africa carry a risk of bilharzia.

The pond snails which harbour bilharzia are a centimetre or more long; they like well-oxygenated, still or slowly moving freshwater, with plenty of vegetation (water-weed, reeds, etc) for them to eat. The most risky shores will be close to places where infected people use water, where they wash clothes. Winds disperse the cercariae though, so that they can be blown some distance, perhaps 200m, from where they entered the water. Scuba diving off a boat into deep off-shore water, then, should be a low-risk activity, but showering in lake water or paddling along a reedy lake shore near a village carries a high risk of acquiring bilharzia.

Water which has been filtered or stored snail-free for two days, or water which has been boiled or treated with Cresol or Dettol, is also safe. Covering your skin with an oily insect repellent like DEET before swimming or paddling is also protective.

Cercariae live for up to 30 hours after they have been shed by snails, but the older they are, the less vigorous they are and the less capable of penetrating the skin. Cercariae are shed in the greatest numbers between 11am and 3pm. If water to be used for bathing is pumped early in the morning, from deep in the lake (cercariae are sun-loving) or from a site far from where people urinate, there will be less risk of infestation. And afternoon swims will be a much higher risk than an early morning

AIDS and venereal disease

HIV and other venereal diseases are widespread in Mozambique. The risks involved in having unprotected casual sex barely need stating. Condoms and femidoms offer a high level of protection against HIV and other venereal diseases, and the additional use of spermicides and pessaries also reduces the risk of transmission.

Hospital workers in Mozambique deal with AIDS victims on a regular basis. Contrary to Western prejudices, health professionals do realise the danger involved in using unsterilised needles, and you are unlikely to be confronted with one in a town hospital or clinic. If, however, you need treatment in a really remote area, where supplies might be a problem, you may be glad to be carrying a few needles and hypodermic syringes.

plunge. Since cercariae take perhaps 10–15 minutes to penetrate, a quick shower, or a splash across a river, followed by thorough drying with a towel, should be safe. Even if you are in risky water longer it is worth vigorously towelling off after bathing: this will kill any cercariae which are still in the process of penetrating your skin.

Only a proportion of cercariae which successfully penetrate will survive and cause disease. Although absence of early symptoms does not necessarily mean there is no infection, infected people usually notice symptoms two or more weeks after penetration. Travellers and expatriates will probably experience a fever and often a wheezy cough; local residents do not usually have symptoms. There is now a very good blood test which, if done six weeks or more after likely exposure, will determine whether or not parasites are going to cause problems and then the infection can be treated. While treatment generally remains effective, there are treatment failures and retreatment is often necessary; the reasons for treatment failures are not yet fully understood, but there now may be some drug resistance. Since bilharzia can be a nasty illness, avoidance is better than waiting to be cured and it is wise to avoid bathing in high risk areas.

Summary points
If you are bathing, swimming, paddling or wading in freshwater which you think may carry a bilharzia risk, try to get out of the water within ten minutes.

• Dry off thoroughly with a towel.

• Avoid bathing or paddling on shores within 200m of villages or places where people use the water a great deal, especially reedy shores or where there is plenty of water weed.

• Ideally cover yourself with DEET insect repellent before swimming.

• If your bathing water comes from a risky source, try to ensure that the water is taken from the lake in the early morning and stored snail-free, otherwise it should be filtered or Dettol or Cresol added.

Thanks to Dr Vaughan Southgate of the Natural History Museum, London, and to Dr G B Wyatt of the Liverpool School of Tropical Medicine, for up-to-date information on bilharzia in Lake Niassa.

Sleeping sickness
This is carried by tsetse flies, which look like oversized houseflies, and have a painful but (sleeping sickness aside) harmless bite. Tsetse flies commonly occur in low-lying game reserves throughout tropical Africa. Sleeping sickness has a patchy distribution, and it only occurs within a small limit of the tsetse fly's range: it cannot be considered a real threat to travellers and it's a treatable ailment. In Mozambique, tsetse flies are common in several game reserves: they bite during the day and are attracted to blue.

Meningitis
This is a particularly nasty disease as it can kill within hours of the first symptoms appearing. The telltale symptom is a combination of a blinding headache and usually high fever. A vaccination protects against the common

and serious bacterial form in Africa, but not against all of the many kinds of meningitis. Local papers normally report localised outbreaks. If you show symptoms, get to a doctor immediately.

Rabies and animal bites

Rabies can be carried by any mammal. The domestic dog is the species which most often passes it to man. The most common route of infection is a bite from an infected animal, but a scratch or a lick on an open wound can do it.

The immunisation against rabies is highly effective, but once symptoms appear rabies is incurable, and the way that you die is so horrible that all doctors advice a post-exposure boost. If you are not immunised and there is any possibility that you have been exposed to a rabid animal, get to a doctor as soon as you can. This should be done promptly, but since the incubation period can be over a month if, for instance, you are bitten on the hand, it's not too late even weeks after exposure. As the incubation period for rabies is determined by the distance between the point of infection and the brain, people who are bitten on the face (as is common with children) have ten days at most and must get help immediately. The message, then, is to be fully immunised against rabies, especially if you intend visiting remote places or handling wild animals. Any wild animals that seem unusually tame should be assumed to be rabid: do not handle them.

All animals bites should be cleaned as protection against general infection. *Scrub* the wound with soap under running water for five minutes (time it with a watch), then liberally apply povidone iodine or 40% (or higher) alcohol – even gin or whisky will do – or aqueous iodine. Cleaning the wound won't necessarily protect you from rabies. Nor will it automatically prevent tetanus infection, a far more immediate concern. If you haven't had a tetanus shot in ten years or you are unsure, get a tetanus toxoid injection *and* a tetanus booster as quickly as possible.

Tetanus

Tetanus is caught through deep, dirty wounds, so ensure that any wounds are thoroughly cleaned. Immunisation gives good protection for ten years, provided you do not have an overwhelming number of tetanus bacteria on board. Keep immunised and be sensible about first aid.

Ticks and tickbite fever

There are several unpleasant illnesses which can follow a tick bite in Africa, including Lyme disease, but the good news is that even if a tick is carrying disease organisms, it will not inevitably infect you. You are less likely to be infected if you get the tick off promptly and do not damage it.

Remove any tick as soon as you notice it on you – it will most likely be firmly attached to somewhere you would rather it was not – grasp the tick as close to your body as possible and pull steadily and firmly away at right angles to your skin. The tick will then come away complete as long as you do not jerk or twist. If possible douse the wound with alcohol (any spirit will do) or iodine.

Spreading redness around the bite and/or fever and/or aching joints after a tick bite imply that you have an infection which requires antibiotic treatment, so seek advice.

INSECTS

Even if you are taking malaria tablets, you should take steps to avoid being bitten by insects, and by mosquitoes in particular. The most imperative reason for doing so is the increasing levels of resistance to preventative drugs. Whatever pills you take, there remains a significant risk of being infected by malaria in areas below 1,800m. Of much less concern, but still a risk, are several other mosquito-borne viral fevers which either are or else might be present in low and medium-altitude parts of Mozambique. Dengue, the only one of these diseases that is anything close to being common, is very nasty with symptoms that include severe muscle cramps, high fever and a measles-like rash; fatalities are exceptional but medical help should be sought. The other diseases in this category are too rare to be a cause for serious concern. Nevertheless, they are difficult to treat, and some of them are potentially fatal. And it is not only mosquitoes that might carry nasty diseases. Leishmania, another difficult-to-treat disease, is spread by sandfly bites. Before you panic, it should be stressed that all these diseases other than malaria are most unlikely to be caught by travellers. I mention them mainly to illustrate that malaria pills on their own do not guarantee your safety against serious insect-borne diseases.

The *Anopheles* mosquito which spreads malaria emerges at dusk, as do sandflies and most other disease-carrying mosquitoes. You will thus greatly reduce your chances of being bitten and contracting insect-borne diseases if you wear long trousers and socks in the evening and cover exposed parts of your body with insect repellent, preferably a DEET-based preparation such as *Jungle Jell*. Sprays or roll-ons of this sort are not available in Mozambique; bring one with you.

The *Anopheles* mosquito hunts mostly at ground level and it can bite through thin socks, so it is worth putting repellent on your ankles, even if they are covered. DEET-impregnated ankle-bands (marketed by MASTA at the London School of Hygiene and Tropical Medicine) are also quite effective. When walking in scrub and forest areas, you should cover and spray yourself by day as well; the *Aedes* mosquito which spreads Dengue is a day-biter. Solid shoes, socks and trousers will, in any case, protect you against snakes, sharp thorns, and harmless but irritating biters like midges.

Like many insects, mosquitoes are drawn to direct light. If you are camping, never put a lamp near the opening of your tent, or you will have a swarm of mosquitoes and other insects waiting to join you. In hotel rooms, be aware that the longer you leave on your light, the greater will be the number of insects with which you are likely to share your accommodation. Once in bed, the most effective form of protection against mosquitoes is a net. Mosquito coils, widely available in Mozambique, will reduce the biting rate, and, even though strains of mosquito have evolved that are skilled at flying in turbulent air, so will a fan. Far better, though, is to carry your own permethrin-impregnated net, which will protect you against everything. Kits are available from MASTA at the London School of Tropical Medicine and Hygiene, and from British Airways Travel Clinics.

To balance the warnings, it should be stressed that the overwhelming majority of insects don't bite people, and of those that do, the vast majority are entirely harmless. Mattresses quite often contain bedbugs and fleas, both of which are essentially harmless.

OUTDOOR HEALTH

Dangerous animals

In the past, the dangers associated with African wild animals have frequently been overstated by the so-called Great White Hunters, and others trying to glamorise their chosen way of life. Contrary to such fanciful notions as rampaging elephants and man-eating lions, most wild animals fear us far more than we fear them, and their normal response to seeing a person is to foot it as quickly as possible in the opposite direction. That said, many travel guides have responded to the exaggerated ideas of the dangers associated with wild animals by being overly reassuring – the likelihood of a tourist being attacked by an animal is indeed very low, but it can happen, and there have been a number of fatalities caused by such incidents in recent years, particularly in southern Africa. Frankly, there are so few large mammals left in those parts of Mozambique which are accessible to tourists that you'd be lucky to see an antelope's hoofprint, let alone be charged down by a herd of angry elephants.

One large mammal that may still be a real cause for concern is the hippopotamus, and even then the chance of encountering one of these in Mozambique is slight. But the hippo is responsible for more human deaths than any other African mammal. This is not because it is especially aggressive, but because its response to any disturbance while it is grazing is to head directly for the safety of the water, and it will trample anything that gets in its way. You should be cautious around any lake or large river unless you know for a fact that hippo are not present. Hippos are most likely to be out grazing towards dusk, in the early morning, and in overcast weather. The danger is getting between a hippo and the water – it would be most unlikely to attack you if it perceived a clear path to safety – so the risk is greater the closer you are to the shore. You should never walk in reed-beds unless you are certain that no hippo are present. On the other hand, you have little to fear on land by approaching a hippo that is already in the water.

Crocodiles are still present along most large rivers in Mozambique, so in the unlikely event that you decide to go wading in the Zambezi or Limpopo, do ask local advice first. As a rule, any crocodile that lives near human habitation and that is large enough to kill a person will have been dealt with by its potential prey, so the greatest risk is attached to swimming or wading in large rivers away from human habitation.

There are campsites in Africa where vervet monkeys and baboons have become a dangerous pest. I am not aware of any such place in Mozambique, but it could happen. It is worth mentioning that feeding these animals is highly irresponsible; not only is it encouraging them to scavenge, but – if the animals become bold to the point where they are potentially dangerous – it may lead to their being shot. If primates are hanging around a campsite, and you wander off leaving fruit in your tent, don't expect the tent to be standing when you return.

Sharks are common along the Indian Ocean coastline, and few if any beaches in Mozambique are protected by shark nets. There is less risk of shark attack on beaches which are afforded a degree of protection by reefs. In reality, the likelihood of being attacked by a shark is infinitesimal, even on totally unprotected beaches, but there is no denying that the risk exists, and unfortunately there's nothing much you can do to lessen it (except, of course, to stay out of the water).

Snakebite

Although poisonous snakes are present throughout Mozambique, they pose little real threat to humans (in South Africa, where there are just as many poisonous snakes, they kill fewer than ten people every year – fewer than the number killed by lightning!). The reason for this is that most snakes are shy and secretive, and will move off at the slightest sign of humans. In three to four years of African travel, I doubt I have seen snakes more than a dozen times, and in all but one instance they slithered off harmlessly.

The one place where you should be conscious of the possible presence of snakes is on rocky slopes and cliffs, particularly where you are scrambling up or down using your hands. This is because snakes respond to seismic vibrations – in most habitats they will sense your footsteps and slither away long before you get near them, but they may not on a rocky slope. You also have a greater danger of cornering a snake, or being unable to get away yourself, in a steep rocky habitat. Finally, rocky areas are the favoured dwelling place of Africa's most dangerous snake, the puff adder. Although this is not a particularly venomous species, it is capable of inflicting a fatal bite. The danger with puff adders is that they are unusually slothful, and the one species of venomous snake that doesn't generally move off in response to human foot treads.

As a general rule, you should wear trousers, socks and solid boots when you walk in the bush. Good boots will protect against the 50% of snake bites that occur below the ankle; trousers will help to deflect bites higher up on the leg. If you see a snake, wait to let it pass. If it rises to strike, the common advice is to stand dead still, as snakes strike in response to movement. All well and good, but on the one occasion where a snake reared at me, and twice when I've been with someone whom this happened to, instinct won over logic and the person concerned beetled off as quickly as possible in the opposite direction. This tactic worked perfectly well.

If the worst should happen, don't panic. Most snakes are non-venomous, venom is only dispensed in about 50% of bites by venomous snakes, and it is quite uncommon for a bite to contain enough venom to kill an adult. The chances are that you will not come to any harm. Keep the victim still and calm; wash the wound with soap then wipe it gently with a clean cloth to remove any venom from the skin surface. Remove rings, bangles or watches in anticipation of swelling. If possible, splint the bitten limb, as movement quickens the rate of venom absorption, or if you have a crepe bandage apply this firmly from the end of the bitten extremity towards and over the site of the bite. Keep the bitten part *below* heart height. The victim should then be taken to a doctor or hospital, where they should be kept under observation. Antivenin will only be administered by a trained heath person if and when signs of envenomation occur. Having a positive identification of the snake will help effective treatment, but you should not attempt to catch it unless you are sure that there is no risk of somebody else being bitten, bearing in mind that even a decapitated head can envenomate.

Finally, note that, after a snake bite, many 'traditional' first aid measures will do more harm than good:

- DO NOT give alcohol or aspirin; paracetamol is safe.

- DO NOT cut, incise or suck the wound; suction devices do not work.

- DO NOT apply a tourniquet.

- DO NOT apply potassium permanganate or ice.

- DO NOT panic – you are unlikely to have been envenomed.

Sun and heat
The equatorial sun is vicious. Although it is impossible to avoid some exposure to the sun, it would be foolish incur it needlessly. Tanning ages your skin and it can cause skin cancer. If you are coming to Mozambique from a less harsh climate, let your body get used to the sunlight gradually or you will end up with sunburn. Take things too far, and sunstroke – a potentially fatal condition – may be the result. Wear sunscreen and build up your exposure gradually, starting with no more than 20 minutes a day. Avoid exposing yourself for more than two hours in any day, and stay out of the sun between noon and 3pm. Be particularly careful of sunburn when swimming or snorkelling. A shirt will protect your shoulders and a pair of shorts will protect the back of your thighs.

In hot parts of Mozambique, particularly along the coast, you may sweat more than you normally would. To counter the resultant loss of water and salt, you should drink more than normal and eat extra salt if you develop a taste for it (salt tablets are useless). Prickly heat, a rash caused by sweat trapped under the skin, is a harmless but highly uncomfortable and common problem when people used to temperate climates first enter the tropics. It will help if you wear 100% cotton clothing and splash yourself regularly with water, but avoid excessive use of soap.

Always wear clothes made from natural fabrics such as cotton. These help prevent fungal infections and other rashes. Athlete's foot is prevalent, so wear thongs in communal showers.

Small cuts are inclined to go septic in the tropics. Clean any lesion with a dilute solution of potassium permanganate 2–3 times daily. Antiseptic creams are not suitable for the tropics; wounds must be kept dry and covered.

CRIME
Theft
Bearing in mind that there is probably no country in the world which is totally free of crime, and furthermore that tourists to so-called developing nations are always going to be targets due to their relative wealth and conspicuousness, I would regard Mozambique to be a relatively low-risk country so far as crime is concerned. When compared to parts of Kenya and South Africa, mugging is a rarity, and I've never heard of the sort of con tricks that abound in places like Nairobi and Dar es Salaam. Petty theft such as pickpocketing and bag-snatching is a risk in markets and other crowded places, but on a scale that should prompt caution rather than paranoia. Walking around large towns at night felt safe enough to me, though it would be tempting fate to wander alone along unlit streets or to carry large sums of money or valuables. On the basis that it is preferable to err on the side of caution, I'll repeat a few tips that apply to travelling anywhere in east and southern Africa:

- Most casual thieves operate in busy markets and bus stations. Keep a close watch on your possessions in such places, and avoid having valuables or large amounts of money loose in your day pack or pocket.

- Keep all your valuables and the bulk of your money in a hidden money belt. Never show this money belt in public. Keep any spare cash you need elsewhere on your person.

- I feel that a buttoned-up pocket on the front of the shirt is the most secure place as money cannot be snatched from it without the thief coming into your view. It is also advisable to keep a small amount of hard currency (ideally cash) hidden away in your luggage so that, should you lose your money belt, you have something to fall back on.

• Where the choice exists between carrying valuables on your person or leaving them in a locked room I would tend to favour the latter option (only one of the hundreds of thefts I've heard about in Africa have happened from a locked hotel room, and that happened in Nairobi where just about anything is possible). Obviously you should use your judgement on this and be sure the room is absolutely secure. A factor to be considered is that some travellers cheque companies will not refund cheques which were stolen from a room.

• Leave any jewellery of financial or sentimental value at home.

Banditry

Mozambique has a long history of banditry. During the civil war, a significant risk of being held up at gunpoint was attached to driving practically anywhere in the country. This risk has abated in the last couple of years, but it still exists, though it is probably only of concern to people driving themselves through Mozambique. A correspondent to the South African travel magazine *Getaway* records two fatal hold-ups in the first three months of 1996, one near the Buzi River and the other 66km north of Maputo. Both incidents occurred at night, reinforcing the widespread advice that it is risky to drive anywhere in Mozambique before dawn or towards dusk.

I've also heard of two incidents of vehicles being hijacked by armed thieves near Inhambane in 1996, and one on the side road to Murrungulu. None of these incidents resulted in fatalities, and all of them occurred during daylight hours. Such incidents are probably fairly random, and they appear to be related to the car-hijacking syndicates that are rife in South Africa, which means that new minibuses, pick-up trucks and 4WDs are probably at greater risk of being hijacked than are older vehicles and saloon cars. For South Africans, the people most likely to be driving in Mozambique, the risk of armed hijacking is probably no greater than it would be in Johannesburg.

There are certainly a few precautions you can take against hijacking. The first and most obvious is never to drive at night, and to set off travelling as early as possible so that you have the maximum available time to deal with unexpected car problems during daylight hours. In Johannesburg, most people now drive around with doors permanently locked and windows raised high enough so that nobody can reach in and open the lock – an obvious precaution in an urban context, perhaps less so in rural Mozambique, but one that can do no harm.

Bribery and bureaucracy

For all that you read about the subject, bribery is not the problem to travellers in Africa it is often made out to be. For backpackers, it really isn't something to worry about. By repute, Mozambican policemen frequently ask for bribes at roadblocks, but nothing of the sort happened to us when we drove through from Komatipoort to Mutare via Maputo and Beira, nor did it to a couple of friends of mine who've recently driven in southern Mozambique.

There is a tendency to portray African bureaucrats as difficult and inefficient in their dealings with tourists. As a rule, this reputation says more about Western prejudices that it does about Mozambique. Sure, you come across the odd unhelpful official, but then such is the nature of the beast everywhere in the world. The vast majority of officials in the African countries I've visited have been courteous and helpful in their dealings with tourists, often to a degree that is almost embarrassing. In Mozambique, I encountered nothing but friendliness from almost every government official I had dealings with. This, I can assure you, is far more than most African visitors to Europe will experience from officialdom.

A factor in determining the response you receive from African officials will be your own attitude. If you walk into every official encounter with an aggressive, paranoid approach, you are quite likely to kindle the feeling held by many Africans that Europeans are arrogant and offhand in their dealings with other races. Instead, try to be friendly and patient, and to accept that the person to whom you are talking probably doesn't speak English. Treat people with respect rather than disdain, and they'll tend to treat you in the same way.

WOMEN TRAVELLERS

Women travellers generally regard sub-equatorial Africa as one of the safest places to travel alone anywhere in the world. Mozambique in particular poses few if any risks specific to female travellers. It is reasonable to expect a fair bit of flirting and the odd direct proposition, especially if you mingle in local bars, but a firm "no" should be enough to defuse any potential situation. To be fair to Mozambican men, you can expect the same sort of thing in any country, and – probably with a far greater degree of persistence – from many male travellers.

Presumably as a result of Frelimo's pro-feminist leanings, Mozambican women tend to dress and behave far less conservatively than do their counterparts in neighbouring countries; we were surprised at how often we saw what were evidently 'respectable' women drinking in bars and smoking on the street, behaviour that is generally seen as the preserve of males and prostitutes in most other parts of East and Southern Africa. Paradoxically, when Ariadne wandered around in shorts it drew far more attention than it would have in any neighbouring country, even the deeply Muslim south coast of Tanzania. I doubt that any Mozambican will be offended by women wearing shorts or other outfits that might be seen to be provocative (Muslims in Mozambique seem far less orthodox than in most countries I've visited, to the extent that one gent practically begged us to take a picture of somebody praying in his private mosque!), but revealing clothes *will* undoubtedly attract the attention of males.

Tampons are not readily available in smaller towns, though you should be able to locate them in Beira and Maputo. If you're travelling in out-of-the-way places, it's advisable to carry enough to see you through to the next time you'll be in a large city, bearing in mind that travelling in the tropics can sometimes cause women to have heavier or more regular periods than they would at home.

Chapter Six

Maputo

Formerly called Lourenço Marques – or LM for short – Maputo is a bustling, attractive port city with a population of around 1.5 million. Situated in the far south of Mozambique on the Gulf of Maputo (previously known as Delagoa Bay, a corruption of the Portuguese Baía da Lagoa), Maputo lies within 100km of the South African and Swaziland borders, and in addition to being the national capital of Mozambique it is also the eponymous capital of the country's smallest, most densely-populated and most southerly province.

With its wide avenidas and engaging Mediterranean atmosphere, Maputo may come as something of a surprise to anybody expecting a city ravaged by civil war. Certainly, it bears little resemblance to the run-down, crime-ravaged slum described to us by several white South Africans – most of whom had not visited Maputo since the 'good old days' of cheap LM prawns, and who were apparently determined to believe the worst of this one-time coastal playground for residents of South Africa's wealthy but landlocked gold-mining regions.

Our first impression of Maputo was that it is just about the cleanest African capital either of us has seen (and between us we've visited at least twenty), remarkably smart and well-maintained, with a practically constant supply of electricity, brightly lit pavements and traffic lights that work, freshly painted buildings and well-maintained surfaced roads – not to mention some of the most orderly drivers on the continent. Window-dressing? Well, of course, no amount of paint and tar can obscure Maputo's endemic poverty – but even if it *is* rather trite or dismissive to say that Maputo's poverty struck me as being no greater than that of, say, Nairobi or Addis Ababa, then it seems equally superficial to toe the party line dictating that Maputo should always be written about in terms of civil war and poverty (mingled in with a few tedious and unfavourable comparisons to LM), whereas it's OK to dwell on the more attractive aspects of equally poor cities elsewhere in Africa.

Arrive in Maputo without prejudice and it is, quite simply, a most likeable city – as safe as any in Africa, and with a good deal more character than most. The jacaranda, flame tree and palm-lined avenidas with their numerous street cafes have a relaxed, hassle-free, Africa-meets-Mediterranean atmosphere that is distinctively Mozambican. Along the avenidas are any number of attractive old buildings in various states of renovation and disrepair, dwarfed at times by the rather incongruous high-rise relics of the fifties and sixties (LM was something of a laboratory for devotees of the Bauhaus architectural style during this period). Maputo has a beautiful location at the mouth of the Matola, Umbeluzi and Tembe rivers on the Indian Ocean, and it boasts a lively nightlife and some of the most vibrant markets in Africa. It is, in short, a compulsive and endlessly rewarding city, and an absolute must on any tourist itinerary of Mozambique. It really isn't all that far from LM in the good old days, except that the absence of apartheid-style laws means that Mozambicans, too, are free to enjoy their capital city.

HISTORY

Delagoa Bay lies to the south of the mediaeval trade routes used by the Swahili, and there is no particular reason to suppose that the area was ever visited by Muslim sailors prior to the Portuguese era. Nevertheless, the evidence suggests that the bay supported a substantial ocean-going fishing community prior to the 16th century, and also that it was the apex of a local trade network running along the eight navigable rivers which flow into it.

In 1502, the Portuguese captain Luis Fernandes sailed a short distance upriver from what was almost certainly Delagoa Bay, at first thinking he was at the entrance to Sofala. He recorded visiting a sizeable African river port, which impressed him mostly for its numerous cattle – large plump beasts that sold for two copper coins apiece. Once he realised that he was not at Sofala, Fernandes gave the bay the name Baía Da Lagoa, in the belief that its rivers all originated in an inland lagoon.

The first European to explore the Delagoa Bay was the Portuguese navigator Lourenço Marques, who visited it in 1544 on the instructions of the Captain of Moçambique and Sofala. Marques noted large numbers of elephants in the area, and he found that the natives of the bay were prepared to trade ivory for a few cheap beads. Shortly after this, King João III renamed the bay after Marques. Over the course of the next century, the bay was visited by a Portuguese ship almost every year. Typically, the ship would spend about four months encamped on Inhaca Island, from where it traded for ivory with the local chiefs on the mainland.

During the second half of the 17th century, the Portuguese ivory trade became increasingly centred around the more northerly ports of Kilwa and Quelimane, which meant that Delagoa Bay often went for years without seeing a Portuguese trading vessel. Portugal's partial abandonment of the southern trade opened the way for English and Dutch traders, to such an extent that five British ships were recorded in the bay at one time in 1685.

The earliest attempt to establish a permanent European settlement on Delagoa Bay was not, as you might suppose, initiated by Portugal, but by the Netherlands. In 1721, on the site of present-day Maputo, the Dutch East India Company established a trading factory and fort, which was abandoned as unprofitable in 1730. Another trading factory was established on Inhaca Island in 1778 by one William Bolts, a British adventurer in Austrian employ. The Austrian settlement was expelled in 1781 when Portugal finally decided to establish a permanent trading post and fort at Delagoa Bay.

In 1781, the Portuguese placed a small garrison on Inhaca Island and set about building a fort on the site of present-day Maputo, but as it turned out, the future capital of Mozambique was to have a less than auspicious start. In May 1782, barely a month after the fort had been completed, the entire settlement burnt to the ground. It was quickly rebuilt, but an argument between the newly appointed Governor of Lourenço Marques and local chiefs forced Portugal to evacuate it in 1783. The settlement was reoccupied under a new governor in 1784, and a stronger fortress was built on the site of the modern one, but the garrison of 80 men was plagued by fever and so when three French gunboats arrived in the harbour in October 1796, the Portuguese settlers fled inland. The fortress was reoccupied in 1800, after which time Portugal retained a permanent presence on the bay.

In the early 19th century, Lourenço Marques was a modest and unremarkable trading outpost; in 1825, the only permanent building apart from the fort was a solitary corrugated-iron homestead. Nevertheless, the settlement stood at the centre of a vast trading network, one that spread along the rivers into the present-day provinces of Mpumalanga and KwaZulu-Natal in South Africa. The trade routes to Delagoa Bay were fiercely contested by various local chieftaincies, especially after the great drought of the 1790s initiated an unprecedented and highly militant phase of empire-building among the Nguni peoples of the lowveld. In 1833, Lourenço Marques was razed and its governor killed by Dingane's Zulu army. After 1838, when the Boers defeated the Zulu army at Blood River, the trade routes to Lourenço Marques became the focus of an ongoing battle between the Swazi and Gaza Kingdoms.

In terms of the development of southern Mozambique in general and Lourenço Marques in particular, the most portentous event of 1838 was not the Battle of Blood River but the arrival at Delagoa Bay of the Boer leader Louis Trichardt. The Boers of the Transvaal were eager to open an export route to Delagoa Bay, not only because it was the closest port to the Boer Republic, but also because it would put an end their dependency on British ports such as Cape Town and Durban. Trichardt died of malaria in Delagoa Bay, but his visit there signalled the beginning of a protracted three-way dispute over the control of what is arguably southeast Africa's finest natural harbour.

The competition for control of Delagoa Bay increased after the discovery of diamonds at Kimberley in 1867 and gold at Lydenberg in 1869. In 1868, the government of the Transvaal claimed that its frontier extended to the coast, a claim that was immediately contested by Britain and Portugal. The result was that the Transvaal and Portugal signed a treaty which not only delineated the modern border between Mozambique and South Africa north of Swaziland, but no less significantly provided for the joint building of a road between the Transvaal and Lourenço Marques.

Unwilling to see the Transvaal establish links with a Portuguese port, Britain immediately and unilaterally annexed the southern part of Delagoa Bay and Inhaca Island to Natal. Portugal called on France to arbitrate over the territorial dispute, and in 1875 it was awarded the entire bay. This was a major blow to the British policy of keeping indirect economic control over the Boer republic – so much so that Britain annexed the Transvaal to its Cape Colony between 1877 and 1881, thereby stalling the development of transport links to Lourenço Marques.

Following the discovery of gold on the Witwatersrand in 1886, Portugal and the Transvaal decided to build a railway line between Pretoria and Lourenço Marques. It was the completion of this line in 1894 which prompted the modern growth of the city. In 1870, Lourenço Marques was a tiny, stagnant trading centre protected by an unimpressive fort. By the turn of the century, the city centre had taken on its modern shape, the port handled roughly one-third of exports and imports from the Transvaal, and the railway carried over 80,000 passengers annually. On 12 November 1898, Lourenço Marques formally replaced Ilha do Moçambique as the capital of Portugal's East African colony. After independence, the city was renamed after the Rio Maputo.

SAFETY

Before we arrived in Mozambique, practically everybody we spoke to in Johannesburg warned us about the soaring crime rate in Maputo. I saw little evidence of this. Doubtless there is a certain amount of crime, but Maputo seems pretty hassle-free by comparison with somewhere like Nairobi, Addis Ababa, Lagos or – dare I say it – Johannesburg.

Before lulling readers into what may be a false sense of security, I should clarify that I met very few travellers who had visited Maputo, which means that our impressions are based largely on our own experience. It is certainly safe to walk around the city in daylight: nobody pays much attention to tourists, and we saw no signs of pickpockets, con artists or other casual thieves on the streets. Crowded places, such as markets and bus stations, should probably be approached with a degree of caution: basically, don't wear flashy jewellery or carry more money than you need, and try not to keep anything of value in a place where it can easily be snatched. We were comfortable walking on the main roads in the city centre at night – they are very well lit for an African city, and there are plenty of other pedestrians around. But, as in any city, it would be asking for trouble to carry large amounts of money or to use alleys or other unlit roads after dark.

If you are travelling to Maputo by public transport, there is a real risk of arriving after nightfall. There are, in my opinion, few riskier or less desirable travel scenarios than wandering around an unfamiliar city at night with your possessions prominently displayed on your back and a map in your hand. Coming from the direction of Johannesburg, trains arrive in Maputo in the early morning, so no problem there; but if you come by road, spend the night in Komatipoort and give yourself a full day to get to Maputo rather than cross the border after noon. Coming from the north, buses from Beira generally arrive in Maputo after dark; and so I would advise travellers to go as far as Xai-Xai, overnight there, and hitch or hop on the first public transport to Maputo the next morning.

There does appear to be a fair amount of property crime in Maputo, particularly against motor vehicles – car parts aren't readily available and so they are subject to a growing shady market. If you are carrying stuff in the back of a pick-up truck, be careful in traffic jams or at traffic lights, as you may be distracted in some way by a couple of people while their friends help themselves to anything that's not secured. You also hear stories, possibly apocryphal, of people grabbing accessories like hubcaps and indicator light covers off cars while they're stalled at traffic lights. It is definitely unsafe to leave an unguarded car parked on the street overnight. Don't stay at a hotel unless it can offer you somewhere safe to park your car. If you are driving to a restaurant or nightclub after dark, the guarded parking lot near the stadium opposite the Feira Popular is reportedly safe, and there is normally plenty of space in the parking lot attached to the Hotel Polana.

GETTING THERE AND AWAY

Getting to Maputo from Johannesburg via Komatipoort is covered in *Chapter Three*. The depot for Panthera Azul buses to and from Johannesburg is on Avenida Mao Tse Tung, while minibuses to Johannesburg and the Ressano Garcia border post leave from the corner of Avenida Albert Lithuli and Avenida 25 de Setembro. Trains for South Africa leave from the Railway Station on Praça dos Trabalhodores.

There are several buses daily between Beira, Maputo and points in between. The most reliable companies are Oliveira's and Virginia, the former leaving from Praça 16 de Junho on Avenida 24 de Julho and the latter from Avenida Karl Marx, near the booking office on the first floor of the Hotel Universo. As mentioned, most buses coming all the way from Beira arrive in Maputo after dark, which makes it advisable to disembark at Xai-Xai and continue to Maputo the next morning.

Heading north from Maputo, some buses to Beira leave at 05.00 and overnight at the Save River while others leave at 13.00 and overnight at Maxixe. If you are heading for Maxixe or destinations further south, it's probably easier to pick up a later bus, but if you want to go all the way to

Beira in one trip, then the earlier bus is recommended to avoid arriving in Beira after dark. If you want to hitch northwards or to find a lift with a truck, the best place to wait is in front of the Jardim Zoologica (zoo) about a kilometre along the Xai-Xai road after it branches from the Komatipoort road some two kilometres out of town.

GETTING AROUND

Taxi cabs are few and far between in Maputo, though you can rely on there always being some at the airport taxi rank, outside the central market, and outside the Hotel Cardoso and Hotel Polana. Taxi fares are negotiable, but you can expect to pay around US$3 for a ride within the city centre and up to US$10 between the city centre and the airport. Buses travel the length and breadth of the city, with major bus stands in front of the Natural History Museum and the large markets.

WHERE TO STAY

Upper range

Maputo's most prestigious hotel ever since it opened in 1922 is the **Hotel Polana** (tel: 49 1001/7, fax: 49 1480), which lies on Avenida Julius Nyerere on a low cliff overlooking the Indian Ocean. The Polana was designed by the renowned architect Sir Herbert Baker, who also created Cape Town's Mount Nelson Hotel and the Union Buildings in Pretoria, where Nelson Mandela was inaugurated as President of South Africa in 1994. Although it fell into a state of neglect during the years of civil war, the Polana was renovated with no expense spared in the early 1990s, since when it has reclaimed its status as one of the most elegant and well-run hotels in southern Africa, combining an Edwardian grace with modern luxuries such as cable television and air-conditioning in all rooms, a gymnasium, a swimming pool overlooking the sea, three restaurants, a coffee shop and delicatessen, a business centre and a kiosk selling South African and other international newspapers. Rooms start at US$165/230 single/double, and suites start at US$350. There is a free shuttle service to the airport, which you should ask about when you book if you're arriving in Maputo by air.

Recently renovated, and second only in status to the Polana, the **Hotel Cardoso** (tel: 49 1071/5, fax: 49 4054) lies on Praça Travessia de Zambeze opposite the Natural History Museum. The Cardoso has arguably the finest location of any hotel in Maputo, on the edge of a cliff with a commanding view over the city centre to the harbour and Catembe. Facilities include a restaurant, coffee shop, book and magazine kiosk, and swimming pool. All rooms are air-conditioned and have cable television, and most have balconies with fine views to Catembe. Prices start at US$120/150 single/double.

The **Hotel Escola Andalucia** on Avenida Patrice Lumumba (tel: 42 3051/ 4, fax: 42 2462) is the training school for Mozambique's hoteliers, and it

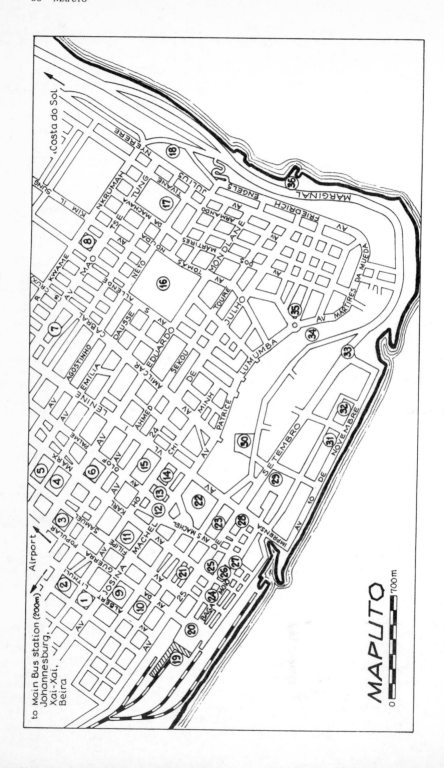

MAPUTO

0   700m

to Main Bus station (200m)
Johannesburg,
Xai-Xai,
Beira

Airport

Costa do Sol

KEY TO MAPUTO

1	Taj Mahal Residencial	19	Railway station
2	Museu da Revolucão	20	Praça Trabalhadores
3	Hotel Moçambique	21	Mercado Central
4	Cemetery	22	Jardim Tunduru
5	Cemetery	23	Scala
6	Hotel Universo and Virginia Buses	24	Central Hotel
7	Fatima's Place	25	Hotel Turismo
8	Panthera Azul (buses to South Africa)	26	Money Museum
9	Map sales office	27	Praça 25 De Junho
10	Stadium	28	Hotel Tivoli
11	Museu Nacional des Artes	29	Feira Popular
12	Praça Independência	30	Stadium
13	Cathedral	31	Zâmbi
14	Hotel Rovuma	32	FACIM
15	Pensão Central	33	Praça Da Travessia Do Zambeze
16	Hospital Central	34	Hotel Cardoso
17	Parque dos Continuadores (José Cabral)	35	Natural History Museum
		36	Clube Naval
18	Hotel Polana		

has a reputation for excellent service. Facilities include a swimming pool, two restaurants, a coffee shop and a free airport shuttle service. All rooms are air-conditioned, and cost from US$95/140 single/double.

The **Hotel Terminus** (tel: 49 1333, fax: 49 1284) is a relatively new establishment situated on the corner of Rua Ahmed Sekou Touré and Avenida Francisco Orlando Magumbwe. Air-conditioned rooms with direct dial telephone and colour television cost US$70/110 single/double.

The **Hotel Rovuma** is after the Polana probably the best known hotel in Maputo. It is being renovated at the time of writing, but should re-open sometime in 1997. Located off Avenida Ho Chi Minh behind the cathedral, the Rovuma will probably charge similar prices to the Cardoso once it re-opens. Tel: 42 0572. Fax: 42 7372.

Moderate

One of the more affordable options in this range is the **Hotel Tamariz** (tel: 42 8608, fax: 42 8609), which is situated in the old part of town, on Rua Consiglieri Pedroso only two blocks from the railway station. Self-contained rooms with fans cost US$38/58 single/double and air-con rooms cost US$57/72. Just around the corner and similar in standard, the **Hotel Turismo** on Avenida 25 de Setembro (tel: 42 6253/4, fax: 42 4937) has self-contained singles/doubles for US$50/75, as well as suites for US$95/115.

Also centrally located, the **Pensão Martins** on Avenida 24 de Julho (tel: 42 4930/5/6, fax: 42 9645) is clean and safe, and has facilities such as telephones and fax, a swimming pool and a good restaurant. Rooms without a bath cost US$45/60 single/double and rooms with a bath cost US$65/80.

There are a few hotels facing the beachfront along Avenida Marginal. The smartest and the closest to the city centre, about 2km north of the Hotel Polana, is the **Kaya Kwanga Club** (tel: 49 2706/7, fax: 49 2704), a very plush, spacious complex with tennis courts, a swimming pool, and a restaurant and pizzeria, and good value with self-contained rooms starting at US$55/70 single/double.

Another 2–3km past the Kaya Kwanga, the **Costa Del Sol** is reputedly the oldest restaurant in Maputo, and certainly worth visiting for a meal, and it has nicely-furnished if rather cramped self-contained doubles for around US$25 as well as a guarded car park. About 500m back towards the city centre, there are large, comfortable double rooms with fans for US$40 at the **Burger King**.

Motorists who are coming from South Africa and who literally want to overnight in Maputo before continuing up the coast are pointed to the **Acijol Guest House** (tel: 47 0562), roughly 5km along the Xai-Xai road. Run by a South African couple, the guest house has rooms for around US$30/40 single/double including breakfast, and facilities include a barbecue area, swimming pool and satellite television.

The **Hotel Tivoli** on Avenido 25 de Setembro had evidently closed shop in late 1996, and there were no signs of renovation.

Budget

There isn't a great selection of budget accommodation in Maputo, and the few options that are on offer are scattered widely around the city, which means that it can be difficult to find a vacant room, especially if you arrive late in the day.

The only place in Maputo that specifically caters to budget travellers, and definitely the best place to head for if you have a tent, is **Fatima's** at Avenida Mao Tse Tung 1317, about five minutes' walk east of the intersection with Avenida Vladimir Lenine. Arriving on public transport, Fatima's is within easy walking distance of the Panthera Azul and Virginia bus depots, but it is some distance from the Oliveira depot and so you are advised to catch a city bus to the corner of Avenida Eduardo Mondlane and Avenida Vladimir Lenine, from where it's a ten-minute walk at most. The hostel is in an ordinary house and although the street number and the word 'Fatima' are painted in red on a post outside, it would be easy enough to miss the entrance coming from the direction of Avenida Vladimir Lenine. Fatima's has dormitory accommodation for US$6.50 per person and private rooms for US$10/15 single/double. Camping is permitted in the garden for US$3.50 per person. Other facilities include good meals for around US$5 (vegetarian dishes are available), multilingual staff, hot showers, a lock-up safe and safe parking. It's also a good place to catch up on current travel information about Maputo and elsewhere in the country.

The cheapest rooms in central Maputo are to be found at the **Hotel Girassol** (tel: 42 1644), a tall circular building with a fading signpost on

Avenida Patrice Lumamba. The rooms are rather sordid, though there is running water in the taps, and at US$5/8 for a self-contained single/double the price is certainly right. If you can, ring in advance, since it is often fully occupied.

The **Pensão Central** (tel: 42 4476), on Avenida 24 de Julho near the intersection with Avenida Vladimir Lenine, is a reliable budget option, and very centrally situated. Rooms vary in size and quality, but they are a uniform US$10/15 single/double. The food is okay, though the selection is limited. There's a limited amount of safe parking.

About four blocks further east along Avenida 24 de Julho, the **Hotel Santa Cruz** is a bit more upmarket but reasonably affordable at US$18/36 for a recently renovated self-contained single/double – a price which is evidently open to negotiation over weekends.

In the same part of town, on the corner of Avenida Eduardo Mondlane and Avenida Karl Marx, the **Hotel Universo** has seen better days, and it's often fully booked, but if you can get a room it's reasonably priced at US$20 for a self-contained double.

The **Pensão Nini**, on Avenida Julius Nyerere, has double rooms at US$15. I've not heard of any traveller who has stayed here, but it looked acceptable – and if you arrive in Maputo late in the day there's a fair chance of finding a vacant room. There's a limited amount of parking behind the hotel.

Another place worth heading for is the **Carlton Hotel** on Rua do Bagamoio, which has large, clean and sparsely-furnished rooms using communal showers and toilets for US$10/15 single/double. This place is conveniently situated for exploring Maputo's main cluster of bars, and it's very close to the railway station – making it the obvious first port of call if you arrive by train.

Another good reason to head for the Carlton is that, if it turns out to be fully booked, you can continue straight to the **Central Hotel** (tel: 43 1652) which is only about 200m along the same road. An attractive old building, if a little run-down, the Carlton Hotel seems reasonable value at around US$20/double. One drawback if you're driving is that you have to park on the street – there is a security guard at night, but I wouldn't personally risk leaving my car in this part of town.

On Avenida Ho Chi Minh, near the intersection with Avenida Albert Lithuli, the **Residencial Taj Mahal** (tel: 73 2122) has recently been renovated, making it relatively good value for money at US$15/20 single/ double.

WHERE TO EAT

One thing you'll never have to worry about in Maputo is finding a decent meal – there are restaurants everywhere catering to all tastes and budgets. The emphasis is on seafood and Portuguese dishes such as the ubiquitous chicken piri-piri, but there is also a good scattering of specialised places ranging from pizzerias and steak houses to Indian and Oriental restaurants.

Several of Maputo's smarter restaurants are along Avenida Julius Nyerere within easy walking distance of the Hotel Polana. The **Ungumi Restaurant** (tel: 49 0951), only a minute's walk from the Polana, is widely regarded as the finest restaurant in town. Main courses mostly cost in the region of US$30–50, though there is a special three-course set menu for lunch costing US$25 per head. The dress-code is smart casual, and reservations are recommended.

A few metres off Avenida Julius Nyerere, along Avenida Mao Tse Tung, the **Sheik Restaurant** is another very upmarket address serving Chinese and international cuisine at around US$15–20 per main course. There is a disco and bar. The **Hotel Polana** itself boasts a number of restaurants, of which the Terraço is recommended for its all-you-can-eat three-course buffet at US$18 per head. The coffee shop serves good pastries and cakes.

Further south along Avenida Julius Nyerere is a cluster of restaurants of which the **A Grelho** (Italian and Portuguese dishes for between US$5 and US$10) and the **Pequimis** (sea food) are recommended. A block south of these, **Javor Quarada** is an open-air restaurant specialising in Mexican and Portuguese dishes for between US$7 and US$10.

Other highly recommended international restaurants include the ones in the **Hotel Cardoso** and **Hotel Escola Andalucia**, the former serving straightforward meat and fish dishes for around US$10, the latter more ambitious Continental cuisine for around US$30; the **Maritimo Yacht Club** on the Avenida Marginal, which does an outstanding Sunday lunch buffet for around US$5; and the beach-facing **Costa do Sol**, about 5km out of town along the Avenida Marginal, which is the oldest restaurant in Maputo and surprisingly affordable (most dishes come in at comfortably under US$10).

Dropping in price, the **Piri-Piri Restaurant** on the corner of Avenida Julius Nyerere and Avenida 24 de Junho serves good Mozambican fare at reasonable prices. Items on the menu include chicken piri-piri, prawn curry and steak, all at around US$5. Around the corner, the **El Greco Pizzeria** does Portuguese dishes as well as good pizzas at similar prices.

The **Taj Mahal** on Avenida Samuel Magaia is the city's best Indian restaurant, and not too pocket-denting with a variety of curries and other Indian and western dishes for around US$6. The **Tai Pan Restaurant** at Rua Consiglieri Pedrosa 343 is recommended, not only for the best Cantonese food in town, but also for offering an excellent view over the city centre. I've also heard good things about the Ethiopian restaurant on Avenida Ho Chi Minh in front of the immigration office.

For steaks and other meat dishes, the **Impala Steak House** on the corner of Avenida Karl Marx and Avenida Josina Machel is recommended, as is the **Rodeo Steak Ranch** on Avenida 25 de Setembro opposite the Feira.

About 50m off Avenida 24 de Julho, along a dirt track facing the Hotel Santa Cruz, **Calu's Take-away** is an open-air restaurant where you can select your own portion of calamari, steak, sausage, chicken or fish and have it barbecued (ask the cook to go light on the salt). The meat is sold by the kilogram – a decent portion should work out at around US$5 including a plate of *shima* (maize porridge).

The **Radio Mozambique Restaurant** on the edge of the Botanical Garden is a good place for a quiet drink outdoors in leafy surrounds and far enough from the street that you're spared the attention of vendors and beggars. Meals are in the US$3–5 range.

For snacks, pastries and breakfasts, there are several cafes and small restaurants along Avenida 25 de Setembro. The **Scala** and **Continental**, which face each other on the intersection with Avenida Samora Machel, have a pleasant street atmosphere, and are popular meeting places. Both cafes serve tea, coffee, prego rolls, hamburgers, fresh bread and pastries, as well as sodas and beers. The more expensive **Ti' Palmo Restaurant** does hamburgers, peri-peri chicken and other fast foods. And there are literally dozens of restaurants catering to all tastes and budgets in the **Fierra Popular**, with the **Coquero**, **Felix** and **Bella Muchacha Restaurants** being particularly recommended. You can also eat in most of the markets, where everything from beer to bread is about two-thirds to half the price of that in normal restaurants.

WHAT TO DO

Maputo lends itself to casual exploration on foot, with several interesting colonial buildings and a buzzing street life. In addition to the two walks described below, it's very pleasant to walk along the seafront along the Avenida Marginal, which is usually pretty quiet, with just a few anglers and other promenaders, and a nice breeze through the palms.

Around the Hotel Polana and Natural History Museum
The Hotel Polana has for decades been the showpiece of Maputo's hotels, situated in the quarter of the same name, east of the city centre on the rise high above the Bay of Maputo on Avenida Julius Nyerere. The Polana survived the period of revolution in a somewhat run-down condition, but was refurbished by a South African hotel chain in the early 1990s and is now restored to its former status.

Heading south from the Polana, turn off the Avenida Julius Nyerere into the first street to the left and walk along the Avenida Friedrich Engels which runs high above the coast. The view extends well beyond the Bay of Maputo to the island of Inhaca. One can walk along the Avenida F Engels almost as far as the presidential palace (where one should be very careful when taking photographs) and then turn right into the Avenida dos Mártires de Mueda, perhaps even enjoying a coffee in the Hotel Cardoso with its fine views of the wide river estuary and the harbour. The open ground next to the hotel has a good view over the city centre.

Near the Cardoso Hotel, on the Praça da Travessia do Zambeze, the

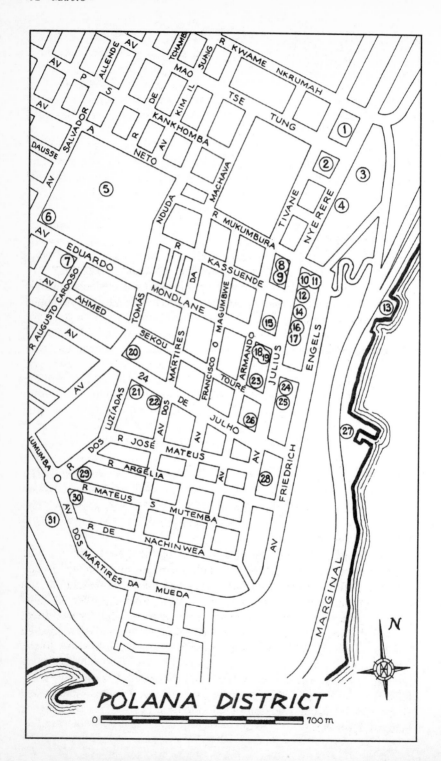

POLANA DISTRICT

0 ▬▬▬▬▬▬▬ 700 m

KEY TO POLANA

1	Ungumi Restaurant	17	Cinema
2	Sheik Restaurant	18	Bookshop
3	Hotel Polana	19	Javor Qarado Restaurant
4	Mobil garage	20	Crystal Restaurant
5	Hospital Central	21	Night Market
6	Restaurant "1908"	22	Geology Museum
7	Pastelaria Florida	23	Church
8	Acanda Restaurant	24	Cafe Mapouto
9	A Grelma Restaurant	25	Pensão Nini
10	Bottle Store	26	Piri Piri Restaurant
11	Ice Cream Parlour	27	Clube Naval
12	La Bussola Restaurant	28	El Greco Pizzeria
13	Praia da Polana	29	Natural History Museum
14	Bank	30	BP garage
15	South African High Commission	31	Hotel Cardoso
16	Pequim Restaurant		

Natural History Museum is housed in a palace built in the Maunelini style (a sort of Portuguese Gothic) and decorated with wonderfully ornamental plaster-work – one of the finest buildings in Maputo. Unfortunately, the collections housed in the museum are somewhat dusty and dilapidated – many of them look like they might have been there since the museum was moved to the building in 1913. One block further on the Avenida Tomás Nduda is the old Maputo synagogue (now the Geological Museum). On the Avenida Patrice Lumumba, the Casa Velha, with the adjoining amphitheatre for open-air performances, is well worth seeing.

The Baixa

The business district of Maputo, the Baixa, is situated at the edge of the wide river to the left and right of the main shopping street, the Avenida 25 de Setembro. Almost all major shops are in or near this street, as are the banks, the airline offices, the main post office, central market, cinemas and the botanical garden. The other busy shopping street is the Avenida Eduardo Mondlane (west end).

The best place to begin a walking tour of the city centre is at the intersection of the Avenida 25 de Setembro and the Avenida Samora Machel, with the Cafe Continental on one corner and the Scala Restaurant and Cinema Scala, built in 1931, on the other. Walk down the Avenida 25 de Setembro in a westerly direction (away from town) and after the next street to the right you reach the Mercado Centrale (central market) a covered building constructed in 1901. It is the prettiest market in Maputo: lively, African and colourful. In addition to vegetables, fruit and everyday household goods, carvings, baskets and other souvenirs are available at the back right-hand side. The surrounding streets have several Asian-owned shops with a decent selection of imported hardware items (flashlights, lanterns, tools etc).

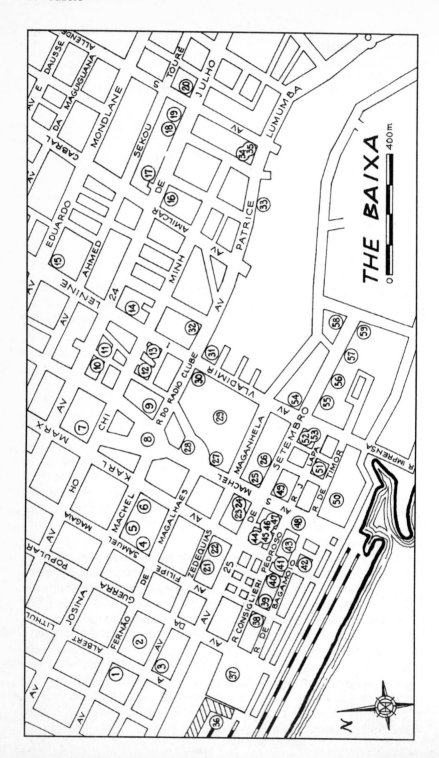

THE BAIXA

0 ——— 400 m

KEY TO BAIXA

1	Coimbro Restaurant	30	Radio Mozambique Restaurant
2	Buses to Johannesburg and Ressano Garcia	31	Parnasa Restaurant
		32	Rico Dunardo Restaurant
3	Stadium	33	Hotel Girassol
4	Taj Mahal Restaurant	34	Techai Restaurant
5	Luis Trichardt Monument	35	Hotel Andalucia
6	Impala Steakhouse	36	Railway station
7	Mercado do Povo	37	Praça Trabalhadores
8	Praça Independéncia	38	Rossio Restaurant
9	Cathedral	39	Central Hotel
10	Forex Bureau	40	Pub Mundo
11	Pensão Central	41	Luso Restaurant
12	Hotel Rovuma	42	Estudio 222
13	UK High Commission	43	Carlton Hotel
14	British Council	44	Hotel Turismo
15	Arco Iris Restaurant	45	Minerva Bookshop
16	Santa Cruz Hotel	46	Tamariz Hotel
17	Calli's Take-Away	47	Standard Bank
18	Pensão Martens	48	Praça 25 De Junho
19	Princesa Restaurant	49	Continental Restaurant
20	Bank	50	Fort
21	Mercado Central	51	Commercial Bank
22	Bank	52	Hotel Tivoli
23	DHL	53	Kalika Restaurant
24	Vitoria Restaurant	54	"33" Building
25	Scala Restaurant	55	Tourist office
26	Post Office	56	Tipalmo Restaurant
27	Samora Machel Monument	57	Theatre
28	Iron House	58	Rodeo Steak ranch
29	JardimTunduru	59	Feira Popular

From here, cross the Avenida 25 de Setembro and walk down the opposite street to the old town. Turning right at the next corner brings you to the Praça dos Trabalhadores, at the centre of which lies a large memorial to Portuguese soldiers killed in World War I. On the edge of the square, the enormous green and white railway station is arguably the most impressive building in Maputo, built by an architect of the Eiffel school, designer of the Eiffel Tower in Paris. Once the terminus of the most important railway line in southern Africa, the shortest coastal connection from the industrial areas and gold mines of the Witwatersrand and Johannesburg and the mines of southern Zimbabwe, the opulent, Victorian-style station is little used these days, which gives it a rather sad appearance, but does not detract from its importance as an architectural monument.

Close to the railway station lies the entrance to the harbour. During colonial times, Maputo harbour was more important to southern Africa than even Durban, a status it seems unlikely to reclaim in the foreseeable future. From the quay, with its huge cranes, there is a view of ships anchored in the Bay of Maputo.

Between the station forecourt and the Avenida Samora Machel is the old town. Most of the buildings constructed in the late 19th century are quite run down but they still have a certain charm. Many still have either wood or iron filigree and covered balconies, reminiscent of the Creole style of Mauritius and La Réunion, and a few have been restored in recent years. From the station, Rua de Bagamoio – formerly known as the 'Street of Trouble' by sailors who frequented its many bars – leads to Praça dos 25 de Junho via the Central Hotel (the oldest in the city), Carlton Hotel, and several bars.

Over weekends, the Praça dos 25 de Junho houses a lively and colourful curio market, where you'll see some of the finest batiks on offer in Mozambique. Around the square are situated the money museum (Museu da Moeda), the renovated bank building and the university administration building with a globe on its spire, as well as the fortress, probably the oldest building in Maputo. The Fortalezada Nossa Senhora da Conceiçáo is a formidable red sandstone building enclosing an area of 3,000m² and constructed between 1851 and 1867 on the site of a smaller fort built in the 18th century. Formerly used as a military museum, the fort is not open to visitors at present.

Next, take the main street back to the corner of the Cafe Continental and Scala and then continue up Avenida Samora Machel to the Jardim Tunduru (Botanical Gardens), a public park with many large shady trees. At the top end of the gardens, it is pleasant to sit in the shade and enjoy a coffee or have lunch. To the left of the main entrance gate, on the Praça de Independencia, is a statue of Samora Machel, the country's first president. Donated by Kim Il Sung of North Korea, the statue of Machel bears a strange and inaccurate resemblance to Chairman Mao. Also near the main gate is the Casa de Ferro (Iron House), a construction of prefabricated metal parts designed by the French engineer Eiffel. Opposite, on the east side of the Tunduru gardens, is the palace in which Paul Kruger, president of the South African Republic, resided after fleeing from British troops at the end of the 19th century and which now houses the Tribunal Supremo.

Continuing up the Avenida Samora Machel brings the tourist to the imposing town hall. On its right is the glistening white Catholic Cathedral, a singularly hideous structure that was completed in 1944. The repellent grandiosity of this cathedral doesn't improve when you discover how the labour used to construct it was recruited. The authorities used to pick up teenage girls off the street and have them examined to establish whether they were virgins. If they weren't, they were assumed to be prostitutes and were given the option of paying a fine they couldn't afford, or else working off the fine by providing labour to help build the cathedral.

Perhaps the most surprising monument in the Baixa, worth seeing if only because it is so incongruous, lies on Avenida Josina Machel on the block immediately west of Avenida Karl Marx. The Louis Trichardt Memorial

Garden, situated on the very spot where this famous Great Trek leader is said to have died of malaria, consists of a stone frieze reminiscent of Pretoria's Voortrekker Monument and a circular pond at the base of which is a ceramic map depicting Trichardt's route from the Cape to Maputo, complete with stylised mosaics of African chiefs in head-dress and bushmen bearing bows and arrows. Alongside the frieze, under the inscription "They Harnessed the Wilds", the story of Trichardt's trek is told in the sort of messianic tones you might expect of a monument opened in 1968 by the South African Nationalist Minister of Education, one J De Klerk. It's odd enough to find this anachronistic piece of 1960s apartheid chic alive and well in 1990s downtown Maputo, odder still that it has apparently been maintained with meticulous care throughout Mozambique's years of civil war and socialism.

There are several museums in Maputo. Aside from those already mentioned above, tourists interested in the revolutionary history of Mozambique should visit the Museu da Revolução on the Avenida 24 de Julho. More interesting, perhaps, is the Museu Nacional des Artes on the Avenida Ho Chi Minh, with paintings and sculptures by Mozambique's most famous artists. There's also a cultural centre (Centro de Estudios Brasileiros) on Avenida 25 de Setembro, with regular exhibitions and performance arts on Fridays, and an irregular exhibition of various artists at the Nucleo de Arte, Rua da Argelia (just off Avenida Julius Nyerere).

NIGHTLIFE

Maputo has always had a repution for being lively by night, and it remains one of the more pleasant African cities for an extended barcrawl. Since the turn of the century, Rua do Bagamoio (formerly Rua Major Araujo) in the old part of town near the railway station has been known to visiting sailors as "Whiskey Road" and the "Street of Trouble", with ten to fifteen bars congregated along its short length. On the evidence of our visit, Rua do Bagamoio is rather more subdued now than in former times (several of the bars were empty, despite it being a Saturday night) but it remains an obvious place to start the evening. The bar in the Central Hotel is one of the busiest, its popularity not unrelated to the fact it sells beers more cheaply than most places, and it also boats a couple of amusing (if undeniably sexist) murals. There are plenty of other bars to choose from.

Another good, earthy place to hang out, whether you want to drink, eat, shoot pool, make friends, watch a strip show, or ride dodgem cars, is the Feira Popular on the east end of Avenida 25 de Setembro. There are literally dozens of bars and restaurants at the fair, as well as variety of rides and other stalls – you'll find your way around easily enough.

The best of all places to drink are the night markets – cheaper, friendlier and more lively than any of the bars we tried. See the section on markets later in the chapter for some suggestions. We didn't feel at all threatened drinking in the markets at night, but it would probably be sensible to carry only as much money as you want to spend.

If you're interested in seeing some live music, the Clube Txova on Avenida Mateus Mutemba has African bands playing every Wednesday, Friday and Saturday night. On Saturdays there is also usually live jazz at the pizzeria in the Botanical Gardens. There is sometimes live music at the Clube Desportivo on Avenida 25 de Setembro.

USEFUL INFORMATION

A magazine called *Mozambique Time Out* contains useful listings of selected restaurants and hotels, with a rough idea of current prices. Published every six months as a supplement to the *Economia* magazine, *Time Out* can be bought for roughly US$2 at most tourist-class hotels as well as at the book shop next to the Jaron Quarada Restaurant and the MNTC office in Johannesburg.

The Empresca Nacional de Turismo office is on the first floor of the Trangilidere de Mozambique building at 1203 Avenida 25 de Setembro. We found the staff to be reasonably helpful, though they don't all speak English and there are no maps or pamphlets of any description on sale. Tel: 42 5011/2

Foreign exchange

The South African rand, Mozambican metical and to a lesser extent US dollar are widely interchangeable in Maputo. Many hotels quote their prices in rands or dollars, and you can pay at most hotels and some restaurants in any of the three currencies (though you'll usually get change in meticais). In markets, shops and local restaurants, the metical is generally the only currency in use. If you're at all budget conscious, it's easiest to pay for everything in meticais, otherwise it's almost impossible to keep mental track of what you're spending.

Rands and US dollars cash can be exchanged for local currency at any bank or bureau de change (cambrio). If you change your cash officially, shop around first, as rates vary greatly. Many hotels, restaurants and private individuals will informally change money, generally at a slightly better rate than the official one. I'm not sure of the exact legality of exchanging money unofficially, but the practice is so widespread and open that it might as well be legal. In any event, banks are only open on weekdays between 08.00 and 11.30, which means that a large number of new arrivals will practically be forced to change money unofficially. I would personally be dubious about changing money on the street, as it leaves you open to con tricks: better to ask at a hotel or restaurant. Provided that you have cash (rands are preferable to dollars), you'll have no difficulty finding somebody to sort you out. When we were in Maputo, the going rate for the South African rand was 2,600 meticais, and we were never quoted significantly more or less.

Travellers cheques can only be exchanged for local currency at banks, and even then only at a few specific branches. The rate for travellers cheques is considerably poorer than that for cash – a difference of around 10% – so it's worth trying all the banks before you exchange money. When we were in Maputo, the Standard Bank on Praça da 25 Junho was offering a far better than any other, but I hear that the private cambrio outside the Hotel Polana is now accepting travellers cheques at a commission of 2% as opposed to the 5% or more that is deducted at banks..

Post office

The main post office in Maputo is in the Avenida de 25 Setembro, an impressive colonial building opposite John Orr's department store. Airmail letters to Europe at present cost around US$0.15. There is an *última hora* (last minute) service where you pay more on the day a flight is going to Europe. Best is the Sunday flight to Paris (letters in on Saturday or Sunday up to 11.30 or until 18.00 at the airport post office).

There is reputedly a serious problem with postal workers opening mail in search of money, so it may be advisable to write your letters on locally printed aerogrammes or postcards. If you want to ship out material, do it from a neighbouring country where your parcel might be safer. Alternatively, use a courier company such as DHL, which has an office on Avenido 25 de Setembro near the Scala Restaurant. Mozambique is more expensive than neighbouring countries as far as shipping costs are concerned.

Telephone

Direct international dialling is possible from the telephone exchange behind the main post office on Avenida Zedequias Manganhela. You can also make international calls from private telephones, provided that the subscriber's bill is paid in US dollars. There is a minimum charge for international calls (three minutes' worth). If you call from a private telephone, the operator can tell you how much of a bill you've run up when you've finished. The exchange has a full set of directories and Yellow Pages.

Books and newspapers

The only place where I could find English-language newspapers was at a kiosk in the Hotel Polana. This stocks a variety of South African papers, including *The Star* on the day of publication, and the weekly *Mail & Guardian* a week after publication. The kiosk also sells the British *Weekly Telegraph* and *International Express*, as well as American publications such as *Time*, *Newsweek* and the *Herald Tribune*. The bad news is the prices, which are ridiculously inflated – *The Star*, for instance, costs around US$3, six times its Johannesburg price.

The book shop attached to the Jaron Quarado Restaurant sells a limited range of paperback novels at around US$15 apiece, as well as a few books on Mozambique and some back issues of glossy magazines. There is also a shelf of secondhand books for sale or exchange at the back of the shop.

Car rental

The main office of Hertz is in the Hotel Polana (tel: 42 3172, fax: 42 6077). Avis is represented at the airport (tel: 46 5140, fax: 46 5439).

Map sales office

There is a map sales office in the National Directorate of Geography and Cartography (DINAGECA) building on Avenida Josina Machel, a block west of Avenida Guerra Popular. It sells a fair range of 1:250,000 sheets but few more detailed maps.

Foreign embassies

Office hours are usually Monday to Thursday 07.30–12.30 and 14.00–17.30, Friday 07.30–12.30 and 14.00–17.00.

Australia:	Tel: 49 3072
Belgium:	Tel: 49 0077
Denmark:	Avenida 24 de Julho 1500
	Tel: 42 0172; fax: 42 0557.
France:	Tel: 49 0444
Germany:	Rua de Mapulanvene 506
	Tel: 49 2714, fax: 49 4888
India:	Avenida Martines da Machava 1630, CP976
	Tel: 49 1605
Italy:	Tel: 49 1520
Japan:	Tel: 49 1001
Malawi:	Tel: 49 1468
Netherlands:	Tel: 49 0031; fax: 49 0429
Pakistan:	Tel: 49 4265
Portugal:	Tel: 49 0316
South Africa:	Avenida Julius Nyerere 745
	Tel: 49 0059; fax: 49 3029
Swaziland:	Tel: 49 2451
Switzerland:	Tel: 49 2432/2744
UK:	Avenida Vladimir Lenine 310
	Tel: 42 0111/2/5/6/7. Fax: 42 1666
USA:	Tel: 49 2797/4146/4482
Zambia:	Tel: 49 2452
Zimbabwe:	Tel: 49 0404

Shopping
Crafts and curios

There's a good craft market, the **Mercado Artesanato**, on Praça 25 de Junho every Saturday morning. This a particularly good place to buy batiks, wood carvings and items crafted from semi-precious stones such as malachite. All manner of basket work, ranging from reed chairs to book shelves, can be bought from street vendors along the Avenida Marginal and Avenida Julius Nyerere north of the Hotel Polana.

Shops and galleries selling Mozambican gifts, arts and crafts include the following:

Afritique, Avenida Mártires da Machave.
Sculpture and paintings by new local artists. Near the Polana, this gallery is run by Naguib, one of the country's most celebrated artists.

ArteDif, Marginal.
Co-operative for the disabled. Leatherwork, sculpture, weaving, ceramics and tee shirts.

Central Market, Avenida 25 de Setembro.
A good place for craft work as well as food. Bargaining is a feature here.

Ceramicarte, Avenida de Angola.
Pottery and ceramic arts for around the home, plus ceramic jewellery.

Classica Shell Shop, at the airport.
As it sounds.

Galeria Vénus, Avenida 24 de Julho / Avenida Vladimir Lenine.
Ceramics.

Gemas e Pedras Lapidadas, prédio Emose, Avenida 25 de Setembro.
Semi-precious stones.

Makonde Artesanato, Rua Consiglieri Pedroso.
Makonde work, arts from the south and local jewellery.

Mozambique Arte, at the airport.
For that last-minute purchase of ivory and ebony! Please don't – but no-one will object if you buy one of the occasional sandalwood pieces to be found here.

Markets

Maputo boasts several interesting markets. The **Mercado Central** on Avenida 25 de Setembro, housed in an impressive building dating to 1901, is a good place to buy a variety of fresh and frozen fish as well as other fresh produce. The **Mercado do Povo**, on the corner of Avenida Karl Marx and Avenida Ho Chi Minh, reputedly sells a variety of groceries and vegetables, though we were more impressed by the volume of squawking poultry on sale and still refer to it as the chicken market. At night, the chickens are tucked away, and the market becomes one of the most lively places for a cheap, informal beer in the city centre.

Also in the city centre are several more informal markets, some of them selling stacks of beer and tinned sodas several metres high: one such place is on the corner of Avenida Ho Chi Minh and Avenida Albert Lithuli. But the mother of all booze markets is the **Barracas de Museu** on Rua dos Lusíados, which only opens at night and sells nothing but drink. A warren-like conglomeration of perhaps 100 bars, this is one of the most extraordinary places to drink anywhere in Africa, and highly recommended provided that you don't carry vast sums of money or valuables on your person.

Further out of town is the main **fish market** on the Avenida Marginal opposite the Club Maritimo. In addition to being the cheapest place to buy fresh fish, this place is of some interest to amateur ichthyologists for the variety of tropical ocean fish that can be seen (even if they are out of their natural habitat). If you're after a good variety of fresh fruit and vegetables, try the **Mercado Janeta** behind the church near the intersection of Avenida Vladimir Lenine and Avenida Mao Tse Tung. It's also a good place for a cheap meal of chicken or fish with rice.

Xipamanine Market, just outside the city centre, is known for its traditional medicines and associated items.

Sport

For a city as large as this, Maputo is a bit lacking in sporting opportunities, but facilities do exist. League Football (soccer) is played at stadiums at Costa do Sol, Desportivo, Machava and Maxaquene. In fact, Maputo – like most of Africa – is football-crazy, with bars importing huge television sets whenever big games are on. There's a golf club out towards the Costa do Sol; squash may be played at the Estrela Vermelha sports club, and at the golf club; and there are several tennis courts, most notably in Tunduru Gardens (Avenida Samora Machel). The major hotels have swimming pools. Other pools can be found at the Clube Naval, Desportivo and Costa do Sol. Clube Naval also arranges fishing trips, as does the Clube Maritimo.

DAY TRIPS FROM MAPUTO

Catembe

Separated by a kilometre-wide stretch of water, Catembe is Maputo's curiously downbeat twin, and the most obvious day trip from the capital. Decidedly low-rise, Catembe's dusty, unpaved streets could be those of practically any small Mozambican fishing village were it not for the skyscrapers dominating its northern skyline. Catembe is reached from Maputo by a ten-minute ferry ride, leaving from the jetty on Avenida 10 de Novembro at 08.30 and every two hours thereafter, and in the opposite direction every two hours starting at 09.30. To the left of the landing jetty at Catembe there is a pleasant restaurant and small beach. The overland buses to Ponta do Ouro on the border with the South African province of KwaZulu-Natal used to depart from Catembe and as soon as the road is improved, they will probably do so again.

Costa do Sol

The best way to enjoy the sea close to the city is to take a trip from the Polana 5km up the Avenida Marginal to the Costa do Sol Restaurant. There is a bus service or one can hitch a ride. From Maputo onwards, one casuarina tree-lined beach after the other lines the coastline. The seabed is very flat, however, and one must wade out a long way to be able to swim. The water is also often cloudy and brown as a result of the river mouth nearby.

In the Costa do Sol restaurant at the end of the street, you can eat well and at a reasonable price, as is the case at the Mediterranean restaurant right on the coast nearer to Maputo or the Minigolfe restaurant on the other side of the road.

Matola

This is the greenest industrial area you're likely to have seen. At the end of the Portuguese colonial period, Mozambique was the fourth most industrialised country in Africa. Most of the industries did not withstand the first years of the socialist People's Republic, and only very few still function properly. The policy of economic reconstruction begun in the late 1980s is intended to change this. You can experience something of the scenery and atmosphere of southern Mozambique if you cross the River Matola from the town.

Matola was outside of the army's protective cordon during the war and consequently it suffered significant damage, so that much of the land is now turned over to agriculture. It is the site of the home and burial place of Chissano, one of Mozambique's leading artists, who committed suicide in 1994. His home, open to the public, contains many of his striking sculptures and carvings, which blend modern and traditional styles.

You can get "I love Matola" stickers ...

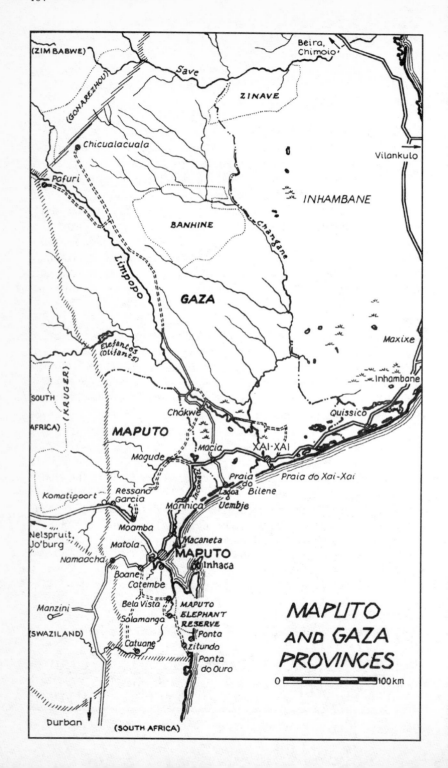

MAPUTO AND GAZA PROVINCES

Chapter Seven

Maputo and Gaza Provinces

With the exception of the capital and the relatively short stretch of coast between Ponta do Ouro on the South African border and Quissico in Inhambane Province, Mozambique's two most southerly provinces encompass a thinly populated area with little to offer tourists: the vast interior of Gaza in particular is one of the most remote, inaccessible and dry parts of the country.

SOUTH OF MAPUTO

The small block of Mozambican territory that lies to the south of Maputo is rather inaccessible from the capital, the notable exception being Inhaca Island, a popular resort lying in the Gulf of Maputo. The main beach resorts in this area, Ponta do Ouro and Ponta Malongane, both lie close to the South African border and are more easily reached from the South African side than from Maputo.

Mozambique's most viable game reserve, the Maputo Elephant Sanctuary, lies on the coast between Maputo and Ponta Malongane. Currently difficult to get to and poorly stocked, this relatively small reserve has been earmarked for a major expansion and restocking programme following the Mozambican government's recent acceptance of a multi-million dollar proposal by an American businessman. The idea is to expand the present boundaries of the reserve to incorporate Inhaca Island and the land in between, thereby creating an upmarket sea and safari venue without rival in Africa. The next five years should see the reintroduction of breeding herds of most large game species, including rhinos, lions and buffaloes, as well as the erection of several lodges, though it seems unlikely that these will be ready for tourism during the lifespan of this edition of *Guide to Mozambique*.

Inhaca Island

Inhaca is the largest island in the Gulf of Maputo, lying about 35km from the city and 24km from the mainland. The island's name derives from that of the Inhaca chieftaincy, the dominant power on the southern mainland of the Gulf of Maputo in the 16th century. Chief Inhaca offered a hospitable welcome to the Portuguese trader Lourenço Marques, and throughout the 16th century he frequently came to the assistance of shipwrecked Portuguese sailors. From about 1550 onwards, a Portuguese ship would set up camp on Inhaca Island for a few months annually, to trade ivory with the chief's town on the mainland. In 1593, one Portuguese navigator settled on the island for a year before he was murdered and his ship looted by a rival chieftaincy. After 1621, Inhaca fell out of favour with the Portuguese: the ships relocated their annual encampment to Xefina Island and they obtained their ivory from the Tembe chieftaincy on the northern part of the bay.

Inhaca is the most accessible of Mozambique's many offshore islands. It boasts an archetypical tropical island atmosphere, with a couple of good beaches, a mangrove-lined north coast, and brightly coloured reefs off the west coast. The reefs of Inhaca are among the most southerly in Africa, due to the water in the gulf being five degrees warmer than elsewhere at this latitude. For those who want to explore the reefs, there is a diving organisation which operates out of the hotel.

The island's main tourist focus is Inhaca village, a tiny settlement dominated by the recently refurbished Inhaca Hotel, which has a salt water swimming pool, tree-lined paths and restaurant. If you have the time, a trip along the north coast to the lighthouse and the Indian Ocean beaches is most worthwhile. The beach directly in front of the hotel is not particularly attractive. If you are prepared to pay the price, a tractor will drive you. On foot, follow the road to the airport which splits just before the airfield. Take the right fork and follow it along the airport perimeter, and wade through the few small rivers and the swampy mangrove area, which can be flooded at high tide, until you reach the mangrove-free coast and a small village with palm huts where you can buy coconuts. Near the fine old lighthouse is the first of the wide beaches, but it is best not to stop here. Make your way further along the beach over the old coral to the eastern ocean side where there is one beach after the other all along the coast. In each direction the walk takes about two and a half to three hours. If this seems too far, take the tractor out and walk back.

Inhaca has been a centre of scientific research for sixty years. An interesting marine research station lies just to the south of Inhaca village, along with a well-kept museum of natural history. For those with a strong interest in the island's ecology, it's worth trying to get hold of a copy of *The Natural History of Inhaca Island* (edited by Margaret Kalk, Wits University Press, Johannesburg), a 395-page book which includes comprehensive species descriptions of the fauna and flora as well as line drawings depicting the more common species.

Getting there and away
Inhaca can be reached by plane for a heavy price, but it's far cheaper to go there by ferry. The public ferry from Maputo costs around US$1.50 per person and takes three to four hours. Timetables are a bit erratic, but in

theory the ferry should leave Maputo for Inhaca at around 07.00 on Sundays, Tuesdays and Thursdays, and start the return trip at 03.00 on Mondays, Wednesdays and Fridays. The ferry crosses in either direction twice on Saturdays, leaving Maputo at 06.30 and 13.00, and returning at around 09.30 and 16.00, which makes it possible to visit Inhaca as a day-trip. The ferry jetty is on the river side of the city centre near the old fort (same jetty as the ferry for Catembe). Tickets may be purchased either at the jetty itself or preferably at the offices of the ferry operators, the Agência Marítima, right at the harbour end of Avenida Karl Marx, and open from 07.30 every day except Sunday.

Letoni Ferries runs a private boat to Inhaca on most days, depending on demand. Normally they leave from Maputo at 09.00 and start the return trip at 15.00. A minimum of six passengers is required and the cost is US$50 per person return. You can contact Letoni Ferries directly at 74 3139 or through Polana Tours on the ground floor of the Hotel Polana at 49 1001.

In calm conditions, the ferry crossing is a most enjoyable experience. As the ferry slowly moves away from the coast at Maputo the skyline becomes more and more impressive. After approximately one hour the hills of Inhaca Island become visible on the horizon, followed gradually by the silhouettes of the palm trees on the neighbouring Ilha Portuguesa. There is no jetty on Inhaca. The ferry anchors at a pontoon not too far away from the island and small boats transfer passengers to the island. The last few metres must normally be waded.

Where to stay and eat

The recently refurbished **Inhaca Island Hotel** is a comfortable and well-situated establishment with rooms for US$95/160 inclusive of breakfast. Meals at the hotel are rather expensive and most people agree that food at **Lucas's Restaurant** in the nearby village is just as good and much cheaper. Scuba and watersport equipment can be hired from the hotel, and a variety of day trips can be arranged for around US$10 per person. Bookings can be made through the Mozambique National Tourist Company or by phoning the Maputo number 49 0551.

There is cheaper accommodation at **Robero's Place**, in the form of basic reed huts costing US$3 per person. This pleasant. low-key resort serves meals and it has basic communal toilets – as well as lots of mosquitoes. There is also a basic campsite at Santa Maria, an attractive and undeveloped corner of the island. The water at the campsite should be purified before drinking. Vegetables, bread and seafood can be bought at a small market near the hotel.

Ilha Portuguesa

The Ilha Portuguesa, opposite the village of Inhaca, is well worth a visit. During Portuguese colonial times it was a leper colony. The island is undeveloped, with a few bushes and palm trees lining idyllic bathing beaches. The beaches tend to be very flat and at low tide large sand banks become visible. When the tide is unusually low, you can cross the channel between the two islands on foot.

The best swimming beach is the one directly opposite the Hotel Inhaca, but it is dangerous to swim out too far as the current is very strong. You can walk round the Ilha Portuguesa in approximately one to one and a half hours. On the other side of the island from Inhaca a large lagoon forms at low tide, surrounded by wide sandbanks. You can camp wild on the island. A small entrance fee is charged.

You can get there by boat from Inhaca – ask at the hotel.

Maputo Elephant Sanctuary

This little-known game reserve covers a lake-dotted stretch of coast roughly 30km southeast of Maputo as the crow flies and about 10km north of Ponta Malongane. Although the reserve has recently re-opened to visitors, it is debatable whether there's any convincing reason to visit it at present: facilities are minimal, landmines are reputedly a threat except along established tracks, and the reserve is arguably of greater interest for its untrammelled atmosphere than its game viewing.

The reserve has suffered greatly from poaching in recent years: the 65 white rhinos that were introduced from South Africa have all been killed, and it is thought that many other large mammals including cheetah, leopard and buffalo are now locally extinct. Elephants are still around, though the 1971 population of roughly 350 animals had been reduced to fewer than 60 in 1994. Because the elephants now live in two large breeding herds, both of which spend long periods outside the reserve and are very shy, they are unlikely to be seen by casual visitors. Hippos and crocodiles are resident in several freshwater lakes, and small antelope such as red and grey duikers, reedbuck, steenbok and suni are still present in diminished numbers. Bird watching is good, with roughly 350 species recorded, aquatic and coastal scrub species being particularly well represented.

The rest camp near the park headquarters is no longer functional, though camping is permitted. Access to the reserve is by 4WD only, and it is better approached from Ponta Malongone than from Maputo. You're advised to speak to the EWT office in Maputo or Johannesburg before heading this way. The resort at Malongone will be able to direct you to the entrance gate. A nominal entrance fee is levied.

It seems probable that some sort of scheme to reintroduce large mammals to the reserve will get under way over the next couple of years, especially if plans to link the reserve to Inhaca come to fruition. It is also possible that the reserve will be linked via the Futi Corridor to nearby reserves in the Maputaland area of South Africa's KwaZulu-Natal Province, depending on whether the World Bank's proposal to create several transfrontier parks in Southern Africa ever goes ahead.

Ponta do Ouro and Ponta Malongane

These two beach resorts lie in the far south of Mozambique very close to the border with South Africa. They are very popular with South African fishermen and divers, but rather inaccessible to people travelling on public transport. The small village at Ponta do Ouro has a couple of basic shops, but otherwise the area is very undeveloped except for the holiday resorts at each beach.

The beach at Ponta do Ouro is ideal for swimming, surfing, line fishing and various water sports. There are diving centres at both resorts where you can hire snorkelling and fishing gear or arrange diving packages. The surrounding dune forest is potentially good for bird-watching, but there is reportedly still a problem with land mines so make enquiries before wandering off the beaten track.

Getting there and away

Either resort is best approached from the south via KwaNgwanase in the Maputaland district of the South African province of KwaZulu-Natal. KwaNgwanase can easily be reached in an ordinary saloon car from either Johannesburg or Durban (it is connected by a surfaced road to the N2 between Mkuzi and Pongola) but beyond that a 4WD vehicle will probably be necessary, particularly in the rainy season. After crossing the border, which lies roughly 20km from KwaNgwanase, you'll reach the first intersection after 4km. Turn right here, and then after further 10km you'll reach a second intersection from where the resorts are signposted. Both resorts lie about an hour's drive from KwaNgwanase, not allowing for the inevitable delays at the border post. The alternative is to drive the roughly 120km to Ponta Do Ouro or Ponta Malongane from Maputo with the option of using the Catembe Ferry to get across Maputo Bay. This road is in poor condition and should only be attempted in a 4WD vehicle.

There is no public transport to either resort, and hitching will require a bit of good fortune except perhaps during school holidays, when the main obstacle to an unscheduled visit is that accommodation will almost certainly be booked solid.

Where to stay

The **Ponta do Ouro Holiday Resort**, set in a sheltered dune forest, offers camping for US$6 per person, two-bed chalets with bedding and gas cooker for US$21 per unit and four-bed chalets with bedding and a gas cooker for US$50 per unit. Luxury chalets with a fridge cost around US$100. Facilities include an ablution block with hot water, a tuck shop, and a restaurant. The **Motel do Mar** in Ponta do Ouro is undergoing renovations at the time of writing, but chalet accommodation should soon be available for around US$100 per four-bed unit.

The well-situated **Ponta Malongane Holiday Resort** has recently been renovated and it re-opened in 1995. It offers camping for US$10 per person, rondawel accommodation without bedding for US$25/double, and self-contained rondawels with bedding, fridge and bathroom for US$35/double or US$65 for a four-bed unit. Four- to six-bed chalets are available for between US$80 and US$110 per unit. There is a restaurant in the resort.

Accommodation and camping at either resort can be booked through the Mozambique National Tourist Company or Mozambique Connections – strongly recommended during South African school holidays.

THE EN1 FROM MAPUTO TO XAI-XAI

Macaneta
Macaneta is the closest beach resort to Maputo and a popular weekend outing with people working in the capital. The major attractions are excellent game fishing and an attractive, clean beach; the sea here isn't particularly suitable for snorkelling, diving or swimming.

Getting there and away
The unsignposted turn-off to Macaneta lies on the EN1, 37km north of Maputo at a village called Marracuene. The road to the resort is rather sandy and requires a 4WD vehicle. Along the way, you will need to cross the Nkomati River by ferry – the trip takes about five minutes and costs US$3 per vehicle. Alternatively, you can catch a boat the whole way downriver to Macaneta Beach for about US$5 per person. The drive from Maputo to Macaneta shouldn't take much longer than a hour. Hitching from Marracuene to Macaneta is easiest at weekends.

Where to stay
The most upmarket option is the **Incomati River Lodge**, which lies on the riverbank in indigenous bush. Accommodation costs US$75 per person per day full board, or US$40 per person self-catering. Bookings can be made by ringing Maputo 42 5322 or faxing 42 1908. The **Complexo Turistico Macaneta** consists of a popular restaurant as well as a few chalets and a basic campsite with washing facilities and cold running water. Chalets cost US$60 per unit and camping costs around US$4/site. Booking is rarely necessary. **Jay's Lodge** is on a private beach and it has secluded campsites with hot showers for US$20 per site (up to four people), as well as four-bed chalets for US$100 per unit. It's advisable to book for Jay's during South African school holidays; this can be done through Mozambique Connection in Johannesburg.

Bilene
The next resort as you head north along the EN1 is Bilene, the former home and burial place of the Gaza chief Shoshangane. Roughly 180km by road from the capital, Bilene overlooks the pretty Uembje Lagoon, which is sometimes separated from the Indian Ocean by a large sandbar. Bilene's

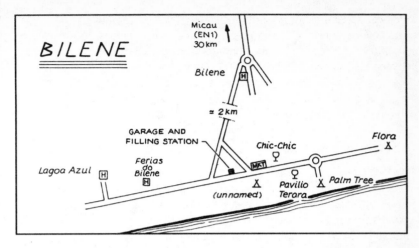

calm waters are popular with watersport enthusiasts, and they offer safe swimming from idyllic white beaches, but the lagoon doesn't offer the good fishing of points further north. As the closest Mozambican resort to Johannesburg, with calm water and beaches that are particularly suitable for family holidays, Bilene tends to be very crowded during South African school holidays. The rest of the time it's practically deserted.

Getting there and away

The signposted turn-off to Bilene is at the village of Micau, about 150km from Maputo along a well-maintained surfaced road. From Micau, a good 30km surfaced road leads to the main roundabout, about 3km from the beach. There are chapas between Micau and Bilene, and hitching should be easy enough, but you want to get to Micau early enough in the day to be certain of getting transport on to Bilene. The village boasts a couple of relatively flash restaurants, but nothing in the way of accommodation.

Where to stay

The **Complexo Turistico Lagoa Azul** has well-equipped self-contained chalets which sleep up to four and cost US$40 per unit during the week and US$50 per unit at weekends. Chalets can be booked through the National Tourist Company in Johannesburg. Similar in price and feel to Lagoa Azul is the **Centro Ferias do Bilene**, which consists of ten brightly painted cottages sleeping one or two people each. The **Hotel Bilene**, on the main roundabout, appeared to be closed when we visited.

There are three campsites along the beach, two of which have a limited amount of relatively inexpensive accommodation. The **Complexo Turistico Parque Flora** is a very attractive spot with camping for US$5 per person, double rondawels for US$15 per unit and four-bed rondawels for US$25 per unit. The nearby **Palm Tree Campsite** charges a steep US$12 per site, and it has a few reed huts ranging in price from US$25 to US$50 per

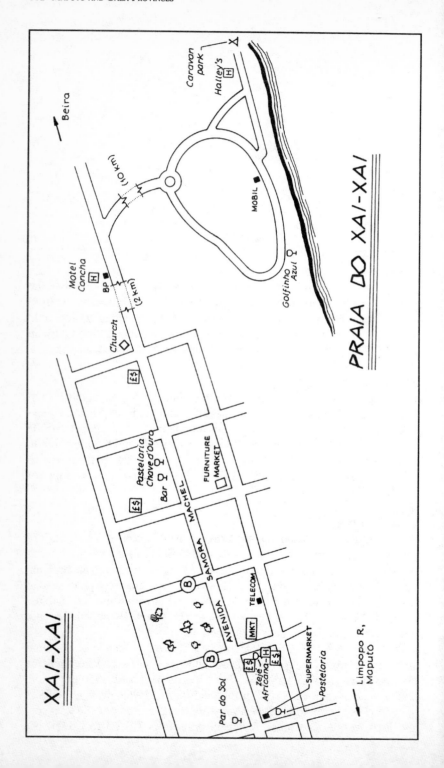

double depending on season. The **nameless site** roughly opposite the market is not particularly good value at US$9 per site, especially as it has no facilities. Accommodation and camping at Lagoa Azul and Palm Tree Campsite can be booked through Mozambique Connections.

XAI-XAI

Xai-Xai (pronounced shy-shy) is the capital of Gaza Province, and also the name of a popular beach resort 10km out of town. Lying on the north bank of the Limpopo, Xai-Xai was founded in the early 20th century as a satellite port to Lourenço Marques and to service local towns, to which end a narrow-gauge railway was constructed 100km inland during 1909–12.

Xai-Xai is a fairly nondescript town – the majority of motorised travellers will probably take one look at it and head straight to the beach. To backpackers, it is of interest as a potential stopover along the EN1 and as the springboard for visits to the nearby beach. Those who do find themselves spending a night in town should take a look at the busy little central market, and at the open-air furniture-making market two blocks away. You might also want to take a peek at the brightly painted church on the edge of the town centre. For birders, a stroll along the lush, marshy fringes of the Limpopo might prove rewarding.

The beach, **Praia do Xai-Xai**, is the sort of idyllic stretch of white sand that is so characteristic of Mozambique (you'd get as bored as I would if I attempted to describe every beach in the country). The sea here is renowned for its excellent game fishing, and for the snorkelling and diving possibilities in the many coral reefs lying within 6km of the shore. There are two points of interest on the shore: the ruined Motel Chonguene about 4km east of the campsite, and the Wenela tide-pool roughly 2km to the west of the main road that loops past the beach. The tide-pool is linked to the sea by an underwater tunnel blow-hole, which you should not even think about trying to swim through. Lined by thick coastal scrub as opposed to the palm trees which characterise beaches further north, Praia do Xai-Xai is surprisingly rich in bird life, with the beautiful green and red Livingstone's lourie being a common resident.

Getting there and away

Xai-Xai town straddles the EN1 roughly 215km north of Maputo – your arrival is heralded by the crossing of a large bridge over the impressive Limpopo River. The road between Maputo and Xai-Xai is surfaced in its entirety and there are practically no serious potholes to worry about. Regular buses and *chapas* connect Maputo to Xai-Xai. You can pick up a *chapa* to the beach from the main city square, or else you could wander out to the turn-off 2km towards Maxixe and try to hitch from there.

The turn-off to Praia do Xai-Xai is clearly signposted on the Maxixe side of town about 200m after the BP garage in front of the Motel Concha. A good surfaced 10km road leads to the main roundabout above the beach. Here, you should take the road to your left down to the beach. After a couple of hundred metres, an unsignposted dirt track to your left leads to Halley's Hotel and the caravan park.

Where to stay

The cheapest accommodation we could find in town was the **Pensão Africana**, but it's a bit of a dump and poor value for money at US$15/20 single/double. Less central, but much better value and conveniently close to the turn-off to the beach, is the **Motel Concha**, which has self-contained doubles for US$25 and suites for US$30. On the beach, **Halley's Hotel** has double rooms starting at around US$35. The adjacent **Xai-Xai Caravan Park** has camping for US$5 per site and US$3 per person. In a protected reed enclosure within the caravan park, **Xai-Xai Diving and Fishing Camp** has dormitory tents with beds, bedding and nets provided for around US$9.

Where to eat

In town, **Restaurante Zéje** serves a variety of fish, chicken and beef dishes for in the US$3 to US$5 range, and the waiters speak a bit of English. The **Pastelaria Chaya Doura** serves similarly priced meals, as well as fresh pastries and rolls, and tea and coffee. You can eat inside or on the street. The umbrella-covered verandah of the **Par do Sol Restaurant** looks like it would be a pleasant place for a chilled beer.

Cheap meals are available at the market, as is a wide selection of fruits and vegetables and crusty bread rolls. There is a well stocked supermarket (frozen meat, pasta, tinned food, wine, beer, fruit juices and most other essentials ranging from margarine to tin foil) on Avenida Samora Machel opposite the Par do Sol Restaurant.

At Praia do Xai-Xai, the best place to eat is the **Restaurante Golfinho Azul**, which serves good fish dishes, chicken and steaks for around US$5–6. There is also a good open-air restaurant in the **caravan park** – the half chicken peri-peri is recommended at US$4.50. The small supermarket attached to Halley's Hotel is not as well-stocked as the one in town.

Beach accommodation is often fully booked during South African school holidays – bookings can be made through Mozambique Connections.

Useful Information

You can exchange money in town at the main branch of the Commercial Bank on Avenido Samora Machel. There is a forex bureau marked on the map. If the rates in town don't look very good, bear in mind that you can pay for practically everything at Praia do Xai-Xai in rands, and this will often work out to be cheaper than would paying in local currency.

Xai-Xai Diving and Fishing Camp organises fishing and diving excursions from the beach.

Chapter Eight

Inhambane Province

The long coastal belt of Inhambane Province is the most developed part of Mozambique in tourist terms, boasting a sequence of idyllic and relatively low-key resorts, most of which are practically unvisited except for during the South African, and to a lesser extent Zimbabwean, school holidays.

The main road through this region is the EN1, which more or less follows the coastline from to south to north. For most of its length, the EN1 runs between 10km and 100km inland of the coast, but it does briefly skirt the beach at Maxixe township, about 450km north of Maputo. The main towns in this region, running from south to north, are Quissico and the coastal ports of Inhambane, Maxixe, Vilankulo and Inhassoro. Aside from the four coastal towns, there are beach resorts at Závora, Tofo and Morrungulo, and on the Bazaruto Islands.

Whereas northern Mozambique boasts a wealth of historical towns and is relatively varied in its landscapes, the south coast is almost entirely of interest for its picture-postcard beaches. This is a great area for snorkelling, fishing, scuba diving and even bird-watching, or just for hanging around on pristine beaches, but it doesn't boast much variety for travellers who aren't equipped for marine activities. If you arrive in Mozambique with a boot full of fishing or diving gear, then practically any beach is worth exploring. For backpackers, the best bet is undoubtedly Vilankulo, where there are inexpensive backpacker-oriented resorts, and you can arrange snorkelling equipment and dhow trips across to the Bazaruto Islands. And if you're not visiting northern Mozambique, then don't miss out on Inhambane, the oldest and most atmospheric town in this part of the country, and one of the most agreeable towns I've visited anywhere in Africa.

The beach resorts along this stretch of coast tend to be booked solid during South African school holidays. During this period, it is advisable to make advance bookings, whether you are camping or looking for a room. A Johannesburg-based company, **Mozambique Connections**, acts as the agency for several of the resorts in this area. You can contact them at PO Box 3781, Kempton Park, 1620; tel: (011) 394 8727; fax: (011) 975 2595. Most South African tourists head straight for one or other of the beach resorts, so school holidays have less effect on room availability in towns

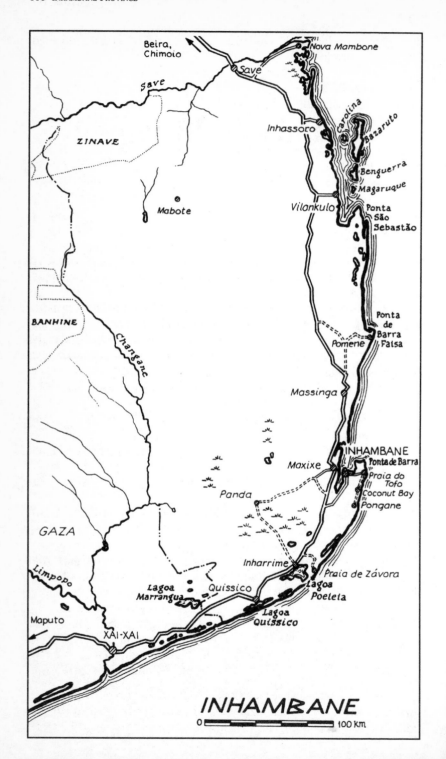

INHAMBANE

0 ▬▬▬▬▬ 100 Km

such as Maxixe, Inhambane and Xai-Xai, or on the backpacker-oriented resorts at Vilankulo.

Getting around

The EN1 between Maputo and Beira is surfaced for most of its length. South of the Save River, the only major stretch of potholes is the 30-odd kilometres north of Quissico, and with a bit of care even this can be navigated by any vehicle in any weather. There are also surfaced roads connecting the EN1 to Bilene, Praia do Xai-Xai, Inhambane, Tofo, Vilankulo and Inhassoro. The roads to some of the more remote resorts (Závora, Coconut Bay and Morrungulo) are unsurfaced and require 4WD, especially after rain, but with the exception of these places you can explore the region covered in this chapter in an ordinary saloon car. If you're thinking of heading from Inhassoro to Beira or Zimbabwe in a saloon car, read the *Getting there and away* section under Beira. Petrol and diesel are readily available at all major towns between Maputo and Vilankulo, but the supply in Inhassoro is rather erratic.

The area covered in this chapter is easily explored on public transport. Buses run the length of the EN1 from Maputo to Beira. For long hauls, the Virginia Bus Line is regarded as the most reliable operator. It runs a daily service in both directions between Maputo and Beira and Maputo and Tete via Chimoio. Buses heading north leave Maputo at 05.00 and arrive in Beira or Chimoio at around 09.00 the following day. The reason why buses heading north take so long is that they have to overnight at the Save River in order to cross the poor stretch of road further north in daylight. In other words, you can get from Maputo to anywhere covered in this chapter within one day. In the opposite direction, buses from Beira and Tete also leave at 05.00, but because they can reach the Save in daylight they continue directly to Maputo, arriving there late in the night.

For shorter hops, you're probably better using the local buses and chapas which connect all towns along the EN1. There are also regular chapas connecting the EN1 to coastal resorts and towns such as Bilene, Praia do Xai-Xai, Inhambane, Vilankulo and Inhassoro.

Once you're out of Maputo, hitching is a possibility; lifts are generally slow in coming, but once you've got a lift it will almost certainly take you all the way to the next town.

QUISSICO

This compact small town lies on the EN1 roughly 100km north of Xai-Xai in an area notable for its several deep-blue freshwater lakes. One of the larger lakes lies immediately southeast of Quissico; there is a good view of it from the EN1 as you leave Quissico for Maxixe, and from the municipal building about 200m off the main road. The lake can be reached along a 10km dirt road which leaves the EN1 just outside town. You could probably

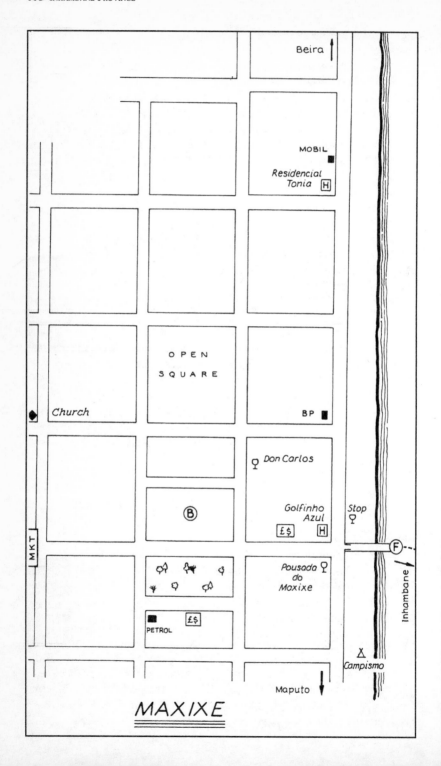

get there more directly by foot (the shore can't be more than 3km from town as the crow flies, but ask for local advice regarding footpaths – there's no danger of getting lost, as the lake lies directly in front of you, but there may be a possibility of land mines if you stray off the established tracks).

Roughly 45km north of Quissico, the EN1 crosses the startlingly beautiful Lake Poelela, reputed to be where Vasco Da Gama first landed in Mozambique in January 1498. You'll get a fair view of the lake from the road, but since there are no facilities in the area and no roads leading to the rest of the lake, the risk of treading on a land mine, however faint, should be viewed as a persuasive deterrent to off-the-beaten-track exploration.

Getting there and away

The surfaced section of the EN1 between Xai-Xai and Quissico is in good condition. The stretch between Quissico and Lake Poelela is heavily pot-holed, though perfectly navigable in a saloon car provided that you drive with due caution. Any bus or chapa heading between Xai-Xai and Maxixe can drop you off in Quissico, and hitching along this stretch of road should be easy enough.

Where to stay and eat

There only place to stay in Quissico is the **Motel Pousada**, which has double rooms for US$12. There is a restaurant and bar attached to the motel, and you can also eat at the wonderfully named **Restaurante Planet Ran Tan Plan** on the opposite side of the EN1. There's a busy market where you can buy fresh rolls and a variety of fruit and vegetables.

ZÁVORA

Závora is the only beach between Xai-Xai and Inhambane which has been developed for tourism, and it has a reputation as an outstanding spot for snorkelling and game fishing. The signposted turn-off to Závora lies a few kilometres north of the bridge across Lake Poelela. The resort is reached via a sandy 15km road, recommended only if you have 4WD. Camping is available at US$6 per person and there are a few bungalows and beach houses ranging in price from US$45 to US$100 depending on the number of beds and the season. You can book through Mozambique Connections.

MAXIXE

Located at the only point where the EN1 actually skims the coast, Maxixe (pronounced Masheesh) is a popular stopover with people making their way between Maputo and Beira. It is also a useful springboard for travellers heading to Inhambane – the two towns lie on opposite sides of the same 4km-wide bay and are linked by a regular dhow service.

Maxixe is not the most inherently interesting of places: its stark grid-like layout and bustling African market-town atmosphere couldn't offer a greater contrast to the seductive Old World sleepiness that envelops Inhambane. In its favour, Maxixe lies on a pretty palm-lined stretch of coast, offers a good selection of relatively cheap accommodation and food, and the view across the water to Inhambane at dusk is well worth stopping the night for.

Getting there and away

Maxixe straddles the EN1 roughly 450km northeast of Maputo, 235km northeast of Xai-Xai, and 60km by road from Inhambane. The road from Maputo to Maxixe is surfaced in its entirety and the only potholed stretch is the one between Quissico and Lake Poelela.

Travellers who are using public transport to get to Maxixe from the south should jump on a bus which leaves Maputo at 13.00. These overnight at Maxixe. Hitching directly out of Maputo probably isn't worth the hassle, but if you are coming from Bilene or Xai-Xai, you shouldn't have to wait too long for a lift. Coming to Maxixe from the north, there are at least two buses daily between Vilankulo and Maxixe, one leaving at around 08.30 and the other at around 13.00.

Where to stay

The best place to stay is undoubtedly the **Campismo De Maxixe**, provided that it isn't full (bookings can be made at PO Box 149 Maxixe, tel: (023) 32251). Accommodation here consists of brick and thatch bungalows with a small verandah and private hot shower for US$25/double, and beach-facing wooden rooms using communal showers for US$18/double. Campsites with electricity cost US$12 for up to two people, and backpackers' campsites (for small tents) cost US$5 for up to two people. There is an additional charge of US$2 per extra person for all accommodation and camping. Motorists who are staying elsewhere in Maxixe can make use of the secure parking at the Campismo for US$2 per vehicle or trailer.

There are three hotels in Maxixe. The most convenient is the **Golfinho Azul**, which lies roughly opposite the ferry jetty. The rooms, which cost US$9/double, are adequate, if a little run-down, and they all have private showers and balconies (note that the balcony door doesn't lock in some rooms). The poorly signposted **Residencial Tonia** has more comfortable self-contained rooms for US$15. The reception and rooms are on the second floor of a high-rise building next to the Mobil garage on the Vilankulo side of town. The **Motel Palmar**, about 1km from the town centre towards Vilankulo, seems reasonable value at US$9 for a self-contained double, but it's not too convenient if you're on foot. Accommodation is in detached cottages, each of which contains two rooms with a shared entrance, so it might be advisable to check the lock on your individual room.

There are also a few rooms in the **Restaurante Pousada do Maxixe**. Doubles cost US$9 (ordinary) or US$13 self-contained.

Where to eat

The **Stop Snack Bar** opposite the Golfinho Azul is an open-air restaurant with tables under thatched canopies, and a great position overlooking the bay to Inhambane. The food here is excellent and reasonably priced (fish or calamari and chips cost around US$4, while meat and chicken dishes a little more) and the waiters speak English. Also recommended is the **Restaurante Don Carlos**, which has a similar menu at similar prices, and an inviting Mediterranean bar atmosphere (missing one vital ingredient when we were there – other customers!). You could eat at the **Restaurante Pousada do Maxixe** – I don't know what the food is like, but I didn't find the musty dining room particularly encouraging.

If you are staying at the Campismo (campsites here have barbecue facilities) and want to prepare your own food, the market has the usual good selection of fresh vegetables and fish, and there are a couple of supermarkets on the block facing the bus station. Shellfish and the like are probably best bought on the beach.

INHAMBANE

The eponymous capital of Inhambane Province lies on a natural bay formed by a deep inlet at the mouth of the small Matumba River. Inhambane is the oldest extant settlement between Maputo and Beira, and it is without doubt the most pleasant and interesting town covered in this chapter. A spacious layout of tree-lined avenues fringed by several eye-pleasing colonial buildings gives Inhambane a strongly Mediterranean character. It is also a remarkably clean and orderly town, with a strangely subdued Old World atmosphere quite unlike anywhere else I've visited in Africa. In short, Inhambane is definitely worth a visit.

Little is known of Inhambane's history prior to the 18th century. It was almost certainly a port of note even before the Portuguese era, and it was visited by several Portuguese traders in the early 15th century. In 1560, Inhambane was selected as the site of a short-lived Jesuit Mission, the first in East Africa, and when the leader of the mission arrived he noted that several Portuguese traders had settled there. By the end of the 16th century it had been incorporated into the Portuguese East African monopoly and had become a regular port of call for Portuguese ivory trading ships. During the 17th and early 18th centuries, Inhambane was, along with Delagoa Bay (Maputo), the most important trade terminus between the coast and interior of what is now southern Mozambique.

In 1727, the Portuguese Commander Bernardo Soares discovered a Dutch vessel trading with the local chiefs of Inhambane. Following this, a punitive expedition led by Domingos Rebello arrived at Inhambane from Sofala, destroying several villages and killing at least two local chiefs as a punishment for trading with another European power. Commander Soares stayed on at Inhambane, where he built a fort large enough to house a

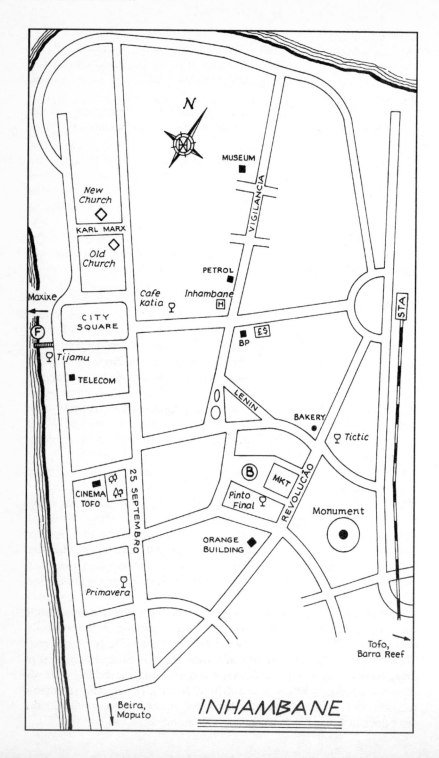

INHAMBANE

garrison of 50 men. Soares' fort was hardly the most impressive defensive structure (a compatriot remarked that "it would have been enough for [the Dutch] to have laid eyes on it to capture it"), but its presence evidently discouraged further Dutch trade, and it laid the foundation for a permanent Portuguese settlement.

Although Inhambane was officially recognised as a Portuguese town in 1763, the local ivory trade was in reality dominated by Indians rather than Portuguese, an aberrant situation which dated to the early 18th century when the port had briefly been leased to an Indian trader called Calcanagi Velabo. Inhambane's Christian population numbered only 200 at the end of the 18th century. Remarkably, several of the parish priests appointed at around this time were of Indian extraction! The town rapidly grew in prosperity during its early years (in 1770, the customs revenue raised at Inhambane was almost equal to that raised at Quelimane), not least because it was the first Mozambican port to establish a trade in slaves. Roughly 400 slaves were exported from Inhambane in 1762, a number which had quadrupled by the end of that decade while ivory export figures steadily dwindled. In 1834, Inhambane was practically razed by Soshangane's Gaza warriors, and most of its traders were killed, but the town soon recovered, and by 1858 it had a population of roughly 4,000 (of which 75% were slaves). Even as recently as 1928, Inhambane was the third-largest centre of population in Mozambique, after the capital city and Beira.

Inhambane today is anything but a bustling trade centre – it is difficult to think of a more sedate town anywhere on the East African coast – but neither has it fallen into the state of disrepair that sometimes appears to be synonymous with the term 'historical coastal town'. Most of the older buildings are clustered around an open square which lies at the jetty end of Avenida Indepencia. Of particular interest is a beautiful 18th-century Cathedral to the north of the square (with what must surely be deliberate irony, the original cathedral and a more modern church are practically the only buildings on the block-long Rua Karl Marx!). The seafront itself is very pretty, particularly at sunset, though it isn't really recommended for swimming. The central market on Avenida Revolução is a lively place, with a good variety of vegetables, fish and local crafts on sale. The Museum on Avenida Vigelençia, two blocks north of the Inhambane Hotel, was closed when we went past, and a peek through the window suggested that it doesn't have too much to offer.

The Inhambane area is noted for its seemingly endless stands of tall coconut palms, and although the town itself lacks a good beach, the peninsula on which it lies boasts several, all within 30km of town. The best developed of these, and the only one that is accessible in an ordinary saloon car, is Praia do Tofo, rated for its surfing, swimming and snorkelling (though currents make it unsafe to swim north of the hotels). There are also camping facilities at Barra Reef, Coconut Bay and Pongane, the latter regarded to offer the best snorkelling in southern Mozambique.

Getting there and away

The surfaced 33km branch road to Inhambane is signposted from the EN1 roughly 450km northeast of Maputo, 235km northeast of Xai-Xai, and 30km south of Maxixe. There is a BP garage at the junction.

Although there are regular *chapas* between the junction and Inhambane, the better way to get to Inhambane by public transport is on a dhow from Maxixe. The two towns are separated by over 60km of road, but they face each other across a bay and are less than 4km apart as the crow flies. Motorised and unmotorised dhows run between Maxixe and Inhambane throughout the day; the cost of a one-way trip is less than US$1. If the cost of accommodation in Inhambane is prohibitive, it's perfectly possible to visit the town as a day trip from Maxixe.

From Inhambane, a good surfaced road covers the 22km to Praia do Tofo. The turn-off to Barra Beach is signposted to the left roughly 15km along this road. The sandy road south to Coconut Bay and Pongane, navigable only in a 4WD, leaves the Tofo road opposite the fish factory on the outskirts of town.

There are a few *chapas* daily between Inhambane and Tofo, and you can pick up shared taxis that take you within 4km of the backpackers resort at Barra Reef. Hitching to Tofo is possible if you walk out of town over the railway track past the small market about 200m along the Tofo road. Unless you get a lucky hitch, Coconut Bay and Pongane aren't realistic goals without private transport.

Where to stay

The only formal accommodation in the town centre is the **Inhambane Hotel**, on the corner of Avenida Indepencia and Avenida Vigelençia. It's a quiet place, rarely used by tourists, but the rooms are pleasant enough and acceptable value for money at US$15/16/17 single/casal/twin. If you ask around, you may be able to find cheaper accommodation at the pink school building near the railway station; ask for the **Escola Ferroviario Alojamento**.

There is a fair range of accommodation at Praia do Tofo, which lies between the Indian Ocean and the freshwater Lake Pembane. The **Complexo Turistico Tofo Mar** lies on the beachfront and has self-contained double rooms for between US$30 and US$45, while the **anonymous hotel** just behind it has similar rooms for US$40. For budget-conscious travellers, the best bet is **Club Americano**, where you can camp for US$6 per person (including a hearty breakfast) or rent a double grass hut at US$12 or a four-bed chalet at US$24. There is a bar and restaurant on site. You can also free camp on the beach in front of the Complexo Turistico, provided that you're prepared to take the attendant security risk.

Barra Reef Backpackers lies at the very north of the peninsula, past the freshwater Lake Malongue. Close to some swamps, and near a reef which offers good snorkelling, the resort offers camping for US$3 per person and basic cabanas for US$3.50 per person. Facilities include flush toilets, hot showers and electricity. The diving school next door rents out snorkelling equipment, and it has a pleasant bar with with cable television and a dartboard. There is food at the diving school, or you can buy fresh seafood on the beach and cook it yourself – there is a kitchen at the Backpackers. You can catch a chapa from Inhambane to within 3km of the site, then walk the rest of the way.

Where to eat

There are a few good restaurants in Inhambane, with prices generally starting at around US$4 for fish dishes up to US$6 for meat and chicken dishes. The open-air **Ti Jamu Snack Bar** certainly wins on location – overlooking the bay in front of the jetty, it's just about the perfect place to sit as the sun sets over Maxixe. On Avenida Revoluçáo, near the market, the **Tic Tic Snack Bar** does very good food, and it offers you the option of sitting indoors or at a table on the street. The **Promavera Restaurant** on Avenido 25 de Setembro also looks good, though there is only indoor seating. We didn't try the food at the **Inhambane Hotel**, but the pavement bar is a nice place for a drink and the beer is cheaper than elsewhere in town.

MORRUNGULO

This is the only beach resort between Maxixe and Vilankulo, and a particularly popular destination with Zimbabweans. The resort lies roughly 100km north of Maxixe and it is reached via a signposted dirt road which leaves the EN1 a few kilometres north of Massinga town. It can normally be reached in an ordinary saloon car provided it hasn't rained for a few days, but the branch road is very sandy in parts and so a 4WD is preferable.

Camping is available for US$8 per person and there are a few very smart self-catering cottages costing US$90 per unit for up to four people. Full-board accommodation costs around US$70 per person. Facilities include organised scuba diving excursions for around US$20 per dive, and you can hire snorkelling equipment for less than US$10. Deep-sea fishing charters start at around US$100.

Booking is essential during school holidays in Zimbabwe or South Africa. Contact Mozambique Marine Holidays in Johannesburg for details, tel: (011) 783 7116 or 883 2033.

VILANKULO

This small but sprawling town, which lies roughly 700km from Maputo and 500km from Beira, has become *the* focal point for backpackers passing through Mozambique, a status which is influenced less perhaps by Vilankulo's attractive coastline and proximity to the Bazaruto Islands than it is by the presence of a couple of excellent backpacker-oriented resorts along the beach north of the town centre.

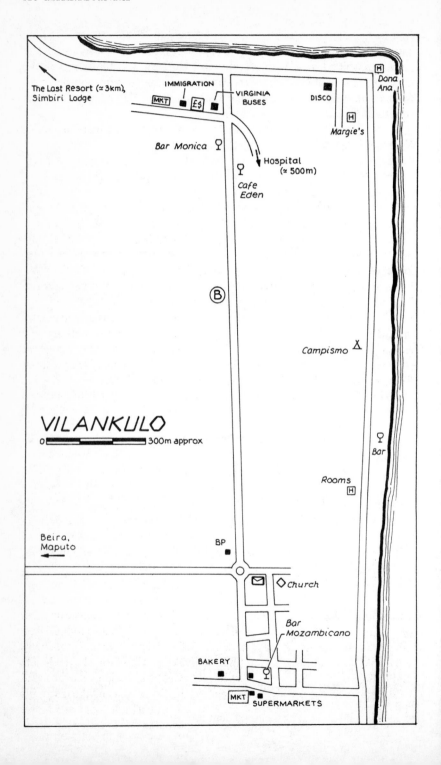

The Last Resort (≈3km),
Simbiri Lodge

IMMIGRATION

VIRGINIA
BUSES

MKT £$

DISCO

Dona
Ana

Margie's

Bar Monica

Cafe
Eden

Hospital
(≈ 500m)

B

Campismo

VILANKULO

0 ⸻ 300m approx

Bar

Rooms

Beira,
Maputo

BP

Church

Bar
Mozambicano

BAKERY

MKT SUPERMARKETS

Getting there and away

Vilankulo lies 20km east of the EN1 along a good surfaced road. The misleadingly signposted turn-off is roughly 220km north of Maxixe – you'll know that you're there when you pass a BP garage to your left and then shortly afterwards reach a large intersection around which lies a cluster of small shops. Take the fork to the right.

Buses between Maputo and Beira stop at Vilankulo, and there are also a couple of buses daily travelling directly between Maxixe and Vilankulo. In the unlikely event that you are dropped off at the junction with the EN1, you shouldn't have any difficulty hitching or finding a ride on a *chapa* through to town.

Shortly after Maxixe, tall coconut palms give way to dense brachestygia woodland. We saw several interesting birds along the road.

LAM flights between Maputo and Beira will land at Vilankulo on request.

Where to stay

Vilankulo probably has the best choice of affordable accommodation of any town covered in this chapter. The only proper hotel, overlooking the jetty, is the **Hotel Dona Ana**, a curious example of Bauhaus architecture – or so I'm told (its peculiar curves and angles look like something that escaped from an episode of the 1960s television programme *The Avengers*). As you might expect, the Dona Ana is a little run-down, but it's not without a certain bizarre charm, and the spacious rooms are indisputably good value at US$8/15 single/double using communal showers, US$9/16 self-contained double, and US$20 for a double suite. There's safe parking outside the hotel, watched over by a man with a bow and arrow (I couldn't decide whether his officious approach every time we got into our own car was best put down to zealous attention to duty, or enthusiastic exploitation of yet another opportunity to bum a cigarette).

Also along the main beachfront, roughly 1km from the Dona Ana, the **Campismo de Vilankulo** is a rather bland and uninviting site enclosed by wire fencing. Camping costs US$3 per person, and there is an additional charge of US$2 per vehicle. A further 500m down the beachfront road, an easily missed sign that simply reads **'Rooms'** signals the entrance to a small complex of huts – very nice huts, it must be said, with spotless shower and toilet facilities, all at the very reasonable price of US$6 per person.

The only other option in the town centre (and not one that will necessarily still be operating by the time you read this) is **Margie's House** (or *Casa Margerida*), which offers immaculate rooms in a private house for US$8.50 per person and camping in the garden for US$4.50 per person. Good meals are available at US$2.50 for continental breakfast, US$4 for a buffet lunch, and US$5.50 for a seafood dinner. To get to Casa Margerida, take the small road leading off the surfaced road between the Dona Ana and the disco; it's the fourth house to the right, and the only one with a high hedge and fence.

The alternative to staying in town is to head out to one of the backpackers resorts along the beach. These lie 3km out of town by road (sandy but passable in a saloon car) or about 20 minutes' walk along the beach from the Hotel Dona Ana. The closest place to town is **The Last Resort**, which has cleared campsites for US$3 per person and simple reed cabanas without beds or bedding for US$3.50 per person. Lying right on the beach, and carved attractively into the natural bush (excellent birding), the Last Resort has a bar and restaurant serving chilled beers and sodas, as well as inexpensive meals.

The newer **Simbiri Lodge** has the disadvantages of being set back from the beach and another 500m or so out of town. Otherwise, facilities are much like those at the Last Resort, and slightly cheaper at US$2.50 per person to camp and US$3 for floor space in a cabana.

Where to eat

In town, the **Hotel Dona Ana** serves good, inexpensive seafood meals. Lunch and dinner cost a straight US$4 inclusive of soup irrespective of what you order as a main course. Actually, this suggests an element of choice which doesn't apparently exist. We assumed we were being offered the choice of linefish or crayfish when both were brought for our perusal prior to being cooked, but after opting for crayfish, we ended up with one plate of each – in hindsight, that's probably what the waiter was trying to tell us. That said, provided that you like seafood, you can be certain of getting a good meal at the Dona Ana, and plenty of it.

The **Bar Mozambique** is a South African run place near the market complete with chilled beers and sodas, a wonky pool table, and an inside wall covered in graffiti. It's also about the only place in town where you get something other than seafood to eat: peri-peri chicken, hamburgers and steaks are all on offer in the US$4 to US$6 price range.

If you're staying at one of the backpackers' hostels, the lazy option is to eat there. A seafood dinner costs US$4 per person, and they also do pancakes, eggs, toast and the like for breakfast and lunch. The alternative is a do-it-yourself barbecue: crayfish and fish can be bought dirt cheap from fishermen on the beach. The main market in town sells the usual variety of fruit and vegetables, and there are several supermarkets outside of the market entrance. The bakery near the market has fresh bread daily at 10.00 and 16.00.

Useful information

Money can be exchanged at the Commercial Bank, with the usual US$5 commission deducted. You'll get a better rate for cash at one of the supermarkets near the market.

The disco near the Hotel Dona Ana often has live concerts on Friday and Saturday nights.

The staff at the Last Resort can help arrange dhow trips to Magaruque and Benguerra Islands. The dhow will cost US$12 per day, and can seat up to six people. Snorkelling equipment can be hired at the Last Resort.

For visa extensions, visit the immigration office near the Commercial Bank.

INHASSORO

Heading north along the EN1, Inhassoro is the final mainland coastal resort before the road veers inland for the 450-odd kilometre trip via the Save River to Beira. Much smaller than Vilankulo, but with a similarly sprawling layout, Inhassoro has an attractive beach and low-key atmosphere that could, in the right mood, keep you lingering on for days.

Getting there and away

Inhassoro lies 13km from the EN1 along a good surfaced road. The turn-off is 50km north of the turn-off to Vilankulo. Buses between Maputo and Beira stop at Inhassoro.

Where to stay and eat

The **Hotel Seta** is an attractive, well-run and surprisingly inexpensive place lying in large, wooded grounds above the beach. It has self-contained doubles for US$20 as well as more basic doubles using clean communal toilets and showers for US$12. The attached campsite costs around US$3 per person. There is a good restaurant and well-stocked bar attached, and safe parking on the property.

About 1km from the hotel, adjacent to the bus station, the **Complexo Salema Mufundisse Chibique** serves filling meals for around US$3. When we were in Inhassoro, this was the only place where you could be served something other than seafood.

BAZARUTO ARCHIPELAGO

The Bazaruto Archipelago consists of a string of small sandy islands lying roughly 15–25km from the mainland north of Vilankulo and south of Inhassoro. One of the few parts of Mozambique that was safe to visit during the closing years of the civil war, the Bazaruto islands have developed an upmarket package-based tourist industry that is largely South African funded and which functions in near isolation from the rest of the country. Most visitors to the islands fly directly there from Johannesburg without ever setting foot on the Mozambican mainland.

The archipelago, gazetted as a National Park in 1971, consists of five main islands. The three largest islands were formerly part of a peninsula which is thought to have separated from the mainland within the last 10,000 years. The largest and most northerly island is Bazaruto itself: 30km long, on average 5km wide, and boasting a few substantial freshwater lakes near its southern tip. South of this are Benguela, the second largest island, and the much smaller Magaruque, the latter almost directly opposite Vilankulo.

The smallest island is a former penal colony covering an area of roughly 2km² roughly halfway between Bazaruto and the mainland. The fifth island, Bengue, is only rarely visited by tourists.

With their white palm-lined beaches, the islands of the Bazaruto archipelago are everything you would expect of Indian Ocean islands. They are of great interest to birdwatchers. Roughly 150 species have been recorded, including several that are rare or localised in southern Africa, for instance green coucal; crab, sand and Mongolian plovers; olive and blue-cheeked bee-eaters; and a variety of petrels, gulls and waders. Lesser flamingoes seen on the islands come from the a nearby breeding colony, the only one known to occur in eastern Africa south of Lake Natron in Tanzania.

An estimated 45 reptile and amphibian species occur on the islands, including two endemics. The freshwater lakes on Bazaruto support a relic breeding population of crocodiles, while the shores of the islands are nesting sites for at least three types of turtle including the rare loggerhead. Mammals present include the localised suni antelope, red duiker, bushbuck and samango monkey. An endemic butterfly species is found on Bazaruto Island.

However, the main attractions of the islands lie off their shores. The surrounding sea, warmed by the Mozambique Stream, is crystal clear and its reefs support a variety of brightly coloured fish, making the area one of Mozambique's finest snorkelling and diving destinations. There are well established diving centres on the north of Bazaruto Island and on Benguerra Island. Visitors to the islands frequently see marine turtles, humpback whales, and bottlenose, spinner and humpback dolphins, as well as large game fish such as marlins and barracudas. The islands are also renowned for their game fishing.

The Bazaruto area supports what is probably East Africa's last viable population of the the endangered dugong. This large and exclusively marine herbivore is a member of the family Sirinia, along with the manatee of the Atlantic Ocean, and its closest terrestrial relatives are elephants and hyraxes. The name Sirinia, a reference to the Sirens of Greek legends, has been given to this family of marine animals because they are considered to be the most likely candidate for the source of the mermaid myth. Dugongs were formerly widespread and abundant in the Indo-Pacific region, and as recently as the early 1970s groups of four to five were commonly seen in places like Inhambane, Angoche and even near Maputo. Dugongs have suffered a drastic population decrease in the last few decades, probably because so many individuals are trapped in fish nets. They are now threatened with extinction except in the seas around northern Australia and the Arabian Gulf. However, dugongs are still seen regularly around Bazaruto – Bob de Lacy Smith had the good fortune recently to see two of them mating in shallow water.

The Bazaruto islands have a long history of human occupation. Prior to the Portuguese occupation of the coast, the islands were almost certainly the site of East Africa's most southerly Muslim trading settlements. By the middle of the 16th century, the islands were lorded over by Portuguese traders, and the surrounding sea was known for producing high quality pearls. The first formal Portuguese settlement was established in 1855, on Santa Carolina. Initially an ivory trading post, the island was later used as a penal colony, but it was evidently abandoned by the beginning of the 20th century. Interesting historical relics include a ruined 19th-century fort on Magaruque and a fully intact but non-operational 100-year-old lighthouse on Bazaruto.

Getting there and away

Because tourism to the Bazaruto islands has developed in relative isolation from that on the mainland, the overwhelming majority of visitors fly to the islands from South Africa as part of a package organised by the lodge they are staying at. People visiting one of the islands as a self-contained trip out of South Africa are thus advised to contact the various lodges (addresses below) or a travel agent to find out what sort of packages are currently available. Return flights from Johannesburg cost around US$400–450 per person. Scheduled flights leave in both directions on Tuesdays and Fridays.

Magaruque and Benguela Islands can be visited by dhow from Vilankulo. The best place to organise a dhow trip is at the Last Resort; the boat and captain will cost around US$12 per day shared by up to six people, and snorkelling equipment can be hired too. The trip takes around two to four hours in each direction, depending on the prevailing winds. In addition to protecting yourself from the sun, take along some warm clothing – the combination of wet and wind can make it a surprisingly chilly trip.

From the mainland, Bazaruto and Santa Carolina Islands are best reached from Inhassoro. Motor boats to these islands can be arranged at the Hotel Seta, which also has safe parking for motorised travellers. If you have booked to stay at Benguela Lodge, and intend to go there overland, the lodge can make advance arrangements for safe parking in Vilankulo and they can get a motorboat to pick you up there.

Where to stay

There are upmarket lodges on Bazaruto, Benguerra and Magaruque Islands. All the lodges charge around US$150/200 single/double full board for visitors getting there by independent means. It's more normal, however, to visit as a fly-in package inclusive of accommodation, and meals. Packages vary in price depending on the duration of your stay and the season, so you are advised to make enquiries at the individual booking offices for the lodge you want to visit. Charges relating to facilities and equipment for various watersports, as well as fishing, snorkelling and scuba diving courses, are not included in the cost of fly-in packages.

The hotel on Santa Carolina was formerly the most popular of those on the islands, but it is now in a derelict state and, although it's sure to be

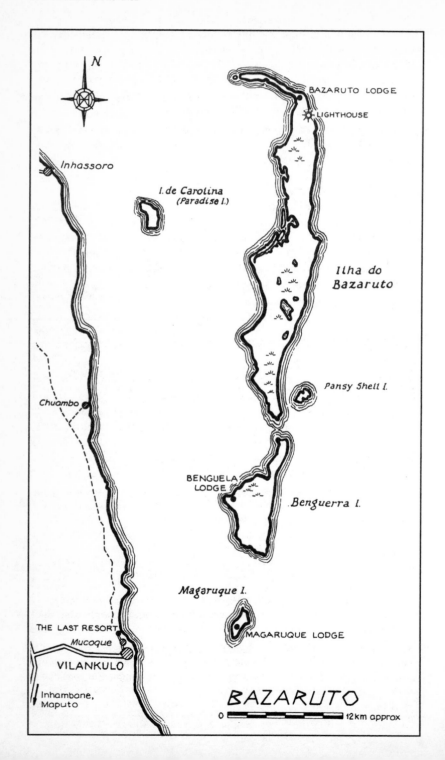

BAZARUTO

rebuilt at some stage, this is unlikely to happen during the lifespan of this book.

Accommodation in any of the lodges can be booked through the Mozambique National Tourist Company, Mozambique Connections or, better still, directly through the individual lodge (telephone and fax numbers below are in South Africa unless otherwise stated):

Benguela Lodge (Benguerra Island). Tel: (011) 483 2734/5, Fax: (011) 728 3767.
Bazaruto Lodge (Bazaruto Island). Tel: (011) 447 3528/4454 or (031) 368 1947. Fax: (011) 880 5364 or (031) 32 9825.
Magaruque Lodge (Magaruque Island). Zimbabwe. Tel: (04) 79 6411. Fax: (04) 70 6148.

Cheaper accommodation can be found at **Sabal Lodge** on Bazaruto Island (around US$35 per person) and at the chalets on Santa Carolina (around US$17 per person, bring all food and water with you). For budget travellers, **Gabriel's** on Benguerra Island used to allow camping for US$5 per person, but it was forced to close in late 1996.

GAME FISHING AND DIVING FROM BENGUELA ISLAND

Bob de Lacy Smith

The Bazaruto area offers some of the most challenging game fishing in southern Africa. Large black and striped marlins are regularly taken between October and December. Prior to the civil war, specimens weighing in the region of 500kg were caught off the islands, and the recent record is more than 400kg. Sailfish can be caught throughout the year, with July and August being the best months for these fine fighters. The largest specimen so far is 55kg. Other game fish to be taken include tuna, all types of bonito, wahoo, king and queen mackerel, dorado, rainbow runner, prodigal son, giant barracuda and several species of kingfish including the mighty giant trevall (*Caranx ignoblis*).

Saltwater fly-fishing has also taken off in the area and regular clinics are held where experts pass on their knowledge to novices. The sport has a growing following and conditions on the islands are ideal. The much sought bonefish occurs in the area, and specimens of up to 8.2kg have been caught by local fishermen, though they have so far evaded the rods of fly-fishermen.

For divers, Two Mile Reef has several interesting dive sites with a maximum depth of 20m. These reefs are completely unspoilt and teem with fishes ranging from tiny coral fish to the mighty potato bass and brindle bass. Manta rays and whale sharks can also be seen by lucky divers. There are many other undived reefs in the area, notably the untouched reefs at Cabo Sebastáo, which offer the experienced diving opportunities to go deeper than 20m.

Bob de Lacy Smith, the owner of Bob's Scuba Centre on Benguela Island, has been resident on the Bazaruto Islands for seven years. Readers seeking further information about diving and fishing opportunities on the Benguela Islands can contact Benguela Tours in South Africa (same phone and fax as Benguela Lodge).

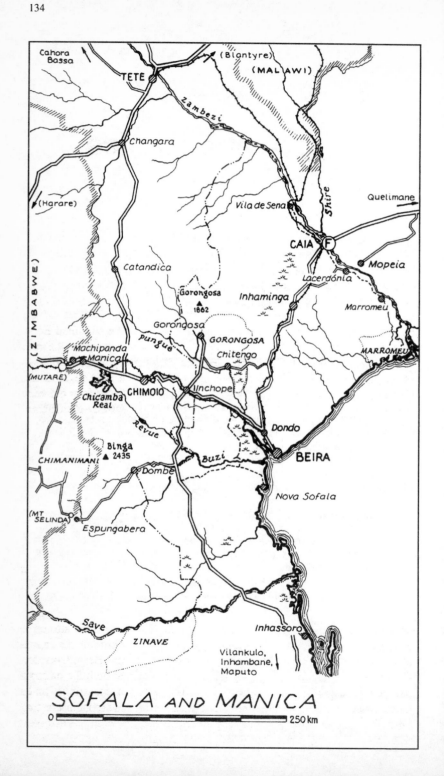

SOFALA AND MANICA

0 ▬▬▬▬▬▬▬ 250 km

Chapter Nine

Sofala and Manica

The central Mozambican provinces of Sofala and Manica are bordered by the Save River to the south, Zimbabwe to the west, the Indian Ocean to the east, Tete province to the northwest and the Zambezi to the northeast. This is an area of relatively limited interest to travellers, and the two provinces have been lumped together in this book largely because they are connected by one of the most important routes in Mozambique, the so-called Beira Corridor between Mutare in Zimbabwe and the Indian Ocean port of Beira.

The interior of central Mozambique has a long history, largely because of its strategic importance to the Swahili gold trade in mediaeval times. For centuries, the Zambezi Valley formed the main trade corridor between the coastal port of Sofala and the goldfields of present-day Zimbabwe. Settled by Muslim traders in the 15th century, the Zambezi Valley later became the first part of the East African interior to be permanently settled by the Portuguese. Many of the region's modern towns were founded even before the Portuguese occupation of the coast. Manica, for instance, stands on the site of the Masekesa gold fair, which operated intermittently from pre-Portuguese times until it was overrun by Nxaba's Nguni warrors in the 1830s, while Tete and Sena on the Zambezi were both founded by Muslims and then occupied by Portugal in the 16th century. Alluring as this may sound on paper, few visible traces of the region's more antiquated settlements remain.

The Beira Corridor assumed a high level of regional importance during the civil war, when it was protected by the Zimbabwean army and was just about the only part of Mozambique which allowed for a reasonably safe passage. Along the Beira Corridor, Chicamba Real Dam is an attractive enough spot but of no more than passing interest, while Chimoio, the capital of Manica, is affably unremarkable. To the north of the Beira Corridor, Gorongosa National Park is sadly depleted of game, and both the national park and neighbouring Mount Gorongosa suffer from inaccessibility and a lack of accommodation or camping facilities. Perhaps the most interesting place in either of these provinces is Beira itself, a city which has acquired a bad name with travellers but which we thoroughly liked and enjoyed.

Getting around

The main roads in this part of the country are all surfaced and in reasonably good condition. Sections of the Beira Corridor were in the process of being resurfaced in mid-1996, but even in its present condition the road can be driven in its entirety in any vehicle. Aside from a few temporary dirt diversions, you can cruise along most of the Beira Corridor at around 80km/hour, keeping an eye open for the very occasional pothole. The Tete to Chimoio road is in a similar condition. The only other routes likely to be used by visitors are the dirt road between Chimoio and Selinda on the Zimbabwe border, which requires 4WD, and the road from Inchope to Gorongosa, which is surfaced and thus should be navigable in any vehicle. Trains between Beira and Mutare run every other day, stopping at all stations en route. They're very slow, very cheap, and facilities are non-existent. There are also plenty of buses and chapas connecting the various towns along the Beira Corridor.

BEIRA

Beira, the capital of Sofala province, is the country's second largest city and its most important port. It is also quite possibly the most unpopular city in southern Africa, at least so far as travellers are concerned. Before we arrived in Beira we spoke to four groups of travellers and heard nothing but negative reports of an unfriendly, depressing, war-damaged slum, with nothing to see and a high incidence of crime against tourists. One of the groups we spoke to – people who had already spent several months travelling down from Uganda – were so put out by Beira that they locked themselves away in a room in the most upmarket hotel in town! Needless to say, we arrived in Beira fully expecting the worst.

As it turned out, within minutes of locking our valuables in a hotel room and hitting the streets, we looked at each other and asked what the fuss was all about. Beira *is* rather run-down, though it appears to me that this is more through neglect than any direct war damage – certainly it bears no comparison to Kampala when I visited it shortly after the end of Uganda's civil war – and the city centre itself is rapidly being restored to something approaching its pre-war condition. There is, of course, a great deal of poverty in Beira, but then so is there in any city in the so-called developing world, the difference being one of prominence: along with Maputo, Beira is one of the few places in Africa to have high-rise slums. As for the reported crime and unfriendliness, all I can say is that we felt perfectly safe wandering around the city centre at night, and we didn't notice any hostility.

What Beira does have is a definite atmosphere, determined by its sticky Indian Ocean air, a quite preposterous mix of mismatched architectural styles, and a buzzing street and cafe life focused around the attractive city square and the bars in the grid of roads near the railway station and port. It's a thriving, pleasant city, and with a bit of common sense I don't think there's anything to fear security-wise. Don't let the bad reports put you off.

History

The region around Beira was the mediaeval gateway to the African interior. For centuries prior to Portuguese occupation, the region's most important trading centre was Sofala, situated about 50km south of present-day Beira amongst the shallow waterways and impermanent sandbars that characterise the stretch of coast near the mouth of the Buzi River. Founded in the 9th century AD, Sofala formed the main link between the inland trade route to the gold mines of Karangaland and the prosperous city of Kilwa (in southern Tanzania), as well as being an important trading centre in its own right. By the 15th century it probably had a population of around 10,000.

In 1500, Sofala was visited by Sancho de Toar, who recognised its pivotal role in the gold trade. Five years later, Portugal erected a small fort and trading factory at Sofala. Although this was done with the permission of the local sheikh, Portugal rapidly set about establishing its own local trade network, bypassing the Muslim traders. Within a year of its foundation, the Portuguese fort was attacked without any marked success by the sheikh and his allies. Portugal responded by killing the sheikh in a punitive attack, and installing a puppet ruler in his place.

The Portuguese occupation of Sofala evidently coincided with a northward migration of the main chieftaincies of Karangaland and a corresponding shift in the main inland trade routes. Combined with the increasing dominance of ivory over gold as a trading commodity, this shift in trade routes caused Sofala to diminish in importance. As early as 1530, the main captaincy of the coast was shifted from Sofala to Mozambique Island. By the 17th century, Sofala was a neglected backwater, with the token Portuguese occupancy largely to prevent the fort from falling to a rival European power. And by the 1750s, the stone buildings of the Portuguese quarter were partially submerged, and Sofala was more or less left in the hands of a few Muslim traders. By the time that modern Mozambique came into being, Sofala's permanent buildings had mostly disappeared beneath the sea, and the ancient port was passed over in favour of Chiluane as the local administrative centre. The stone fort at Sofala was dismantled and its bricks were used to build Beira Cathedral.

Beira itself is one of Mozambique's more modern cities, founded in 1884 on the sandy, marshy shore near the mouth of the Pungue River as a base for the rich prazero Joaquim Carlos Paiva de Andrada. In the late 1880s, the British imperialist and founder of Rhodesia, Cecil John Rhodes, attempted to annex the Beira area, but his attempts at warmongering garnered no support from the British government and in 1891 the area was formally incorporated into Mozambique. The town centre was laid out in 1887, and at the same time a permanent garrison was installed. Beira was granted city status in 1894. Serious development of the port started in 1891, when it was leased to Andrada's Mozambique Company, and it accelerated after 1898 following the completion of Rhodes' railway line to Rhodesia.

In its early days, Beira was a scruffy shanty town with a reputation as the most drunken, lawless settlement in Africa. At the turn of the century, the city boasted some 80 bars and a population of only 4,000, roughly a quarter of which consisted of Europeans, mostly of Portuguese or British origin. The town did not have the most amenable of settings: the company that built the railway line to Rhodesia lost 60% of its European staff to malaria in two years, and the surrounding area was so untamed that lions were frequently seen walking through the main street. The sand on which the town was built was so deep that 40km of trolley lines had to be laid to allow residents to transport goods to their homes. The trolley lines later served as public transport, before they were torn up in 1930.

Beira's rapid expansion was curbed after rail links were completed between Rhodesia and South Africa in 1903. Nevertheless, the figures produced by the 1928 census show that by this time Beira was well-established as the country's second city, with a population of almost 23,694 – more than half that of Lourenço Marques, and well over double that of the next largest town in Mozambique. The city today has a population of around half a million.

Getting there and away
From the south

The road heading north from Inhassoro to Beira has a few very bad stretches – nothing to worry about if you are driving a 4WD or using public transport, but a potential problem if you are driving a saloon car. It is important to get an early start, as the full 450km drive from Inhassoro to Beira will take at least ten hours, longer if you have a flat tyre or any other technical problem, and you most certainly do not want to be driving on this road after dark (aside from the risk of banditry, you'd almost certainly drive into a pothole sooner or later). If you don't think you can make it all the way in a day, you could cut an hour off the trip by staying at one of the rooms attached to the roadside bar in Pande, a small settlement about 10km south of the Save River – there is no other accommodation between Inhassoro and Beira.

Before we drove to Beira, we had heard so many bad reports about this road that we very nearly decided not to risk it and to take a bus. Having taken the plunge, we – again – wondered what all the fuss was about. From Inhassoro to the Save River, there is an excellent surfaced road which you can cruise along at a comfortable 80km/hour or so. After crossing the Save (and paying the nominal toll-fee), the surfaced road is in fair condition as far as the Buzi River, though it's worth keeping your speed down to around 60km/hour due to the occasional large pothole. And remember to cut your speed whenever a vehicle approaches in the opposite direction – Sod's law dictates that the nastiest potholes will save themselves for that moment when oncoming traffic restricts your ability to weave around the road.

The worst bit of road begins roughly 50km north of the Buzi River and it continues until about 30km before Inchope, the village at the junction of the EN1 and the Beira Corridor. This stretch probably only covers about

30km, but even in a 4WD it will take longer than an hour to get through. Heavily mined during the civil war, there are several patches which are so severely potholed that you need to follow dirt lanes on the side of the damaged tar. If it hasn't rained for a few days, you can get through in just about any car, provided that you have reasonable clearance and that you drive very slowly (at low speed, there's no real danger of damaging a tyre or rim, but there are countless opportunities for cracking an unprotected sump, which means that you need to be very conscious of the height of the centre of the car in relation to the wheels). After rain, the road can be covered only in a 4WD. The situation changes from week to week, and the best place to seek current advice is at the Hotel Seta in Inhassoro, but broadly speaking, and a week of unseasonal weather excepted, a saloon car should get through during the dry winter months (May to September) but it may have problems in the wet summer months.

If you are using public transport, the best thing to do, whether you're heading to Beira directly from Maputo or from somewhere in between, is to catch one of the buses that travel the whole way between Maputo and Beira. These stop at all large towns along the way, but unlike local buses they don't stop at every possible opportunity to pick up passengers. The recommended bus service is the Virginia Bus Line, which leaves Maputo at 05.00 from outside the Hotel Universo on Avenida Karl Marx, overnights at the Save River to avoid crossing the worst stretch of road in the dark, and normally arrives in Beira before 12.00 the following day. You can check exact timetables and prices at the booking office on the first floor of the Hotel Universo in Maputo. The full trip costs US$20. Other buses leave Maputo from the main bus station at 13.00, spending the night in Maxixe, and normally arriving in Beira after dark the next day – not a good idea.

In the opposite direction, Virginia buses from Beira to Maputo leave at 05.00 and, because they will have crossed the bad stretch of road by midday, they will continue driving until they reach their final destination – generally late at night. Again, you don't really want to be wandering around Maputo in the dark, so it's better to get off at somewhere like Maxixe or Xai-Xai and continue south the next day.

LAM flies between Maputo and Beira on a daily basis. There are no scheduled passenger boats between Maputo and Beira, but it may occasionally be possible to organise a ride with a cargo boat. Ask at the Marítima agency at the port end of Avenida Karl Marx in Maputo – tel: 42 6146.

From the west

The road connecting Beira to the Zimbabwean town of Mutare via Chimoio is in good condition, and the 300km trip shouldn't take longer than four hours in a private vehicle. There is also a good road connecting the Beira Corridor to Tete; the junction is roughly halfway between Chimoio and Manica.

Coming from Mutare or Tete on public transport, it is emphatically worth avoiding arriving in Beira in the late afternoon or evening. If there's any

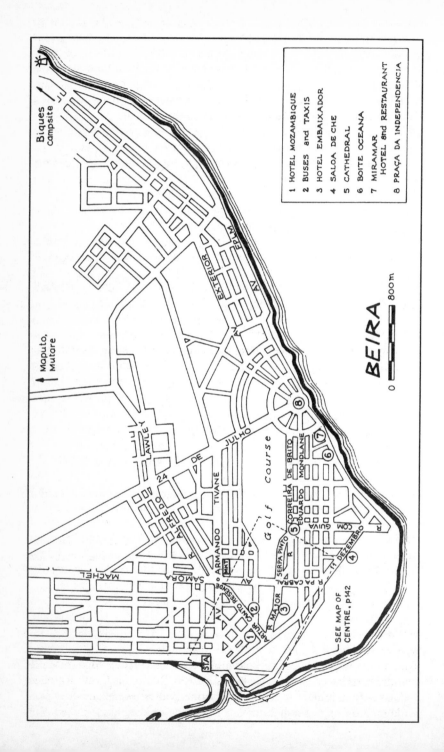

BEIRA

1 HOTEL MOZAMBIQUE
2 BUSES and TAXIS
3 HOTEL EMBAIXADOR
4 SALOA DE CHE
5 CATHEDRAL
6 BOITE OCEANA
7 MIRAMAR
   HOTEL and RESTAURANT
8 PRAÇA DA INDEPENDENCIA

danger of this, I suggest that you spend a night in Chimoio, then catch the first public transport to Beira the next morning. Chapas to Beira leave Chimoio from the bus terminus opposite the railway station. On the opposite direction, chapas and buses to Chimoio leave Beira from the central bus station on Rua Artur Canto Resenda. There are regular chapas between Chimoio and Machipanda on the Zimbabwe border – watch out for thieves. Hitching is a realistic possibility along the Beira Corridor.

The rail service between Beira and Mutare runs in each direction every other day. It's very slow and uncomfortable, and few travellers use it.

LAM flies between Harare and Beira a few times a week.

From the north
There are no bus services covering the 1,055km road which connects Nampula to Beira via Quelimane. Your options are to spend the best part of a week on the back of various trucks (covered in further detail in *Chapter Eleven*) or to fly. LAM fly to Beira from Nampula and Quelimane at a cost respectively of around US$150 and US$100. If you are thinking of driving this stretch, a 4WD is essential and you should check whether the ferry across the Zambezi is operating.

Orientation
Arriving by bus, your trip will terminate either at the central bus station in the traffic island on Rua Artur Canto Resenda, or else at the market on the junction of Avenida Samora Machel and Avenida Armando Tivane. If the former, not only are you in a central position but there are also usually a few private taxis at this rank. If the latter, you'll feel like you've been abandoned in the middle of nowhere, but in fact you're only five minutes' walk from the town centre – walk across Samora Machel Avenue and follow Avenida Armando Tivane for about 100m and the first road to your left is Rua Artur Canto Resenda, which after an odd little kink and about 200m will bring you to the central bus station.

The city centre is divided in two by a mangrove swamp called the Chiveve, which is crossed by several bridges, including one at the city centre end of Rua Artur Canto Resenda between the central bus station and Praça do Metical, the main banking square. To the south and east of the Chiveve is the old town, with many houses dating from the turn of the century, the main city square (Praça da Municipalia), the Mercado central, the main post office, and a number of hotels and restaurants.

Where to stay
Upper range
The most upmarket accommodation in Beira is the **Hotel Mozambique** (tel: 329351, fax: 325060) which lies just off Rua Artur Canto Resende and has air-conditioned self-contained rooms with hot water and television for US$55/65 single/double.

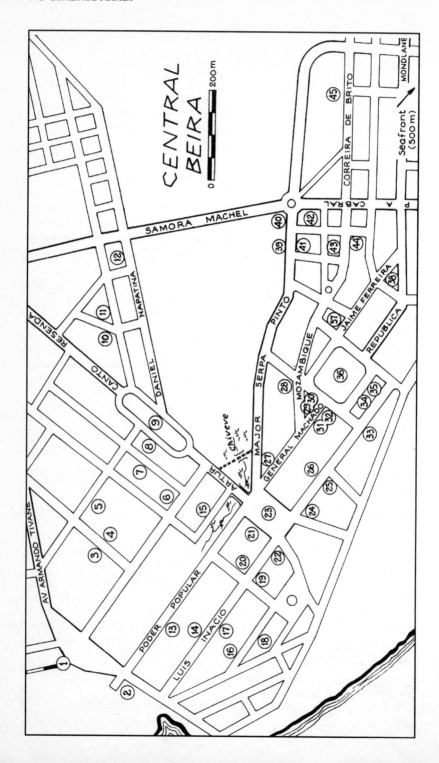

KEY TO BEIRA

1	Railway station	24	Casa Portugal
2	Casa Infante de Sagres	25	BP garage
3	Imperial Restaurant	26	LAM
4	Bar	27	Mrs Mondlane's Flat
5	Bars	28	Telecommunications
6	Monaco Restaurant	29	Scala Restaurant
7	Bar	30	Post Office
8	Phoenix Restaurant	31	Supermarket
9	Buses and Taxis	32	Capri Restaurant
10	"2 + 1" Take-away	33	Tourist Office
11	Pensão Sofala	34	Riviera Restaurant
12	Pensão Messe	35	Marble building
13	Arcadia Restaurant	36	Praça da Municipalia (City Square)
14	Pensão Beirense	37	City Market
15	Hotel Mozambique	38	Infante Residencial
16	Pique Nique Restaurant	39	Mobil garage
17	Beira Hotel	40	Petrol station
18	Cinema	41	Hotel Embaixador
19	Cinema	42	Standard Bank
20	Luso Restaurant	43	Ice cream parlour
21	Bank	44	Restaurant Chines
22	Bank	45	Small church
23	Praça do Metical		

The **Hotel Embaixador** (tel: 323121, fax: 323788) on Rua Major Serpa Pinto is similar in standard, though a little more run-down. Standard self-contained rooms cost US$30/35 single/double, while rooms with air-conditioning are about US$10 more. Air-conditioned apartments are available.

The **Hotel Dom Carlos** (tel: 711158) lies a few kilometres out of town opposite the lighthouse. It appeared to be closed when we were in town; presumably it's being refurbished. The **Hotel Beira**, opposite the Pensão Beirense, was temporarily closed when we were in Beira.

Moderate

The **Hotel Infante Residencial** (tel: 323042) on Rua Jaime Ferreira is clean, pleasant and conveniently located. Large carpeted self-contained doubles with a fan, telephone and small balcony cost US$24. Rooms with air-conditioning cost around US$30.

The **Hotel Miramar** (tel: 322283) lies one block behind the seafront restaurant of the same name near the Praça da Indepencia. It's is a little out of the way, but reasonable value for money, with large, rather dank self-contained doubles for US$20.

Budget

The **Pensão Sofala** is indisputably cheap at US$4/6 single/double, and it is located very close to the bus station, which is useful if you arrive late at night or plan on an early start. Unfortunately, the pensão is also a dump of the highest order, and I would be slightly wary of leaving anything of value in the rooms. If you walk to this pensão from the bus station, you'll see it signposted well in advance opposite the 2+1 Take Away. Your first impression might be that it is closed but if you continue several metres down the road, you'll find the reception in a discrete and anonymous bar with a raised verandah.

Much better than the Sofala and almost as convenient is the **Pensão Beirense** on Rua Luis Inacio, which has basic but spacious doubles with private toilet and baths (but no running water) for US$8. Similar in standard, the **Pensão Messe** on Rua Daniel Napatima has acceptable doubles for around US$10. One correspondent, writing in 1995, mentions a similarly priced **Pensão Carlotta** near the railway station, but even after traipsing around this part of town several times, I couldn't find it.

Mrs Mandate, a Mozambican women who speaks fair English, has recently started putting up travellers in her flat for a cost of US$5 per person. The block of flats she lives in is on Rua General Machado facing the Praça da Metical next to a bank. The flat number is 103, and it's on the tenth floor.

If you have your own tent, there are a couple of places to camp near the beach. At **Clube Náutico** (tel 313093), on the coast about 3km east of the Praça da Indepencia near Macuti Hospital, there is a clean site with slightly suspect security for around US$4.50 per person.

A better bet is **Biques Camping**, which lies on the beach about halfway between Clube Náutico and the lighthouse (tel: 312853). In addition to a campsite (around US$4.50 per person), Biques has a good bar and restaurant. The chalets which are currently under construction should be operational by the time this goes to print. Biques is a long walk from the city centre, so it's advisable to catch a *chapa* heading to Estoril and ask to be dropped at Biques (pronounced bee-keys).

Where to eat

In most respects, Beira's merits and demerits may well be a subjective matter, but few would deny that it boasts a remarkable selection of good, reasonably priced restaurants. Top of the list is the **Restaurante Pique-Nique**, which lies in the southwest corner of the city centre opposite the disused National Cinema. The service and food here wouldn't look out of place in a European city: some might say that the red-velvet carpet, crushed flock wallpaper, and tuxedoed English-speaking waiters seem something of an affectation, but my opinion where Mozambique is concerned is that you should enjoy your comforts where you can afford them. In any case, what counts is the food, which is excellent and not too expensive at around US$5–7 for a main course.

In the same league is the **Arcádia Restaurant** on Rua Poder Popular. Alternatively known as Johnny's Place, after its founder Johnny Kamamis, the Arcádia has been one of Beira's top restaurants for over three decades and no visit to the city would be complete without a meal there. You can eat inside, or at a table on the street, and, again, the prices are not prohibitive – we had a lethally hot but delicious half-chicken peri-peri and a generous portion of fried fish for a total of around US$8 excluding drinks.

The **Restaurante Imperial** near the railway station has a good reputation, and the menu and prices are similar to the Arcádia. Also recommended in this part of town is the **Restaurante dos CFMC**, which lies within the station building and is known for good game meat and local dishes.

Less central, the **Miramar Bar and Restaurant** is on the seafront a few hundred metres west of Praça da Indepencia. The sea-facing verandah is a pleasant place to down a couple of beers as the sun sets, and the food is of a similar standard and price to the Arcádia. About a block further west, and also overlooking the beach, the **Bote Oceana** has a popular disco, a large bar, and good meals. There are also two highly rated upmarket restaurants on the seafront, the **Cutty Sark**, which specialises in Italian dishes, and the seafood-oriented **Clube Náutico**.

If you're looking for something cheaper, try the **2+1 Take Away** opposite Pensão Sofala, which does a variety of basic meals for about US$3 and tangy prego rolls and burgers for US$1. Primarily a take-away, there are a couple of tables where you can sit outside, and we found it a reliable spot for a chilled soda break in our meandering through town.

For a lingering breakfast or afternoon tea, there's a choice of three *Salõa de chá* on or near Praça da Municipalia, the **Riviera**, **Cafe Capri** and **Scala**. All of these places serve fresh bread, a range of pastries, and tea and espresso coffee (out of a sachet). The Capri also has a little kiosk selling imported chocolates and other tempting odds and ends.

If you're putting together your own food, the Mercado Central is also on Praça da Municipalia, and there's a good supermarket just off the square on Rua General Machado between the Capri and the Scala.

The main concentration of local bars is in the triangle of roads between the railway station and Rua Artur Canto Resendo. It's follow your nose stuff: there are at least ten bars in this area, and you'll sooner or later stumble into the one that screams 'you', but for what it's worth, the bar about 50m up the road from the Monaco Restaurant was the liveliest and among the cheapest when we were in town, and it has a good PA and some magnificently incongruous and mismatched murals.

There's an ice-cream parlour tucked away on an alley behind the Embaixador Hotel. In addition to ice-cream, it serves syrupy fruit juice and sells a variety of imported chocolates and biscuits.

Useful information

The tourist office, signposted on the first floor of a building on Rua Luis Inacio, was closed when we looked in on a Friday afternoon. A peek through the window revealed as bare a desk as you could imagine; perhaps the staff had locked away the glossy pamplets and information sheets while they were attending a crucial cobweb-fighting strategy meeting.

The LAM office is on the ground floor of the shopping mall on Rua Luis Inacio between Praça do Metical and Praça da Municipalia. The staff here speak some English and seem very helpful.

There are three or four banks dotted around Praça do Metical, and there is a bureau de change on Rua General Machado between Praça do Metical and the Scala. The Standard Bank lies off Rua Major Serpa Pinta a block up from the Embaixador Hotel. If you want to exchange foreign currency, shop around for rates as they tend to vary a bit.

There is a public swimming pool opposite the Hotel Mozambique.

Things to do

If you like your entertainment to come planned and packaged, there isn't an awful lot to occupy yourself with in Beira, but it's pleasant city to explore with several notable buildings and an attractive seafront. The city centre boasts an intriguing mixture of architectural styles, ranging from early 20th century colonial buildings – many in an advanced state of disrepair – through 1950s constructions in the Bauhaus style to some bizarre and ostentatious modern buildings.

A good place to start any exploration of the city centre is Praça da Municipalia, which is ringed by old colonial buildings, notably the marble Municipal Hall, with a tile mural of Sofala castle, and the old fort and jail, which now serves as the city market. A short walk away, on Rua Luis Inacio at the corner of Praça do Metical, the red-brick Casa Portugal is one of the best surviving examples of a turn-of-the-century Portuguese dwelling. Praça do Metical, named after the country's currency, is appropriately ringed by banks housed in buildings of various vintages.

From Praça do Metical, walk up Avenida Poder Popular to the recently restored Casa Infante Sagres, a fine old colonial building covered in mosaic murals. From here, a short and bumpy dirt road leads to Praça dos Trabalhadores (Workers' Square), the port, and the adjacent railway station. Completed in 1966, the railway station has been described in the tourist literature as "one of the most beautiful modern buildings in Africa" and by my favourite correspondent, Andrew Chilton, as "a hideous example of imperial overlord modern school architecture". Full marks to Andrew on this, I'm afraid.

Return to Praça da Municipalia and follow Avenida Republica into Avenida Eduardo Mondlane. A short distance along the road (just off our city centre map), the Beira Cathedral is in my opinion the most beautiful building in the city, erected between 1907 and 1925 using stones taken from the Portuguese fort at Sofala. There is a pretty chapel along the same road, as well as one a block up on Rua Correia de Brito. In addition to housing Beira's main cluster of old ecclesiastic buildings, this part of town was formerly the most upmarket residential area, and there are several pleasing old houses, some beautifully maintained, others utterly derelict.

A brisk 30-minute walk along Avenida Eduardo Mondlane brings you out at Praça da Indepencia, a large open circle on the seafront. From here, you can follow Avenida 27 de Abril back towards town, with the crumbling seafront wall and the rusting hulks of several ships to your left – possibly taking a drink or meal break at the Mirimar Restaurant, an open-air place facing the sea a few hundred metres down the road from Praça da Indepencia – then walk up Rua 11 de Dezembro back to the city centre.

Further afield, the site of the historic city of Sofala lies at the southern end of the bay, approximately 40km from Beira, on a lovely tropical beach. Today little remains of the former glory of Sofala, once the gateway to southern Africa. Sofala is accessible by road from Buzi which one can reach by small boat (*chata*) or, more safely, by ferry (Tue, Fri, Sat, Sun).

THE BEIRA CORRIDOR AND GORONGOSA

The strategic importance of the Beira Corridor, which consists of a 300km long railway line and a parallel road and oil pipeline, grew after Zimbabwe achieved full independence in 1980, leaving South Africa and Namibia as the last bastions of white rule in Southern Africa. Zimbabwe and the various other states neighbouring South Africa formed the SADCC (Southern Africa Development Co-ordination Conference), with the declared aim of reducing the region's economic dependence on the apartheid regime. For landlocked countries such as Zimbabwe, Zambia and Botswana, a crucial factor in achieving this goal was to have access to a sea port which was not under South African control.

Beira was the obvious choice, due to its proximity to the Zimbabwe border. However, by the mid-1980s, years of neglect had caused Beira's harbour to silt up to the point where it was practically unnavigable, while the rail link to Zimbabwe had become a regular target for terrorist attacks by Renamo. The Mozambican army was too weak to protect against these attacks, so Zimbabwe's defence forces took responsibility for defending the Beira Corridor. After large amounts of foreign aid were used to make Beira harbour operational, Zimbabwe and Zambia steadily increased their imports via Beira during the late 1980s – although neither country ever came close to being independent of the South African transport system.

Gorongosa Mountain and National Park

The Parque Nacional da Gorongosa extends over the brachestygia-covered plains north of the Beira Corridor to the southeastern base of Mount Gorongosa. Formerly regarded as one of southern Africa's finest wildlife reserves, with more game than the much larger Kruger National Park in South Africa, the area became a central battleground when Renamo had its headquarters near Mount Gorongosa, and there is now little wildlife left. The day may well come when Gorongosa is once again the showpiece of

Mozambique's reserves, but it won't be in this millennium. At present, my understanding is that the park isn't formally open to visitors and that uncleared mines pose a serious risk to exploration. This could conceivably change during the lifespan of this edition – the EWT in Johannesburg or Maputo would be your best source of current information.

The 1,862m high Mount Gorongosa, which lies outside of the synonymous national park, is an isolated massif rising almost 1.5km above the surrounding plains. Covered in montane forest, Gorongosa has acquired something approaching legendary status with South African birders as the only place south of the Zambezi where the attractive and vociferous green-headed oriole can be seen. It also supports a variety of other interesting forest birds, though as things stand it's a destination suitable only for dedicated and self-sufficient birders.

Getting there and away

The surfaced 62km road to Gorongosa town leaves the main road through the Beira Corridor at Inchope. The unsurfaced turn-off to Gorongosa National Park and what remains of Chitengo Safari Lodge departs eastwards from this road about 40km towards Gorongosa. To get to Mount Gorongosa, continue along the tar road until it terminates at Gorongosa town, then ask to be shown the rough motorable track which passes the southeastern base of the mountain. There are some very rough footpaths up to the forest zone. It would be unrealistic to explore this area without a 4WD, a tent, and sufficient food.

Where to stay

Chitengo Safari Lodge was attacked during the civil war, and recent reports suggest that the building isn't in a fit state for habitation. There are at present no plans to renovate the lodge or to build one elsewhere in the park, and it seems unlikely that any will be discussed until the current mine clearing operation has been completed and animal populations have started either to recover or to be replenished from elsewhere. It is possible that camping will be permitted at some point soon.

Chimoio

The capital of landlocked Manica province, and Mozambique's fifth-largest city, Chimoio is the archetypal small southern African town. Portuguese signposts aside, there is nothing about Chimoio (pronounced Shimoio) that is distinctively Mozambican; in fact, with its fresh mid-altitude climate and drearily uniform grid of streets, you could as easily be in Zimbabwe or Malawi, countries which have in common a distinct lack of towns with any discernible character.

Chimoio may not be the sort of town you'd make a special effort to see, but it's agreeable enough, and its location, roughly 40km from the junction of the Beira Corridor and the Tete road and 100km from the Zimbabwe border, makes it a route focus of sorts, and the obvious place to spend a night if you enter Mozambique from Mutare late in the day. The only real tourist attraction around Chimoio is Cabeca de Velho, a vast granite outcrop shaped like an old man's face in repose. Visible from the city centre, and less than 3km away as the crow flies, the outcrop might make a rewarding day walk. There are reportedly good views from the top.

Getting there and away
There are regular chapas and buses between Chimoio and Beira, taking roughly three hours, and also between Chimoio and the border taking about half that time. Virginia buses between Maputo and Tete all stop at Chimoio, and there are also regular buses running directly between Chimoio and Tete. Trains between Mutare and Beira stop at Chimoio.

Where to stay
The only accommodation we could find in the city centre was an **unsignposted hotel** at Avenida 25 de Setembro 670 (the number is above the entrance) around the corner from the Concorde Restaurant. Recently refurbished, the rooms here are nicely furnished and they have hot running water, but they seem a bit steeply priced at US$30/double.

Much more affordable – in fact, as good value for money as you'll find anywhere in southern Mozambique – is the **Moinho Motel**, 2km out of town off the Beira road. The main building of this hotel, shaped like a mill, contains a ground floor bar and restaurant and a few eccentrically shaped rooms on the first and second floors. There is also a row of more conventionally rectangular rooms at the back. All rooms are self-contained with hot showers, and they cost US$13.50/double. There is safe parking. If you're coming on public transport from Beira or the south coast, you could ask to be dropped at the turn-off to the motel before you reach the town centre. Otherwise, it's a 30-minute walk from the bus station. Follow the main road out of town across the railway line with the stadium to your right for about 400m until you hit the intersection with the main Beira–Mutare road. Here you must turn left, towards Beira, until after about 1.5km you'll see the hotel signposted to your left (and the windmill rising above the surrounding shrubs and trees). The motel is about 400m from here, next to a pleasant reed-hut village.

Another affordable option, and considerably more central, is the **Bamboo Inn**, which is noisy and basic but very friendly and cheap at US$5/double. To get there, walk up to the small market (top right corner of the map), then turn left out of town, following a bend in the road, and continue on for about ten minutes.

The final option is the **Manica Executive Lodge**, a spanking new and very plush set-up lying about 200m off the main Beira–Mutare road. Self-contained rooms cost US$50/60 single/double, and facilities include a good restaurant, a bar, safe parking and a swimming pool.

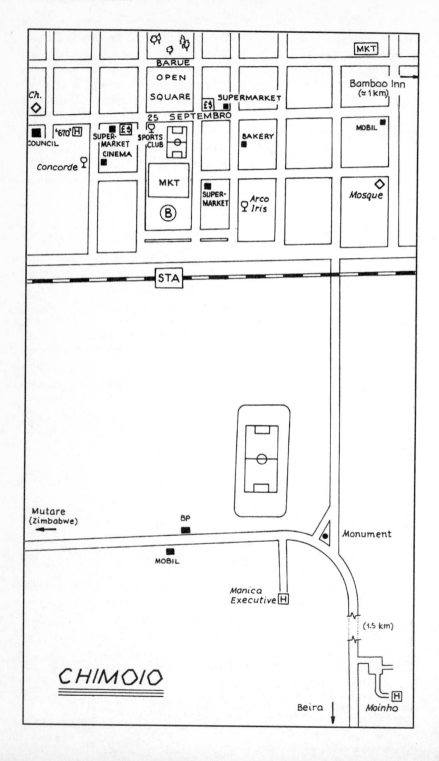

Where to eat

If you're staying at the Moinho Motel, look no further – the food here is excellent, reasonably priced at around US$4 to US$5 for a main course, and the portions are immense. There's also a nice bar in the main building.

In town, the best place to eat is the Sports Club Bar next to the small stadium, which serves a variety of meat, fish and chicken dishes for around US$4. Cheap ice-cream cones and freshly baked bread are available at the Arco Iris Solõa de Chá. The market sells a good selection of fruit and vegetables, and there are a couple of reasonable supermarkets.

Useful information

If you've just entered from Zimbabwe, a priority will probably be to exchange some foreign currency, which you can do at the main branch of the Commercial Bank on Avenido 25 de Setembro or at the private Bureau de Change on the same road. Around the market, you'll find plenty of people willing to change cash – in this part of Mozambique, Zimbabwe dollars will get you the best rate, but be warned that there are some slick operators around. At weekends, there are sometimes concerts in the small stadium next to the market.

Chicamba Dam

Lying between Chimoio and the Zimbabwe border is an area of thick brachestygia woodland and undulating hills with good views of the Vumba Mountains to the south. In the middle of this distinctively African landscape lies Chicamba Dam, remarkable as much as anything for being the only functional tourist attraction in the Mozambican interior south of the Zambezi. Chicamba Dam is popular with bass fishermen (the resort is often full during Zimbabwean school holidays) while the surrounding wooded hills have an isolated, low-key charm, and would be of great interest to bird-watchers. Otherwise there's not a great deal to say about the dam – there are dozens of similar places in South Africa and Zimbabwe – except that it's a more inherently attractive stopover than Chimoio, and that it might make for a welcome mid-altitude break from the sweaty coast for backpackers who are covering the whole of the coastline. If that sounds like damnation with faint praise, let me put it this way: I could happily have spent a week relaxing and birding in the area, and just as happily have lived my life without ever seeing Chicamba Dam.

Getting there and away

The dirt turn-off to the Casa Msika Motel is clearly signposted from the main road through the Beira Corridor roughly 47km from Chimoio and 20km from Manica. The resort lies about 5km from the main road.

The **Casa Msika Motel** lies on the lake shore. It has chalets costing US$24/double and campsite where you can pitch a tent for US$2.50 per person. There is a restaurant and bar on a raised wooden platform on the edge of the lake.

Mount Binga

The country's highest mountain is not difficult to climb but it is not easily accessible from the Mozambican side. The 2,436m-high mountain is situated in the Chimanimani Mountains right on the Zimbabwe border and from the Zimbabwe side it is easy to reach.

In order to climb Mount Binga start at Mutare in Zimbabwe, then go 150km south to the small town of Chimanimani. From the town there is a good dirt road to the entrance of the Chimanimani Mountain Park, where there is a campsite with showers and toilets as well as the park headquarters. The normal route to the hut via Bailey's Folly takes one to one and a half hours without a pack, and about two hours with a pack. The hut is situated above a spectacular high-lying valley surrounded by the Chimanimani mountain ridge. From the hut to the summit takes about another two and three-quarter hours.

The climb down to the floor of the valley is splendid, under trees with wide spreading branches. After this you cross the very picturesque Bundi stream and then climb to the small ridge followed by the final stretch up to the summit. The view from the summit stretches beyond the descending mountains of the Mount Binga Massif well over Mozambique.

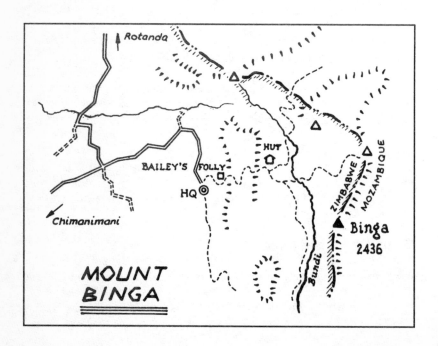

Chapter Ten

Tete Province

The province of Tete in western Mozambique must rank as one of the most peculiar relics of the colonial carve-up of Africa: a wedge-shaped Portuguese territory protruding into what was formerly the British Central African Protectorate. Today Tete is bordered by Zimbabwe to the west, Zambia to the north, and Malawi to the east. Only the southern border is shared with other parts of Mozambique.

Looking at a map, one would probably consider Tete to be a part of northern Mozambique. In reality, the province and its eponymous capital city have much closer economic links and are more easily accessed from the south, largely because they are isolated from the four provinces of the northeast by Malawi and the Shire River. Tete's virtual separation from the rest of Mozambique and its importance as the most straightforward route between Blantyre and Harare have resulted in several other mild anomalies; we found, for instance, that considerably more English is understood in Tete itself than in any other town in Mozambique.

Tete probably sees more traveller through-traffic than the rest of Mozambique's provinces combined, once again a function of its location as opposed to any great inherent charms. Practically every traveller who crosses between Malawi and Zimbabwe uses the so-called Tete Corridor (the road which bisects Tete and which was known during the civil war as the 'Gun Run') but very few spend even one night in Mozambique, let alone explore the province. Tete town is also the main gateway to southern Mozambique for travellers coming from Malawi.

As seen from the window of a bus between Blantyre and Harare, Tete is not the most inviting of areas: a dry, dusty badland covered in puny acacia scrub and punctuated by the occasional small thatched village which only makes you wonder how anybody can live in this harsh, arid climate. Lying at a low altitude on the south bank of the Zambezi, the town of Tete manages to be both dusty and almost intolerably humid. As seen in the harsh light of the day, it's a town with little to no aesthetic appeal, though in the softer light of the evening the old town and riverbank take on an altogether more pleasant hue.

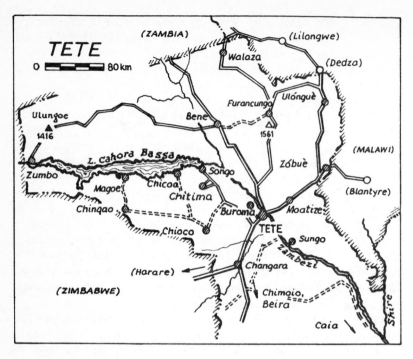

Away from the main road, Tete Province boasts at least one worthwhile and straightforward excursion in the form of the vast Cahora Bassa Dam and the nearby town of Songo – the latter with a remarkably fresh highland climate after the claustrophobic humidity of Tete. More off the beaten track, but also of interest, is the attractive mission at Boroma, which lies on the west bank of the Zambezi some 60km upriver from Tete.

TETE

The eponymous capital of Tete Province, often and with some justification claimed to be the hottest town in Mozambique, is situated on the southwest bank of the Zambezi roughly 650km upriver from its mouth and at an altitude of only 175m above sea level. Remarkably, the large suspension bridge at Tete is the only permanent crossing of the Zambezi anywhere in Mozambique, hence the town's importance as a regional transport hub.

Tete is a settlement of some antiquity. Even before the Portuguese arrived in East Africa, it lay at the junction of the Zambezi and three of the four main trading routes from the Sofala area into the African interior. The site of the modern town was probably occupied by Muslim traders in the 15th century, when it formed the main link between the coast and the gold fairs of Karangaland. Tete was settled by a few Portuguese adventurers in 1531, and by 1630 it supported around 20 *mazungo* households.

Contemporary reports suggest that Tete was rather makeshift in appearance until around 1767, when it was made the seat of administration for the Zambezi Valley and a garrison of 100 soldiers was posted there on a permanent basis. By the end of the 18th century, Tete's city centre consisted of roughly 30 stone houses enclosed by a 3m high wall, as well as a hospital, trade factory, governor's residence and council building.

Tete today is quite modern in both appearance and outlook. The city expanded greatly in size and population during the construction of Cahora Bassa Dam, and it is now one of the largest towns in the Mozambican interior, with a population of around 50,000. It is, in all honesty, a town of limited interest to tourists, and for many its few attractive qualities will be outweighed by the oppressive humidity of the Zambezi Valley. The old part of town is not without a certain decrepit charm: there are some beautiful old houses here, though most are in urgent need of restoration. The oldest building in town is the disused cathedral, which reportedly dates back to 1563. The most unlikely building is a domed gazebo on the riverfront, presumably where the Portuguese colonists enjoyed their sundowners. Also worth a look is the old slaving fort near the municipal market, though it now protects a couple of water tanks so it may be difficult to get inside, and a second fort on the riverfront below the bridge.

An attractive feature of Tete is the row of bars and restaurants that lines the riverfront – this is, after all, the one place in Mozambique where the Zambezi is readily accessible to casual visitors, and even if the riverbank around Tete itself is somewhat denuded of natural vegetation, it would be a shame to visit Mozambique and not spend at least one evening drinking in sight of Africa's fourth largest river. More adventurously, you could ask around to find a fisherman to paddle you along the river in a dugout: the papyrus beds near the town support a good variety of birds, and you wouldn't need to go more than a kilometre or so upriver to stand a good chance of seeing hippos and crocs.

Getting there and away

Tete will be the first port of call for travellers who are visiting southern Mozambique from Malawi. A good surfaced road connects Blantyre to Tete via Mwanza and Zóbuè – in a private vehicle, the 225km drive shouldn't take more than three hours, allowing for delays at the border. Using public transport, the simplest way to get to Tete is with one of the daily buses between Blantyre and Harare, but you could also do the trip in hops.

A scenic and well-maintained surfaced road connects the Tete and Beira corridors. This 270km road branches southwards from the Tete Corridor at Changara, 95km from Tete on the road towards the Zimbabwe border, and it connects with the Beira corridor 270km further south, roughly 20km west of Chimoio (the capital of Manica Province). Virginia Bus Lines run daily buses between Tete, Chimoio and Beira, and there are also regular chapas along this road.

When you are ready to leave Tete, you'll find that Virginia buses to

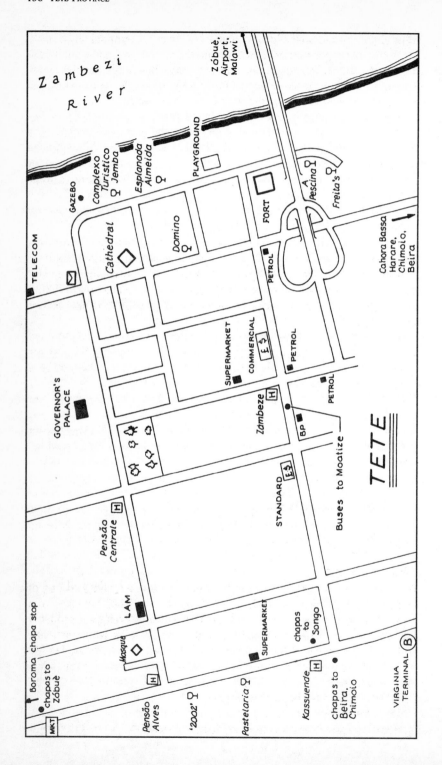

Chimoio, Beira and Songo leave from the Virginia Bus terminal on Avenida 25 do Junho, chapas to Beira and Chimoio leave from in front of the Hotel Kassuende, chapas to Songo and Chitima leave from opposite the Hotel Kassuende, and chapas to Zóbuè on the Malawi border leave from in front of the market near the slaving fort.

LAM flies from Tete to Lichinga and back every Wednesday. There are flights in both directions between Tete and Beira every Monday and Wednesday. The airport lies about 5km out of town towards Zóbuè. There are no taxis in Tete, but any bus travelling between Tete and Moatize, a small town 20km to the east, can drop you at the entrance to the airport. Buses to Moatize leave Tete from in front of the Hotel Zambeze.

Where to stay
The five-storey **Hotel Zambeze** must once have been something of a showpiece, but these days it is rather run-down and the top-floor restaurant and bar area floods whenever there's heavy rain. Still, the rooms have been reasonably well looked after, and they are acceptable value at US$18/20 for a self-contained room with air-conditioning, and US$9/11 for a more basic room.

The **A Pescina** complex on the riverfront has pleasant air-conditioned doubles for US$18. You can also camp in the grounds for US$1.50 per person, but bear in mind that camping in this muggy climate could be a rather stifling experience.

The **Pensão Alves Melo** near the municipal market has basic but acceptable rooms for around US$5 per person as well as air-conditioned doubles for US$15. Unfortunately, it's as often as not full. The nearby **Hotel Kassuende** seems overpriced with very basic rooms for US$8/10 and air-conditioned doubles for US$30.

Due to open in early 1997, the **Pensão Central** is being constructed by the same American who owns the Restaurante Freita's and it promises to be the best value for money in Tete, with self-contained air-conditioned doubles for around US$15. The restaurant and bar will presumably be up to the standard of the Freita's.

Where to eat
Whatever else it may lack, Tete certainly has an above average selection of restaurants and bars, most of which run along the riverfront. Set back from the river at the southern end of town, the **Restaurante Freita's** is probably the best in town, with a wide selection of dishes ranging from pasta and pork to the more predictable chicken and fish. The chips here are the best we had in Mozambique and the chicken piri-piri is strongly recommended. Most dishes cost less than US$5. The all-night disco on Fridays and Saturdays is the most popular in Tete.

The **A Pescina** complex next door is also highly recommended. It has a particularly varied menu, with most dishes in the US$3.50 to 4.50 range, and the restaurant is air-conditioned. Other attractions include a pool table, table tennis and the (normally empty) swimming pool which gives the complex its name. Although the complex lies right on the river, a high wall obscures the view and blocks any breeze.

Also on the riverfront, but north of the bridge, the **Esplanada Almeida** is a pleasant place for a cold beer, but the food is relatively ordinary and judging by the smell, it's positioned right next to a popular ablution spot.

Attractive flowering gardens and relatively fresh air conspire to make the **Complexo Turistico Jemba** the best place to enjoy a sundowner in full view of the Zambezi. It has a varied menu, and is the only place in Tete that serves pizzas. There's a loud disco in the complex at weekends, though far enough away from the bar and restaurant that it's not too intrusive.

The **Pastelaria** with the red and white striped awning on Avenida 25 de Junho is a good place to enjoy a relaxed, varied breakfast. In addition to a selection of pastries, doughnuts, fresh bread and espresso coffee, the Pastelaria stocks chilled fruit juice and refrigerated chocolates, and it serves good burgers, prego rolls and egg or cheese sandwiches.

Most of the hotels mentioned above serve meals, but they're ordinary by comparison with the proper restaurants.

BOROMA MISSION

On of the most interesting excursions out of Tete is to Boroma, site of one of the country's most attractive missions. Boroma was an important source of alluvial gold even before Portuguese times, though it had been exhausted long before the mission was founded in 1891. The centrepiece of the mission is a large and beautiful church on a hill overlooking the river, abandoned by the missionaries shortly after independence, but recently reoccupied by an Italian priest. The Boroma area is also a good place to see hippos and crocs, and it should offer good birdwatching.

Getting there and away
A few vehicles run between Tete and Boroma daily, generally leaving Tete before 08.00. To pick up transport to Boroma, follow Avenida 25 de Junho out of town past the old slave fort and market for five to ten minutes until you see a large blue signpost pointing to Boroma. The point where vehicles wait is about 100m past this signpost, immediately after the road bends to the left. The road to Boroma should only be attempted in a 4WD, and it may be closed due to flooding after heavy rain.

Where to stay
There is no formal accommodation at Boroma, and with an early start it would be easy enough to visit the mission as a day trip out of Tete. If you have a tent, you should be allowed to pitch it near the mission.

CAHORA BASSA DAM

Situated on the Zambezi in the north of Tete Province, Cahora Bassa Dam is the fifth largest dam in the world and it dams one of Africa's ten largest bodies of water, covering an area of 2,660km². Construction of the 300m wide and 160m high concrete wall started in 1969, and despite Frelimo's attempts at sabotage, it was completed in 1974.

Cahora Bassa is potentially Africa's largest supplier of electric power and a vital source of foreign revenue for Mozambique. The five turbines, housed in a rock-hewn cavern of cathedralesque dimensions, have a total capacity of 2075MW, roughly ten times the power requirement for the whole of Mozambique. When the dam was built, the idea was that it would supply large amounts of hydro-electric power to South Africa. Sadly, by the end of the civil war only two of the dam's turbines were still functional, and no electricity from Cahora Bassa had reached South Africa since part of the power line was destroyed by Renamo in 1986. The lines are currently in the process of being restored, and it is expected that the dam will be sending electricity to Johannesburg by April 1997.

Now partially submerged, the Cahora Bassa Rapids were the obstacle which prevented Livingstone's Zambezi expedition from opening up the Zambezi as "God's Highway" into the African interior, and which led to the explorer turning his attention to the Shire River in what would eventually become the British enclave now known as Malawi. Covering a distance of roughly 80km, and marked by two near vertical drops of 200m, the rapids had been known to the Portuguese and other traders for several centuries before Livingstone arrived at the Zambezi – the phrase 'Cahora Bassa' means 'where the work ends' in the local dialect, a reference to the fact that rapids were an impassable obstacle for boatsmen sailing up the Zambezi.

Livingstone had used a path which arced around the rapids in the course of his epic trans-African hike, the journey which preceded and inspired the Zambezi Expedition, so it is something of mystery why he never thought to look at the rapids for himself, and steadfastly dismissed local advice that they would be impassable. Even when his boat, the *Ma-Robert,* was confronted by the rapids on 9 November 1858, Livingstone refused to believe they couldn't eventually be surmounted, though he was finally persuaded of this in November 1860, when he attempted to ascend the rapids with five dugout canoes, a number of which overturned, taking many of the expedition's notes and drawings with them.

Probably the first person to navigate the rapids was a rather enigmatic and obscure figure remembered in the annals of the Royal Geographic Society by the name of Mr F Monks (though his real surname was evidently Foster). In 1880, Monks did a solo canoe trip between the confluence of the Gawayi and Zambezi Rivers and the port of Quelimane. Although he left no substantial journal of this trip, he did leave behind an impressively accurate topographical map of the Zambezi and several of its tributaries as far downriver as Tete. Monks disappeared into the African interior a few years after this, never to be heard of again. As a footnote, the first people known to have kayaked the full length of the Zambezi from its source near the borders of Zambia, Zaire and Angola are two young British travellers, Rupert FitzMaurice and Justin Matterson, who did the trip to raise money for charity towards the end of 1996.

An interesting story associated with Cahora Bassa is that of the legendary silver mines of Chicova, which were shown to Portuguese explorers in the early years of the 17th century. In 1617 and 1618, the period when Madeira occupied the fort at Sena, an estimated 450kg of silver was brought there, allegedly from Chicova. The odd thing is that the mines were 'lost' shortly after Madeira left Sena, and despite the attempts of several fortune hunters since, they have yet to be relocated. If the mine ever did exist, then it's probably now submerged by Cahora Bassa, or close to its southern shore.

The closest town to the dam, Songo, was purpose-built in the style of a Portuguese village while the dam was under construction. By 1974 it had a population of almost 15,000. Located in the cool, breezy highlands immediately south of the dam, Songo is well worth visiting in its own right, with a spacious layout and green, flowering gardens that blend attractively into the surrounding woodland. The approach road to Songo is one of the most spectacular in Mozambique, and the well-wooded, boulder-strewn hills that surround the town offer a refreshing contrast to the humid air and stark landscape of Tete. The Songo area also promises excellent birdwatching, and there are plenty of roads along which you can explore it (though do bear in mind that straying from roads could be risky; this part of Mozambique was heavily mined during the civil war).

Travellers cannot visit the dam without authorisation. It is straightforward enough to get authorisation once you arrive in Songo, but it would nevertheless be a better idea to get a *credençial* in advance (you can do this at the HCB office on Avenida 25 de Junho in Tete), if only because visitors who arrive at Songo without permission may be required to leave their passports at the police checkpoint about 5km before the town for the duration of their stay. Alternatively, contact Mr Nhamposa, HCB's chief of Public Relations at Songo (tel: 82221/2/3/4).

Getting there and away

Songo lies 150km from Tete along an excellent surfaced road. The turn-off to Songo is roughly 25km from Tete along the road towards the Zimbabwe border. It isn't signposted but it's the only major junction along this stretch of road. The drive from Tete to Songo can comfortably be done in two hours in a private vehicle.

Virginia Buses travel between Tete and Songo twice a day. In theory, these buses leave Tete at 08.00 and 14.00, but this timetable is evidently not adhered to with any rigidity. On the morning we went to Songo, the 08.00 bus had already left when we pitched up at the Virginia depot at

07.45, and the afternoon before that, the 14.00 bus was still at the depot when I made enquiries at about 15.00. In other words, you're advised to get to the bus depot well in advance of the scheduled departure time. If you miss the bus, a few chapas leave for Songo daily from in front of the Hotel Kassuende. You could also take a chapa to Chitima (marked on some maps as Estima), a small town at the base of the mountains about 15km from Songo, and pick up a lift to Songo from there.

Where to stay and eat

The **Pousada Sete Mentes**, the only hotel in Songo, is a pleasant and reasonably inexpensive place with a good restaurant. The restaurant at the airport serves really good chicken and chips for US$4.

With permission from the HCB, you should be allowed to camp near the wall of Cahora Bassa, bearing in mind that there are no facilities.

There is also a very basic resthouse in Chitima. It isn't signposted, but it's easy enough to find since it's right behind the bar where chapas stop to pick up passengers.

ZUMBO

Lying on the Zambian border at the confluence of the Zambezi and Luangwa Rivers, Zumbo was once an important gold fair, said to have been founded in 1715 by Francisco Pereira, a Goan trader and refugee from the Rozvi attack on Dambarare. By 1750, a lively trade in gold with the Rozvi had led to Zumbo becoming the largest Portuguese town on the Zambezi, with a Christian population of almost 500 including 80 Europeans. By 1764, when it was granted municipal status, Zumbo was possibly the most prosperous settlement in Portuguese Africa.

Zumbo's decline can be linked to the political tensions that gripped the upper Zambezi area in the late 18th century, combined with the great drought that started in 1895. After being attacked several times, Zumbo was fortified in 1801, and at the same time a Portuguese garrison moved in. This was not enough to prevent further attacks and so the town was evacuated in 1813. The fair was reoccupied in 1820, but following the resurgence of drought conditions and the looming threat of the Ngoni after they deposed the Rozvi dynasty in 1836, Zumbo was permanently abandoned by Portugal.

In 1859, the British explorer Richard Thornton passed through the ghost town that had once been described as the metropolis of the whole trade of the rivers. Thornton recorded seeing the ruins of some 200 stone houses lining the river bank over a distance of three kilometres. A more recent report confirms that a fort of unknown antiquity, built around a 500-year-old fig tree, was still in use at Zumbo during World War II. Though Zumbo is well off any beaten track today, it may well be of interest to self-sufficient travellers with private transport – and if anybody does head out this way, I'd be most interested to hear about it.

Chapter Eleven

Zambézia

Zambézia, in central Mozambique, is the most populous province in the country, and the most agriculturally rich, with many areas receiving an average rainfall of around 2,000mm. Paradoxically, this province also suffers from what are possibly the worst transport links in Mozambique, and despite its pivotal position it is only likely to be visited by travellers who are making their way overland between Beira in southern Mozambique and Nampula in the north.

The overland trip from Beira to Nampula is among the most taxing in Mozambique, and most travellers will choose to punctuate it with a stay at Quelimane, the capital of Zambézia. Fortunately, this ancient river port is, relentless humidity aside, one of the more pleasant cities in the country, with surprisingly good tourist facilities and easy access to the nearby beach resort at Zalala.

Apart from Quelimane, Zambézia has little to offer travellers. The attractive town of Milange is only likely to be visited by travellers entering Mozambique from Malawi. A more accessible part of the western highlands of Zambézia is the area around Gurué, a spacious small town with a beautiful situation at the base of Mount Namuli, Mozambique's second highest peak.

QUELIMANE

Quelimane is Mozambique's fourth largest town, with a population of roughly 140,000. The settlement that eventually became Quelimane was founded on the north bank of the Qua-Qua River after it was discovered that this relatively small waterway was linked to the Zambezi by a channel that emerged near modern-day Mopeia. For centries, the Qua-Qua offered safe and easy access to the Zambezi, at least when compared to the vast and labyrinthine Zambezi Delta to its south, but the channel connecting the two rivers silted up during the great drought of the 1820s and has since fallen into disuse.

Quelimane was almost certainly founded by Muslim traders, probably at around the same time as Tete and Sena. The first Portuguese trading

ZAMBÉZIA

0 ▰▰▰▰▰▰▰ 125 Km

factory at Quelimane was established in 1530, and the town appears on Portuguese maps dating from 1560. Quelimane grew in importance as the ivory trading routes up the Zambezi replaced the older gold trade routes out of Sofala. Reports dating to the 1590s depict it as an attractive small town, surrounded by plantations and protected by a wooden fort.

Like many other coastal settlements, Quelimane benefited greatly from the growth in the slave trade during the latter part of the 18th century. It also became a major supplier of food to Mozambique Island during this period. Quelimane's oldest stone buildings date from the 1780s, and in 1812 the town was made a separate Captaincy with its own customs house. By the 1820s, Quelimane was the most important slaving port in East Africa, but its municipal status was discontinued in 1826 due to the lack of government control over the free trade in slaves. The main results of this

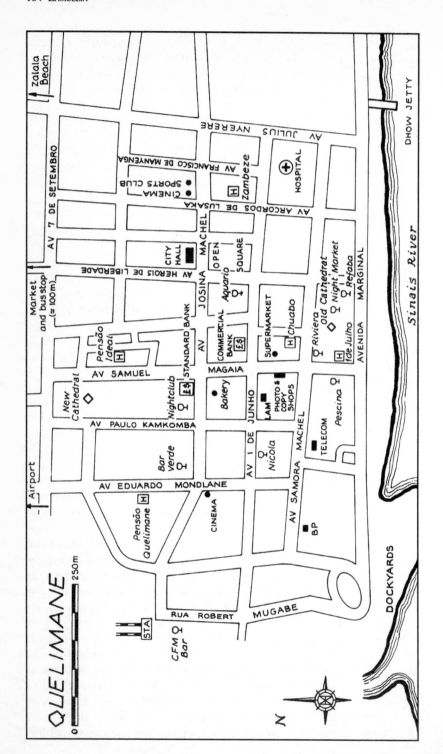

action were that the local slave trade was driven underground, and that many visiting ships avoided Portuguese settlements altogether, preferring to enter into clandestine trade with Muslim settlements elsewhere on the coast. Quelimane nevertheless remained a prosperous settlement, mainly through its importance as a supplier of agricultural produce. David Livingstone was officially appointed the British Honorary Consul to Quelimane in 1858, even though his main interest in the town was as a base from which to explore the Zambezi.

Quelimane today has a more modern and low-rise appearance than you might expect. There is no old town as such: most of the older looking buildings in the city centre evidently date to the early 20th century, and we couldn't see any trace of the old forts and customs house. Built in 1776, the old waterfront cathedral is still in reasonable condition, though it has fallen into temporary disuse (except as a breeding ground for some impressively large rats) due to a leaky roof. Nevertheless, it remains an appealing building, and the caretaker will probably let you poke around inside if you ask. There are several old plaques on the wall and floor, including five tombstones marking the graves of former priests. The night market next to the cathedral is also worth visiting – a couple of dozen reed-and-bamboo bars surrounding a rather incongruous and normally empty discotheque.

Getting there and away
If you are driving from Beira to Quelimane, prepare yourself for at least a day of ruts and potholes, relics of intense mining during the civil war. Twelve hours for the 450km journey is good going, and very strenuous. The condition of the road means that a 4WD vehicle is a necessity, especially during the rainy season.

There is no public transport along most of the road between Beira and Quelimane, so you'll probably be dependent on getting a lift with a truck and you should expect this to take the best part of two days with an overnight stop at Caia. From Beira, take any vehicle heading towards Chimoio and ask to be dropped at Dondo, 28km west of Beira. Once you have found the huge crowd of people sitting by the northbound road that branches from the Beira Corridor at Dondo, you will know that you have found the right departure point. When eventually a truck arrives, be prepared for a scramble and then, once aboard, switch off for the ten-hour journey to Caia, the small village on the south bank of the Zambezi near the confluence with the Shire River.

There is no bridge at Caia, but a vehicle ferry crosses back and forth throughout the day between 07.00 and 18.00. You will probably have to overnight at the river before picking up transport to Quelimane the next day. Either you can bed down in the huge truck yard with the other passengers, or else you can stay in the peculiar double-storey reed hotel on the north bank of the river. The only other accommodation along this road is a pensão at Inhaminga, a small town 85km south of Caia where there is also a large mission. Inhaminga is the obvious place to break up the trip if you're not in a rush.

Travellers covering the road between Quelimane and Beira from north to south should first take a bus from Quelimane to a small village near Nicuadala (I don't know the name of this village, but if you go to the bus station and ask for a vehicle heading to Beira you'll be put on the right bus) which is the conventional place to pick up vehicles heading further south.

For motorised travellers, there are a couple of potentially interesting diversions from the Caia area. To the east, a rough road follows the course of the Zambezi about 50km downriver to Lacerdonia (formerly known as Chupanga) where Mary Livingstone, wife of David Livingstone and daughter of Robert Moffat, was buried in the mission grounds. This road continues eastwards from Lacerdonia to the village of Marromeu on the fringes of the Zambezi Delta.

Roughly 50km upriver of Caia, the rather remote outpost of Vila de Sena was formerly one of the two most important Portuguese outposts on the Zambezi, and it quite possibly stands on the same site as the trading post of Seyouna mentioned in a 12th-century Arab document. The 3,660m-long railway bridge at Sena, completed in 1935, was the longest bridge in the world at the time it was built, and it would still be the longest bridge in Africa had it not been sabotaged by Renamo during the civil war. The Sena Bridge is unusable at the time of writing, but I understand that it will eventually be rebuilt.

Getting to Quelimane from the west and north is rather more straightforward. From Milange on the Malawi border there is at least one chapa daily to Mocuba on the main Beira–Nampula road. From Nampula, there are regular buses and chapas to Quelimane, most of which stop overnight at Mocuba. There's plenty of transport between Mocuba and Quelimane.

Where to stay
The last thing you'd expect to find in Quelimane is a plush tourist-class hotel, but that's precisely what the **Hotel Chuabo** is. Easily the most upmarket hotel in northern Mozambique, the eight-storey Chuabo has well-maintained air-conditioned rooms in the US$100–130 range. The top-floor restaurant is notable for the view over the river and cathedral more than the food.

The **Hotel Zambeze** is a reasonable mid-range hotel undergoing extensive renovations at the time of writing. Rooms with a fan cost US$13/25 single/double and rooms with air-conditioning US$16/28.

The **Pensão Ideal**, an unsignposted pink building more or less opposite the new cathedral on Avenida Filipe Samuel Magaia, is one of the best value budget hotels in the country – clean air-conditioned doubles cost US$10, and rooms with fans US$7.50. We'd heard good things about the restaurant, but it struck me as being very ordinary considering what's on offer elsewhere in town. Also fair value for money is the **Hotel 1 de Junho**, on the river end of the same road, which has large clean doubles with a fan for US$15. Grossly overpriced by comparison is the **Pensão Quelimane**, an unsignposted and rather grand-looking white building on Avenida Eduardo Mondlane, which charges US$15/22 single/double for an ordinary room and US$27/37 for one with a private bathroom.

Where to eat

We spent a fair amount of time in the **Cafe Riviera**, the unsignposted building with reflective glass windows on the corner of Avenida Samora Machel and Filipe Samuel Magaia. Is it possible to overpraise this place? The comfortable air-conditioning and clean modern furnishing wouldn't be that out of place in a South African shopping mall, and the food is quite superb – fresh spongy chocolate cake, a variety of pastries, ice-cream, cheese sandwiches, good hamburgers and real espresso coffee. It also does meals such as chicken curry for around US$4. Definitely the top eating spot in northern Mozambique.

Also very pleasant is the **Restaurante Refaba** on the riverfront next to the night market. There's generally a good breeze here, and although the food is standard Mozambican fare (chicken, meat or fish with chips for around US$4–5) the portions are substantial and the quality is well above average.

The restaurant on the eighth floor of the **Hotel Chuabo** is worth a try, though you should check the menu at the ground floor reception to see what's on offer – generally a selection of three or four different meals, with a good chance of something unusual like prawn curry or pork cutlets. Meals cost around US$5. The view from the restaurant is exceptional.

The **Pescina** (Swimming Pool) opposite the Hotel 1 de Junho serves chilled beer and cheap if unexciting meals, and you can take a table on the roof, where there's a good breeze. Use of the pool costs a rather prohibitive US$3. You'll no doubt be pleased to hear that Sunday night is Bingo night.

The **Cafe Nicola** serves beer and simple snacks such as prego rolls. There's also reasonable food at the **Hotel Zambeze** and ice-cream at the open-air **Restaurante Aquario** facing the main square.

ZALALA

Zalala Beach, 27km from Quelimane, is the obvious place to head for if you want to break up the slog between Beira and Nampula in relatively rustic surrounds. The surfaced road to Zalala passes through one of the most extensive coconut palm plantations in Africa, and the wide sandy beach itself offers good swimming and surface.

No more than 100m from the beach, the Complexo Turistico Kass-Kass (tel: 212302, fax: 212132) consists of several chalets each of which has two double bedrooms for a very reasonable US$15 per unit. These could be full over the weekend, so ring first. Alternatively, you can camp in the grounds for US$2.50 per tent. There's decent food and expensive beers in the restaurant.

To get to Zalala, follow Avenida Julius Nyerere out of Quelimane city centre. The road to Zalala is unsurfaced immediately as you leave the city centre, but the tar starts about 1km towards Zalala near a cemetery. In a private vehicle, you can't go wrong if you just stick to the surfaced road. If you're looking for a lift, the best place to wait is opposite the cemetery. There are regular chapas and it's easy enough to hitch, especially at weekends.

ALONG THE QUELIMANE–NAMPULA ROAD

The 525km road connecting Quelimane to Nampula is in poor condition for most of its length, though the last 100km or so before Nampula had been freshly tarred in late 1996 and there's reason to hope that it will be extended further south over the next couple of years. As things stand, you really need a 4WD to cover this road, or at least a vehicle with good clearance, and the full journey will probably take eight to ten hours. Plenty of buses and chapas cover this road, though few make it the whole way through in a day. Vehicles travelling from Quelimane to Nampula generally overnight at Alto Molócuè, 187km before Nampula, while vehicles travelling from Nampula to Quelimane generally overnight at Mocuba, 148km before Quelimane.

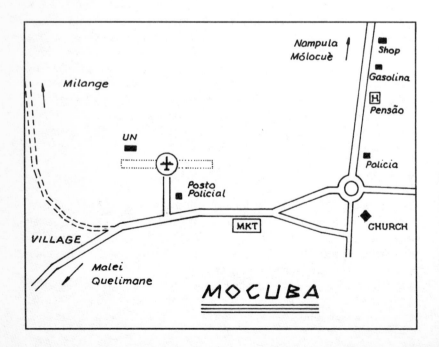

Mocuba

Mocuba is a nice, airy town at a sufficiently high altitude to stay relatively cool. It is mostly of interest to travellers as the junction of the road between Nampula and Quelimane, and the road west to Milange on the Malawi border. Vehicles to and from Quelimane stop in the market place, those to and from the north stop at the bridge at the north end of town. To get to Milange, you need to take the dirt road parallel to the tarred road just past the UN airstrip. This then turns right and heads northwest. It's quite easy to miss. The only pensão in Mocuba is rather run-down and decidedly overpriced at US$15/double.

Alto Molócuè

This dusty, scruffy small town sprawls around the Molócuè River exactly halfway between Mocuba and Nampula. The leafy administrative part of town, situated on a hill overlooking the north bank of the river, has a few interesting buildings dating to the early 20th century, notably a very pretty church, a peculiar house that was evidently converted from a fort, and a

run-down town hall with a large and decidedly pointless parking area in front of it. The hotels, restaurants and municipal market are in the small commercial centre, clustered around a triangular town 'square' to the south of the river about 500m from the administrative centre.

The best accommodation is at the **Pensão Santa Antonio**, where you have the choice of a clean double room with a fan and private balcony for US$10 or a self-contained double with a fan and fridge for US$25. The **Pensão Fambo Uone** is rather scruffy by comparison and no cheaper at US$10 for a spacious double without a fan. The food at the Santa Antonio isn't up to much, but there's an anonymous bar and restaurant about 50m from the square, in the opposite direction to the market, where we shared an excellent whole chicken and chips for US$8. A limited range of fresh fruit is on sale at the market, and there's a good bakery between the market and the square.

Vehicles heading towards Nampula or Quelimane leave Alto Molócuè from the square in the commercial centre. Vehicles heading to Gurué via Nauela leave from the traffic circle about 500m out of town along the road that passes the church.

GURUÉ

The highland town of Gurué makes for an interesting off-the-beaten-track diversion from the main road between Quelimane and Nampula. Situated amongst rolling hills and tea plantations at the base of the 2,419m-high Mount Namuli, Mozambique's second highest peak, Gurué has the highest rainfall of any town in Mozambique and an atmosphere quite unlike that of any other part of the country. Gurué would look and feel pretty tropical if you arrived there fresh from the European winter, but after a few weeks on the muggy coast of Mozambique it has a wonderfully fresh and invigorating climate.

The Gurué area is promising walking country. The sizeable town centre sprawls along the higher contours of a small hill offering great views up to Mount Namuli and down to a wood-lined dam. Several roads lead out of town among the tea plantations and to the footslopes of Namuli, where there are still a few well-maintained estate properties. As is the case elsewhere in Mozambique, a degree of caution is advised before attempting any serious off-road walking – mines may well remain a risk, and you should certainly check out the situation before attempting to ascend the slopes of the mounition. One good day walk would be to follow the road to Alto Molócuè out of town for roughly 5km, where there is a large, isolated and apparently abandoned old church standing on a hill.

Getting there and away
Gurué can be approached in two ways from the Nampula–Quelimane road, either directly from Alto Molócuè via Nauela along a little-used but

reasonably well maintained and very beautiful 80km road, or else from Nampevo via Errego along a 125km road that is reportedly in better condition though not as scenic. In a private vehicle, the direct route from Alto Molócuè is the better option if you're coming from the direction of Nampula, while the Nampevo route is better if you're coming from the direction of Mocuba.

Using public transport, there's considerably more traffic along the road from Nampevo to Gurué. Unaware of this, we approached Gurué from Alto Molócuè and waited for three or four hours before catching a lucky lift with a couple of businessmen who were using the scenic route to drive from Nampula to Lichinga. Had this vehicle not come past, I very much

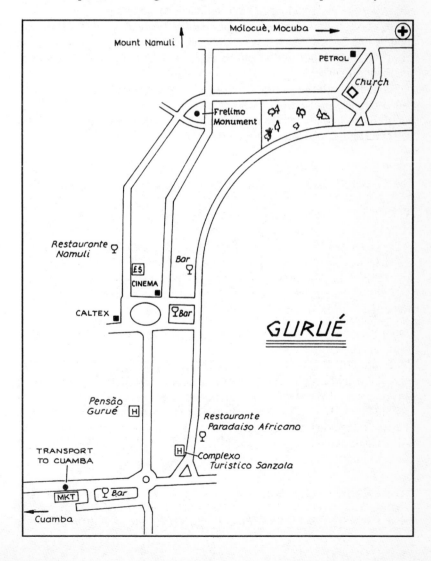

doubt that we would have got through. That said, it took us some time to find the right place to get a lift, which meant that we were only in position at around 05.30 – it's quite possible that a chapa would have been waiting for us had we arrived there before 05.00. If you want to try this route, I suggest that you get out of your hotel room before 04.30: it's a good 10–15 minute walk to the right spot, which you'll reach by walking to the church and then following the road that curves past it out of town for about 500m.

The road to Gurué via Nauela passes through some of the most attractive scenery in Mozambique: dense, green brachystegia woodland, rolling hills, and some monumentally contorted granite outcrops. Nauela itself is an intriguing place, with a small fort and large church as well as a few terminally run-down colonial buildings. The surrounding countryside is very beautiful. There's no accommodation, but you should be fine with a tent. One option, then, would be to take a lift as far as Nauela (a few vehicles go here daily from Alto Molócuè) and spend some time there before trying to find transport on to Gurué.

Gurué could also be approached by catching the train between Cuamba and Nampula, and getting off at Mutuali, from where there are usually a couple of trucks daily to Gurué via Lioma. In the opposite direction, vehicles to Lioma and Cuaba leave from in front of the market before 05.00.

Where to stay and eat
The **Pensão Gurué** is an adequate place with large, clean double rooms for US$12.50 using communal baths and US$15 self-contained. The food is excellent – we had a great plate of spicy chicken stew with boiled potatoes for US$3.50 each.

The only other accommodation is at the **Complexo Turistico Sanzala**, which has cramped and dingy self-contained doubles for US$10. We didn't try the food, but the flowering garden is a pleasant place to drink a cold beer or two. There are a couple of other bars and restaurants in town, but nothing out of the ordinary.

Chapter Twelve

Niassa Province

Sometimes referred to as the Siberia of Mozambique, Niassa is the country's driest and least densely populated province, but also one of its most scenic and climatically pleasant. The western border of the province is dominated by Africa's third largest body of water, the 585km-long Lake Malawi, still called by its colonial name of Lago Niassa in Mozambique, and by the wild, brachystegia-covered mountains that form the eastern escarpment of the Great Rift Valley.

Although few travellers currently explore Niassa, the province is the main gateway into Mozambique for people coming from Malawi, with border crossings by rail between Liwonde and Cuamba, by road between Mangochi and Mandimba, and by boat between Likoma and Cóbúe. The rail crossing in the south of the province is the one currently favoured by most travellers, many of whom then take a train straight out of Niassa to Nampula. However, as more people become aware of the road and boat crossings further north in the province, and facilities on the lake shore improve, Niassa may yet realise its enormous potential for relatively off-the-beaten-track exploration.

Oddly, Niassa is more accessible from neighbouring Malawi than it is from other parts of Mozambique. There are only two access roads to Niassa from elsewhere in Mozambique. The reasonably well maintained 310km unsurfaced road between Cuamba and Lichinga, the provincial capital, is the more accessible route, covered by several chapas and buses daily. The rough 750km road between Pemba and Lichinga via Montepuez and Marrupa is only suitable for self-sufficient 4WD drivers, though it could make for an exciting hitching trip for patient backpackers.

CUAMBA

Cuamba is an important route focus, lying at the junction of the railway line between Malawi and the coast of Mozambique, and the main roads north through Niassa and south via Gurué to Quelimane. Considering that it is currently many people's introduction to Mozambique, Cuamba is a

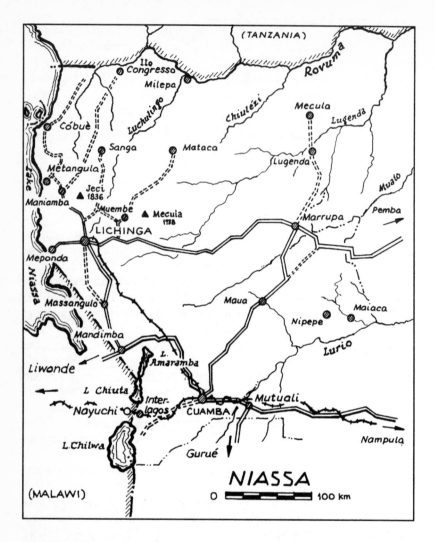

pretty humdrum sort of place; a dully uniform grid of flame-tree lined avenidas salvaged from complete anonymity by the granite hills that surround it. In its favour, Cuamba's proximity to Malawi means that it has the most affordable beers and sodas in northern Mozambique. Other notable features of the town are a predominance of bicycle shops – presumably influenced by the quirky and mysterious trade patterns that characterise northern Mozambique – and that it has its own electricity supply, derived from a hydro-electric scheme established in 1988 with Norwegian aid.

Getting there and away

Many travellers enter Mozambique from Malawi using the rail service between Liwonde and Cuamba.

A daily passenger train has recently started operating between Cuamba and Nampula. In either direction, the train leaves at around 06.00, takes about eight hours and costs less than US$4. The seats are reasonably comfortable and when we used the service it wasn't prohibitively crowded. That said, it's advisable to buy a ticket a day in advance and to arrive at the station at around 05.00 to be certain of getting a seat.

There are at least two buses daily between Cuamba and Lichinga, leaving Cuamba at around 05.00 from the opposite side of the railway line to the town centre, and Lichinga at the same time from the central market. Several chapas and trucks also do this trip every day, with the last vehicles typically leaving at around midday. The 310km trip between Cuamba and Lichinga takes about six to eight hours in a bus, a bit longer in a truck or chapa.

Cuamba can also be approached from Gurué in the south. There's not much traffic along this route – we got through in a day, but it's difficult to say how much this was due to luck. Vehicles heading from Gurué to Cuamba generally leave from in front of the market between 04.30 and 05.00. On the morning we did this trip, we missed the only vehicle heading straight through to Cuamba and so had to take a lift as far as Lioma, where we waited for four hours for a truck to Mutuali, a small town on the Lichinga–Cuamba railway line. We arrived in Mutuali at 13.00, literally as the train to Cuamba was pulling in, which meant that I was unable to confirm the rumour that there is a pensão in Mutuali should you get stuck there overnight. There is definitely no formal accommodation in Lioma, but I doubt you'd have a problem finding a room in a private house or somewhere to pitch a tent. The best advice I can give travellers heading this way is to be at Gurué market by 04.30 at the latest. Provided that you can get a lift as far as Mutuali and you arrive there before midday, you can safely bet on picking up the train to Cuamba.

People who are driving their own vehicle between Cuamba and Nampula might think about using the route through Gurué and Molócuè – it's a longer road but much more scenic and in better condition.

Where to stay and eat

The **Hotel Vision 2002** is the only place in town with pretensions to upmarket status, and it's pretty good value, with clean air-conditioned doubles in the US$20–25 bracket. The menu is the most varied in Cuamba, and reasonably priced, with most dishes in the US$5–7 bracket. Be warned, however, that on the night we ate here we waited an hour-and-a-half to be served prawns that were decidedly on the edge and chips that had evidently been left to cool in the kitchen for an hour or so – an unacceptable waste of US$7, even allowing for the fact that the hotel was in the process of being refurbished by newly installed Dutch management.

There are several cheaper lodgings in Cuamba. The **Pensão Sáo Miguel** is the obvious standout, offering clean double rooms with a fan for US$13 (communal bathroom) or US$15 (self-contained). The restaurant here has

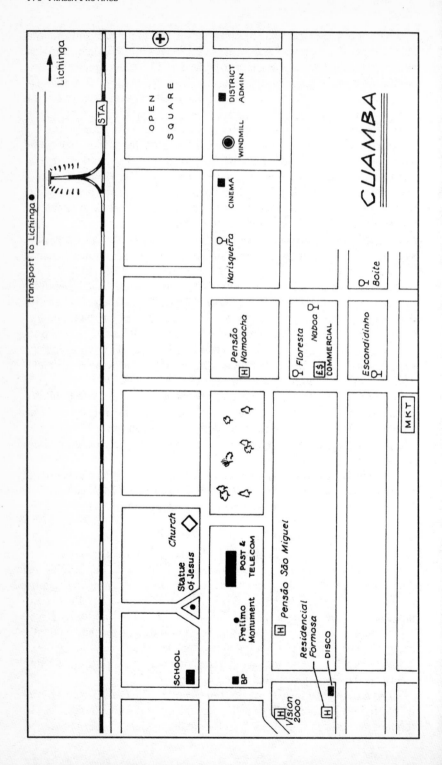

an enticingly varied but ultimately rather misleading menu, since all that they served on the day we visited was chicken and chips for around US$3.50. On the plus side, the patio is a pleasant place to sip on the cheapest beers in northern Mozambique.

The **Residencial Formosa** looks rather tired by comparison, and the ground floor disco doesn't bode well for a quiet night. That said, solo travellers may still prefer to stay here, since the single rooms are relatively good value at US$6. People travelling in tandem will pay US$12 for a twin or US$15 for a double (no fan or private bathroom).

The **Pensão Namaacha** might also be worth a try. It was full on both occasions we looked in, which is always a good sign, and you will have to walk past it on your way between the railway station and the other hotels.

Aside from the restaurants at the hotels, there are several other restaurants and bars dotted around town, though most don't seem to serve any food. Exceptions are the **Restaurante Narisqueira**, which has the usual fish or chicken with chips, and the **Restaurante Escondidinho**, which has a more interesting menu but is very hot and stuffy inside.

MANDIMBA

Situated on the Malawi border almost exactly halfway between Cuamba and Lichinga, Mandimba is notable mostly for being the best place to cross between Malawi and Mozambique by road (see *Chapter Three*). In other respects, it is a thoroughly nondescript town, sprawling messily along the main road for a kilometre or so. Mandimba's one saving grace is the unusually cheap and pleasant resthouse, behind the petrol station, where you can get ice-cold beers and sodas in the bar, a promising looking restaurant, and double rooms for US$5. Buses travelling in either direction between Cuamba and Lichinga generally stop at the market in Mandimba between 09.00 and 10.00. Should you arrive in Mandimba from Malawi between 10.00 and 14.00, you will still stand a good chance of catching a lift in either direction on the back of a truck. If you arrive later than that, expect to spend the night in Mandimba.

MASSANGULO

This atmospheric small town lies about 2km off the main Cuamba-Lichinga road, roughly 65km north of Mandimba. Situated at the base of a pretty mountain, and dominated by an extraordinary mission church, Massangulo could be an attractive place to spend a couple of nights, particularly if you like walking. The Yaileka Resthouse behind the market has cheap if rather basic rooms. Most vehicles heading between Cuamba and Lichinga don't divert to Massangulo, but you can ask to be dropped at the signposted turn-off and walk from there – it shouldn't take longer than 30 minutes.

LICHINGA

Formerly known as Vila Cabral, Lichinga is the capital of Niassa and the main gateway to the Mozambican shore of Lago Niassa. Lichinga lies at an altitude of 1,277m on the plateau to the east of the lake, giving it a refreshingly breezy climate. Fringed by the unusual combination of exotic pine plantations and more characteristically tropical vegetation such as mango trees and leafy plantains, Lichinga has a markedly different atmosphere to any other of the larger towns in Mozambique. Nevertheless, it's a rather poky little place with poor and generally overpriced facilities, and little in the way of tourist attractions.

Lichinga has long been the best place to change US dollars cash into meticais. When we were in town, the going rate was US$1 = MT 12,500

(as opposed to around MT 11,500–12,000 in Maputo, Beira or Nampula). You'd be safer changing money in an upmarket hotel or shop than on the street.

Getting there and away
LAM flies between Nampula and Lichinga several times a week. There is also a return flight between Tete and Lichinga every Wednesday.

The unsurfaced road between Cuamba and Lichinga is generally in good condition. There are, however, a couple of makeshift bridges along the way which would definitely require high clearance and possibly even 4WD. The road has been known to become impassable during the rainy season, though I understand that recent roadworks mean that this is unlikely to happen again in the foreseeable future.

There are two buses daily from Cuamba to Lichinga, leaving in either direction at around 05.00.

Unusually for Mozambique, most transport out of Lichinga leaves from in front of the central market, so that for once you are spared the hassle of walking a couple of kilometres out of town at an obscenely early hour to find the vehicle you want.

Where to stay
The **Pousada Lichinga** is the most upmarket establishment in Lichinga. The large, clean doubles can hardly be called good value at US$20, especially as you must still use communal bucket showers and toilets, but they are still the most pleasant rooms in the town centre.

The **Hotel Chiwindi** deserves some sort of award for the sheer gall of asking US$8/16 single/double for a dingy, dirty room and access to even less savoury toilets. Give it a miss unless everything else is full.

The **Residencial Rival** is probably the best value for money in Lichinga, with reasonably clean self-contained doubles for US$12. Unfortunately, it is often full – though we managed to get a room on our third attempt.

The blue **Resthouse** next to the market is the sort of cheap, simple family-run lodge that comes a dime a dozen in Tanzania or Malawi but is all too rare in Mozambique. Cell-like rooms cost US$5/6 single/double. The communal showers and toilets leave a little to be desired, but you can't complain at the price.

The **Kuchijinji Motel** lies about 3km out of town on the road to Meponda and the airport. Rooms cost around US$15 per person including breakfast. There is a restaurant but no bar, so bring your own drinks.

Where to eat
The best place to eat in Lichinga is the **Pousada**. The set menu is OK, without justifying the charge of US$7.50. It is perhaps better to order the same dish as a snack (around US$3) or to stick to the excellent snack menu (quarter chicken and chips, chouriço sandwiches and prego rolls).

The options for eating out in Lichinga are otherwise rather limited. The food at the Hotel Chiwindi is unexceptional, overpriced and, as seems to be the custom in Niassa, the chips are generally served cold. The Snack Bar next to the Residencial Rival is all bar and no snacks, as is the Restaurante Planalto opposite the water tower.

The Salõa Cabalereira Take-Away opposite the market does at least have a menu. The million dollar question is *when* they actually serve food: our attempts to eat here at a few different times of the day invariably resulted in much head-shaking, pointing at watches, and no food. Still, the beers are cold and cheaper than elsewhere in town.

LAGO NIASSA

Lake Malawi is the third largest lake in Africa, measuring 585km from north to south and up to 100km from east to west. The bulk of Lake Malawi lies in the country with which it shares a name, but large stretches of the eastern shore are territorially part of Mozambique and Tanzania. During colonial times, Lake Malawi was known as Lake Nyasa and Malawi was called Nyasaland. For some reason this colonial name has remained unchanged in Tanzania and Mozambique, where the lake is still known respectively as Lake Nyasa and Lago Niassa.

Lago Niassa is a remarkable body of water, lying at the southern end of the Rift Valley system, an immense geological scar that cuts through Africa all the way from the Red Sea in the north. Much of the lake is hemmed in by the dramatically mountainous Rift Valley escarpment, which in places towers more than 1km above its waters. The thrillingly clear water of Lake Malawi probably protects a greater variety of fish than any other lake in the world. At least 500 fish species have been recorded – a greater tally of freshwater species than for the whole of Europe and North America – and it is thought that a similar number of species still await formal scientific discovery. Lake Malawi is particularly notable for its amazing variety of cichlids, a group of highly colourful fish that look after their offspring by holding them in their mouths until they are large enough to fend for themselves.

It should be said, particularly for people who are visiting Mozambique as part of a longer trip through Africa, that the Mozambican stretch of the lake offers little that cannot be done more easily and cheaply in the better developed Malawian sector of the shore. The attraction of this part of the lake is that it is still really off the beaten track, for which reason there remains a genuine sense of exploration attached to visiting it. Another feature of the eastern lake shore is that, because it faces west, it is the best place to see the dramatic sunsets for which the lake is famous.

As things stand, there are three points of access to Lago Niassa. Meponda lies almost directly east of Lichinga along a good 65km road, making it the easiest place to get to from the provincial capital. Metangula lies roughly

140km from Lichinga by road, making it more time consuming to reach, though it has better facilities than Meponda. Cóbuè is another 80km north of Metangula, and of note mostly as the best place to cross between Malawi and Mozambique over the lake.

Meponda

This is the closest lakeshore settlement to Lichinga. Little more than a glorified village with a few mostly derelict concrete buildings, Meponda lies on an attractive sandy beach that arcs for a kilometre or more below low wooded hills. At present there is no formal accommodation at Meponda, but it seems that a lodge will be constructed in the near future. For now, there would be nothing stopping you from camping on the beach or, if you don't have a tent, from sleeping under one of the open-sided reed shelters in the beachfront salõa de chá, which also serves beers, sodas and basic meals such as fish and chips or chicken and rice.

To get to Meponda, follow the Metangula road out of Lichinga for about 5km until you reach the signposted turn-off, from where it's 60km to Meponda. The descent to the lake passes through tall brachystegia woodland and several small villages where you will see several examples of the distinctive huts and raised grain stores that are characteristic of Niassa. Public transport to Meponda leaves from the market in Lichinga. The trip takes about two hours.

Metangula

The largest settlement on the Mozambican shore of Lago Niassa (which isn't saying a great deal), Metangula was formerly the main slave terminus on the eastern side of the lake, the counterpart to the slaving emporium of Nkhotakota in Malawi. Today, Metangula is rather an out-of-the-way place, consisting of a small town centre with a few shops and a run-down pensão. More attractive than staying in Metangula itself would be to head 8km along the lake shore to Chiwanga, where there a small beach resort with a few reed huts and space for camping, as well as a restaurant and bar. The Australian who runs the hotel at Cóbuè also has plans to develop a small campsite and hut complex at Metangula. Called The Knoll, this should be operational by mid-1997.

There is a good 120km road from Lichinga as far as Maniamba, then a rougher 28km road to Metangula: a 4WD vehicle is required. To find a truck heading this way, go to the market in Lichinga, preferably before 05.00. You will probably have to walk the 8km from Metangula to Chiwanga.

Cóbuè

The small town of Cóbuè lies on a beautiful part of the Lago Niassa shore, roughly 80km north of Metangula and facing Likoma Island, a Malawian territory surrounded by Mozambican waters. An Australian has recently opened a lodge at Cóbuè called **Hotel Santo Miguel**, with rooms for around US$10, as well as a more basic campsite called **Njafuwa Beach Camp**. Coming from the south, there are infrequent trucks between Metangula and Cóbuè, but the more comfortable mode of transport is by fishing dhow. Coming from Likoma Island in Malawi, dhows formally act as public transport to Cóbuè, taking about an hour to make the 10km crossing.

It is permitted to visit Cóbuè from Likoma for up to 24 hours without a Mozambican visa, but a visa *is* required for a longer stay, or if you plan to travel further afield in Mozambique. At the time of writing, visas must be obtained in advance (this can be arranged at the High Commission in Lilongwe or the Consulate in Blantyre). The immigration officer in Lichinga has recently agreed to allow visas to be issued at Cóbuè, but this plan hasn't yet come into operation, for which reason I wouldn't recommend that you arrive at Cóbuè without a visa unless you have independent confirmation you will be able to get one on the spot.

OFF THE BEATEN TRACK IN NIASSA

Niassa is reputedly still home to large numbers of wild animals, including substantial numbers of elephants, buffaloes and lions. At the time of writing, there is no real tourist development in the province, and the reserves are only accessible to self-sufficient travellers who have a reliable 4WD and the appropriate spares.

Inland from the lake, some 80km from Metangula, lies the **Sanga North Game Reserve**. Hunting guides are available, but there are no facilities unless you can get help from the locals. Safari or hunting groups must first obtain permission from the Department of Forestry and Veterinary Services in Maputo. Photographic safaris, in particular, will be welcomed. At Ilo Congresso, up on the border with Tanzania, can be found various sites of historical interest.

Near Mecula, in the far northeast of the province about half-way between Lago Niassa and the ocean, borders the vast **Niassa Game Reserve**. Again, there are no facilities or provisions for food here, but local guides are available. It must be stressed that hunting is forbidden in this reserve.

Further south, on the road from Cuamba to Marrupa, the mission at Muau and the even more remote mission at Nipepe both have beautiful churches decorated in traditional style. The Marrupa area is reportedly rich in game, and there is some tentative talk of running safaris into the area within the next couple of years. Maiaca, near the border with Nampula province, is another good location for spotting wild animals, principally elephant, buck and hyena. Again, there are no facilities, but camping is possible by the river, a subsidiary of the Lúrio.

18th century church at Quelimane

Above: *The Church of Senhora Baluarte at Ilha do Moçambique is the oldest European building in the southern hemisphere.*

Below: *A private mosque sits among the reedhouses on the outskirts of Lichinga.*

Above: *The hills outside Gurue, with Mount Numuli in the background*

Below: *Children in reed homesteads*

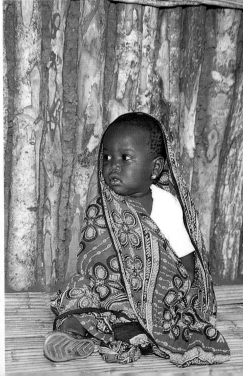

A SEA-FARING NATION

Above: *Fishermen at Vilankulo*

Below: *Dhows near the ferry at Maxixe, where boats are boarded for Inhambane*

Chapter Thirteen

Nampula Province

Bounded by the rivers Lúrio to the north and Ligonha to the south, the province of Nampula is comprised largely of open savannah broken up by any number of isolated and imposing rocky outcrops, mesas and plateaux. The provincial capital, also called Nampula, is the largest and most prosperous city in northern Mozambique, and an important route focus – it would be practically impossible to travel through northern Mozambique *without* stopping over in Nampula at least once.

Historically, the most important town in Nampula Province is Ilha do Moçambique (Mozambique Island) which was the Portuguese capital in East Africa for almost four centuries prior to 1898, when it was superseded by Lourenço Marques. For those with a historical bent, Ilha do Moçambique is without doubt the most alluring travel destination in Nampula, if not in the whole of Mozambique: an absorbing and atmospheric warren of dense alleys and beautiful colonial buildings, many of which date to the earliest years of the Portuguese occupation.

Nampula boasts few other tourist attractions. The rocky outcrops that dominate the landscape reputedly offer some of the best free-face rock climbing in Southern Africa, but pending further tourist development, this is of academic interest to anybody but experienced and fully equipped rock climbers. The Indian Ocean port of Nacala, roughly 100km north of Ilha do Moçambique, has largely superseded the older port in economic terms but it is of limited interest to visitors – the nearby beach at Fernáo Velosa is highly rated by snorkellers, but, once again, you could only snorkel here with your own equipment. Also of interest is the ancient Muslim port of Angoche, situated on one of the finest beaches in the country and boasting a small turn-of-the-century 'old town'.

NAMPULA

Nampula is the commercial heart of northern Mozambique, a relatively lively and prosperous city with good shops and reasonable facilities for visitors. An important transport hub, Nampula is likely to be visited at

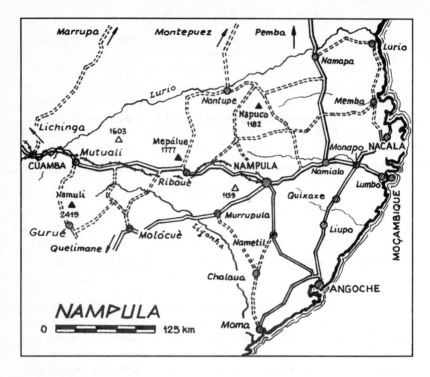

some point by most people who travel through northern Mozambique. Otherwise, it is of limited interest to visitors – a southern African everytown which, the linguistic dominance of Portuguese aside, has little to distinguish it from a dozen other similarly sized towns in Zimbabwe or Malawi.

The main cluster of older buildings is focused around the Praça de Destacemento Feminino, but of these only the early 20th-century cathedral vaguely warrants a second look. Of greater interest is the museum, which has a good ethnographic collection dominated by a number of old musical instruments and some very weird face masks. The Makonde co-operative behind the museum is a good place to see Makonde carvers at work and to buy or (for a small negotiable fee) photograph Makonde masks and carvings. Just outside Nampula lies a large basalt outcrop resembling a profile of a face looking at the sky. Known as "the old man", local legend has it that this outcrop materialised upon the death of an old king of Monomotapa in 1570.

It's worth knowing that the private cambrio on Avenida Paolo Samuel Kamkomba offers the best rate for US dollar travellers cheques we encountered in Mozambique – the same as the cash rate with a commission of less than 1%.

Getting there and away

LAM flies between Nampula and Beira and Maputo on most days. There are less frequent scheduled LAM flights between Nampula and the other four provincial capitals north of the Zambezi: Pemba, Quelimane, Lichinga and Tete. The airport is about 4km out of town and about 1km off the road to Pemba. There are no taxis but it's reasonably easy to hitch.

Nampula is connected by a good surfaced road to Pemba and Nacala, and except after heavy rain the road between Nampula and Ilha do Moçambique will also be passable in most vehicles. A 4WD will be required to drive between Nampula and Cuamba. The direct route between Cuamba and Nampula is reportedly in worse shape than the longer but more scenic route via Gurué. A 4WD is also currently advisable if you want to drive between Nampula and Quelimane, though the 100km of road closest to Nampula has recently been resurfaced and it's possible that the tar will be extended south as far as Quelimane in the next two or three years.

The best option for backpackers who are heading to Nampula from Niassa Province or Malawi is the recently installed daily rail service between Cuamba and Nampula. Trains leave in either direction at about 06.00 and take roughly eight hours. The seats are comfortable, though you risk having to stand for at least part of the way if you don't arrive at the station an hour or so before the train departs. Tickets cost less than US$4 for the whole trip. You're advised to bring along something to eat and drink, since all that's available along the way are mangoes or whatever other fruit is in season. The alternative to the trains is to go by road via Gurué – an interesting and scenic trip covered more fully in *Chapter Eleven*.

There is plenty of transport between Nampula and Pemba, Nacala and Ilha do Moçambique. The best option to Pemba is the daily Transnorte bus which leaves in either direction at 05.00 sharp. There is also a daily bus to Nacala, leaving at the same time. All chapas and buses between Nampula and Pemba, Nacala or Ilha do Moçambique leave from and arrive in Nampula at the junction of Avenida Paulo Samuel Kamkomba and Avenida de Trabalho.

There is at least one bus daily in either direction between Nampula and Quelimane. Buses heading to Quelimane generally stop overnight at Mocuba and buses heading to Nampula stop overnight at Molócuè. It is also possible to do this trip in hops using the regular chapas that connect Nampula to Molócuè and Mocuba, and Mocuba to Quelimane. Most transport along this road, including the bus, leaves Nampula at around 05.00. The best place to wait for vehicles is at a stop situated, with the obliqueness that seems to be characteristic of Mozambicans where public transport is concerned, about 20–30 minutes' walk from the railway station and town centre along the Quelimane road. In other words, to be sure of getting a seat on the bus to Quelimane you need to be out of your hotel room by 04.15 at the latest.

Where to stay

Nampula probably has a greater number of hotels and pensãos than any other similarly sized town in Mozambique. For budget travellers, a cluster of three affordable pensãos lies near the intersection of Avenida Paulo

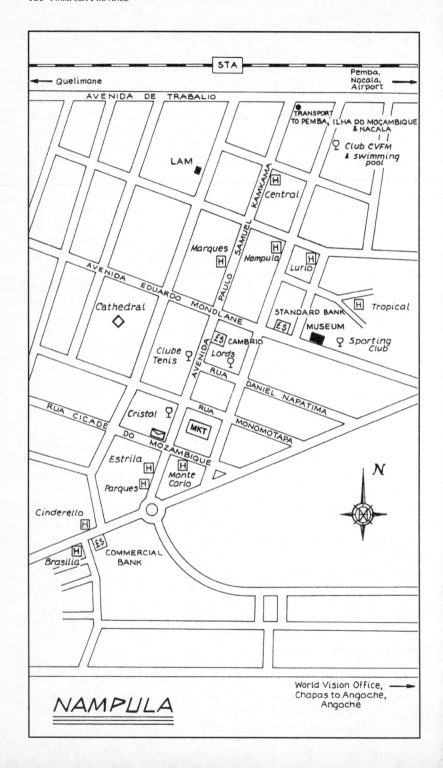

NAMPULA

Samuel Kamkomba and Avenida de Indepencia. The **Pensão Marques** is currently the most popular of these places; by Mozambican standards it's little more than an above average dump at below average prices, but it is nevertheless good value at US$4/7 single/double with a fan. The rooms at the **Pensão Centrale** are perhaps a bit cleaner and airier than those at the Marques, and they're cheaper at US$3 per person, but they have one major disadvantage in that there aren't any fans. The **Pensão Nampula** is similar in price, but it struck me as the least attractive of the three places.

There are three more upmarket pensãos at the far end of Avenida Paulo Samuel Kamkomba, all with rooms in the US$13–15 range. The rooms at the **Pensão Estrila** have little to recommend them: admittedly, they are relatively attractively furnished, but this doesn't compensate for the fact that they're very hot and stuffy and lack fans. It is also difficult to think of a compelling reason to stay at the **Residencial Monte Carlo**. Much better, at least on the face of it, is the **Pensão Parques**, a very well maintained building that was full whenever we looked in. Near the traffic circle at the end of Avenida Paulo Samuel Kamkomba, the **Pensão Brasilia** also seems sensibly priced at US$10/15 single/double for a clean room with a fan, and US$15/20 for an air-conditioned room.

The best upmarket option is the well-maintained **Hotel Tropical**, which has self-contained air-conditioned rooms for US$30/40 single/double. Bookings can be made directly (Nampula 212232) or through the Maputo office (tel: Maputo 427466, fax: 427464). The nearby **Hotel Lúrio** is very run-down and poor value at US$20/30 single/double.

Where to eat

There is a good selection of restaurants in Nampula. First choice is probably the **Clube Tenis**, which has a smart, pleasant outdoor restaurant serving everything from steak and chicken to prawns at reasonable prices; dishes start around US$5. Another attraction for some will be the pool tables. The beers and sodas here are relatively pricey.

The **Sporting Club** next to the museum also has several outdoor tables. The menu is more limited than at the Clube Tenis, but the food is still very good and relatively inexpensive. The beers here are amongst the cheapest in town, and it has the only functional coffee machines in town.

The **Club CVFM** has an air-conditioned restaurant which, although the food is nothing special at around US$5 for most dishes, does offer some relief from the humidity in hot weather. The club's swimming pool has a high-diving board and lies in peaceful bougainvillea-draped gardens. Entrance to the pool costs US$3.50.

Other places you could try are the restaurant at the **Hotel Tropical**, which serves good meals in the US$5–8 range, and **Lord's Restaurant** on Rua Daniel Napatima. The cheapest place to eat is probably the restaurant below the **Pensão Centrale**.

NAMIALO

The small town of Namialo lies at the junction of the main road between Nampula and Pemba and the turn-off to Nacala and Ilha do Moçambique. Travellers heading between Pemba and either Nacala or Ilha do Moçambique may well choose to spend a night in Namialo, whether they've come from Pemba and feel like a meal and wash before continuing their travels the next day, or they are heading to Pemba and want to catch the Transnorte bus which leaves from Nampula at 05.00 and passes through Namialo at around 08.00.

If you do spend a night in Namialo, the **Pousada Hotel** on the main road has large, slightly run-down double rooms for a reasonable US$7.50. Remarkably, given that it is an archetypically dusty and unappealing African junction town, Namialo boasts a couple of good restaurants. The Restaurante Tropical, the unsignposted green building about two blocks from the Pousada along the main road towards Nampula, serves large, tasty helpings of fish or chicken and chips for around US$4, and it has a fridge stocked high with beers, sodas and imported cartons of fruit juice. The newer restaurant around the corner is even better, according to a Portuguese resident of the area, but unfortunately it was closed for the day when we were in town.

All public transport in and out of Namialo stops at the bus station roughly opposite the Pousada.

MONAPO

Monapo lies 38km east of Namialo and roughly 3km before the roads to Nacala and Ilha do Moçambique part way. Monapo is noted for its cashew factory – it's a good place to buy cashews cheaply – but there is no obvious reason why you would want to spend a night in Monapo, and so far as I'm aware, nowhere to stay if you do.

ILHA DO MOÇAMBIQUE

The town of Moçambique, on the small coral island of the same name, is not only the oldest European settlement in East Africa, but arguably also the most bizarre. Declared a UNESCO Cultural Heritage Site in 1992, Ilha do Moçambique, known to locals simply as Ilha (pronounced *ilia*), must surely rank as northern Mozambique's most alluring travel destination both for its singular atmosphere and for its wealth of beautiful old buildings.

Linked to the mainland by a 3.5km-long single-lane causeway, the crescent-shaped island measures a mere 2.5km from north to south and is at no point more than 600m wide. Despite its small size, the island supports a population of roughly 7,000, and as the most important Portuguese settlement on the east African coast for the best part of four centuries, it boasts several of the oldest extant colonial buildings in the southern hemisphere.

Ilha do Moçambique was, like Sofala and Angoche, an important Muslim trading centre even before the Portuguese landed on the east coast of Africa. The island's name is probably derived from that of Moussa Ben Mbiki, said by some to have been the incumbent sheikh when Da Gama first landed there in 1499, and by others to have been the founding father of the island's Muslim settlement.

Prior to the Portuguese occupation, Mozambique Island was renowned as a centre of ship building; in 1502, a Portuguese navigator Vincente Soares had a boat assembled there. Portugal occupied the island in 1507, two years after they occupied Kilwa and Sofala, and immediately built a hospital, church and small fort. With its long tradition of boat building, and easily defendable position at the junction of the East African coast and the all-important route to India, Mozambique Island soon became the focus of Portuguese naval activities and the most important stopover for Portuguese ships waiting for the monsoon winds. This rapid rise to prominence caused Portugal to abolish the Captaincy of Kilwa in 1513. In 1530, the Captaincy of Sofala was renamed the Captaincy of Moçambique and Sofala, and the island effectively became the capital of Portuguese East Africa, a status it was to retain for close on four centuries.

By the mid-16th century, some 70-odd officials, ranging from a judge and doctor to priests and soldiers, were listed on the official payroll of the island. Depending on how many ships were docked at the island, it supported up to 1,000 Portuguese at any one time. Food was in short supply, and although some was imported from Comoros and Madagascar, many provisions were bought through the Muslim traders who had abandoned the island for Sancul on the facing mainland following the Portuguese occupation.

Mozambique Island was the site of the earliest battle between European powers to take place in Africa, when the Netherlands attempted to seize it as an East African base for the Dutch East India Company in 1607/8. The island was also attacked by Omani Arabs in 1671 and by France in 1793–7. Mozambique Island was the most important port south of Mombasa from the early 16th to late 19th centuries. It probably peaked in prosperity during the 18th century, when it handled some 70% of the ivory exported from the Mozambican coast.

Mozambique Island began a slide into economic decline during the late 19th century. This phenomenon was rooted in two causes: the general southward drift of the economy towards Lourenço Marques and the Portuguese 'discovery' of the far superior natural harbour at nearby Nacala. The declining importance of the island was acknowledged as early as 1898, when it was superseded as national capital by Lourenço Marques, even though it was still handling approximately 20% of the total goods shipped out of Mozambique. As recently as 1928, Mozambique Island was still one of the five largest urban centres in the country, supporting a population of

7,000. However, it was by this time losing even its local economic significance, following the completion of the more modern port at Nacala. In 1935, the reigns of local government were moved from the island to the new provincial capital of Nampula.

Ilha do Moçambique may now be something of a backwater, but it is also one of the few old towns in Africa which has by and large kept its historical appearance. Portuguese architecture dominates, though very few buildings on Ilha do Moçambique are in the expansive classical style seen at somewhere like Ibo, most probably due to the small size and dense population of the island. Among the more interesting buildings are the fortress of São Sebastão, the former governor's palace, and the Church of Senhora Saude.

The old town, a maze of narrow alleys lined with fading whitewashed buildings and little changed in shape since the late 18th century, has a mood not unlike that of some of the older Swahili island towns of the Tanzanian and Kenyan coast: Lamu, say, or even more strikingly, the old quarter of Mombasa. An unexpected factor, but one that serves only to underline Mozambique's kinship with the rest of the Swahili coast, is the overwhelming Muslim presence. Every historical source that I'm aware of states that the Muslim population was forced to relocate to the mainland during the four centuries when Mozambique Island was the Portuguese centre of operations in East Africa. Probably the Muslims drifted back across to the island after the capital was moved to Maputo in 1898; possibly even more recently, in the wake of what was effectively the Portuguese evacuation of Mozambique in 1975. Whenever and however it occurred, the Muslim reoccupation of the old town has created a strong but possibly rather deceptive sense of historical continuity, one which has the effect of reducing four centuries of Portuguese occupation to something of a passing episode.

Getting there and away

From Nampula, your best bet is probably to catch a bus towards Nacala and change vehicle at Namialo or Monapo – there are regular chapas to Ilha do Moçambique from either of these towns. You can refer to the Nacala section for details of transport between Nacala and Ilha do Moçambique, and for details of getting to Ilha do Moçambique from Pemba (much the same as for getting to Nacala from Pemba). Transport out of Ilha do Moçambique leaves from next to the causeway.

Where to stay and eat

The **Hotel Pousada do Mozambique**, situated between the old town and the fort, is the only place to stay on the island. It's a rather run-down but nevertheless quite pleasant Bauhaus-influenced building, with breezy, sea-facing rooms for US$7/10 using communal bucket showers and US$10/12 with a private bathroom. There's a rumour that this hotel will be taken over by a large international chain, in which event you can expect a rise both in standards and in price. The restaurant serves acceptable fish and chips for around US$3.50, but not much else.

The sea-water **Pescina** (swimming pool) on the waterfront near the hotel has a restaurant which serves a large plate of prawns for US$7 and fish and chips for a similar price to the Pousada. The only other place to eat is the eminently avoidable **Restaurante Ancoura D'oura** opposite the Palace Museum.

Around the island
São Sebastão

Dominating the northern tip of the island, the fortress of São Sebastão has often been described as the most formidable fortress in Africa. Measuring up to 20m high, it was built with dressed limestone shipped from Lisbon between 1546 and 1583 as a response to the Turkish threats of 1538–53. The shape of the fort has changed little over the intervening centuries, though all but one of the three original gates, the one beneath the buttress of Santa Barbara, was filled in before 1607, and its condition is remarkably similar to that described by the English sailor Henry Salt in the 1800s. The fortress was in active use as recently as the liberation war, when it was used as a Portuguese barracks. It remains in remarkably good condition, and its wells are still the only source of fresh water on the island.

There must be few other buildings which have played such a decisive role in shaping the course of history as has São Sebastão. On 29 March 1607, nine Dutch ships appeared off the shore of Mozambique Island, causing the Portugese inhabitants to withdraw to the fort. The Dutch navy landed on the island and occupied it for about a month, but, unable to capture the fort, it withdrew on 13 May. A year later, the Dutch returned to Mozambique Island with a formidable fleet of 13 ships carrying 377 guns and 1,840 men. Again, they seized the island, and again, three months after landing, they were forced to withdraw, incapable of capturing the fort.

Had São Sebastão been a less imposing fortress, it is almost certain – given that Portugal was by this time a waning naval power – that Mozambique Island would have become the Dutch East India Company's East African base, with incalculable ramifications on the eventual course of events that shaped modern southern Africa. In all probability, a Dutch victory in 1607 would have signalled the end of Portugal's influence in the region. Furthermore, with Mozambique Island as their African base, it is unlikely that the Dutch East India Company would ever have founded the reprovisioning station on the Cape of Good Hope that was eventually to become Cape Town and give birth to the Afrikaner nation.

The fortress of São Sebastão has witnessed several other important events in Mozambican history. In February 1618, the acting Captain of Moçambique and Sofala was stabbed fatally on the steps of the fort by his eventual successor, a culmination of the ongoing intrigues that surrounded the three-

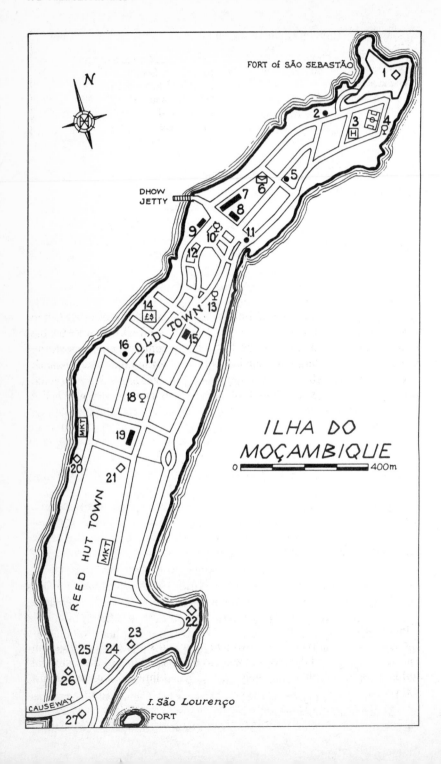

FORT of SÃO SEBASTÃO

DHOW JETTY

ILHA DO MOÇAMBIQUE

0 ⊏▬▬▬▬▬▬▬▬▬▬▬▬⊐ 400m

OLD TOWN

REED HUT TOWN

CAUSEWAY

I. São Lourenço
FORT

KEY

1	Church of Senhora Baluarte	15	Mercado Centrale (closed)
2	Secondary school	16	Primary School
3	Pousada Hotel	17	Park with bandstand
4	Pescina	18	Pastelaria
5	Cinema	19	Hospital
6	Post Office and Telecommunications	20	Mosque
		21	Church (1896)
7	Palace Museum	22	Catholic Cathedral
8	Sacred Art Museum	23	Mosque
9	Old Customs House	24	Cemetery
10	Restaurante Ancore D'Oura	25	BP Garage
11	Statue	26	Small Mosque
12	Central Square	27	Church of Senhora Saude and old cemetery
13	Escondidinha Restaurante		
14	Commercial Bank		

yearly appointment to this most profitable of the various postings available in Portugal's Indian Ocean empire. In 1671, an Omani naval attack on Mozambique Island followed a similar course of events to the earlier Dutch attacks, as the Omanis occupied the island for several weeks but were unable to drive the Portuguese out of the fort – an outcome which had a strong influence on the modern-day boundary between Mozambique and Tanzania.

Apart from Sáo Sebastão, the only 16th-century building to have survived to the present day is the Church of Nossa Senhora Baluarte, which lies within the fortress. Built in 1522, this small church is the oldest standing European building in the southern hemisphere. The main body of the church has changed little since the 16th century, though the covered porch and pulpit both date to the 18th century. The eminent archaeologist James Kirkman, writing about 30 years ago, remarked that Senhora Baluarte is notable for its several gargoyles as well as a Manoeline frieze around the roof and the Royal Arms of Portugal situated above the entrance, but these features seem either to have been removed in the interim or else they are obscured by the lamentably run-down condition of the building. On the floor of the church, a stone plaque marks the tomb of the Portuguese Bishop of Japan, who was buried there in 1588. There are several other graves of bishops outside the main building, dating from between 1592 and 1969. Several human bones of unknown origin are stored in a box in the church.

The old town

The island can be divided into two parts: the old stone town or museum zone to the north and the reed hut zone to the south. Most of the historical buildings lie in the old town, which has changed little in shape in the last 300 years.

When the Dutch evacuated Mozambique Island in 1607, they burned the old town to the ground, destroying the old Muslim quarter as well as two

churches and the hospital, and sparing only the Portuguese-held fortress of
Sáo Sebastão and the church that is protected within its walls. In 1671, the
Omani Arabs again razed much of the old town following their short-lived
occupation of the island, for which reason the only extant 17th-century
building in the old town is the former Jesuit College of Sáo Paulo. Situated
near the jetty, this large red building with its impressive spire was constructed
in 1619. It served as a college until 1763, when it was converted to a
governor's palace following the decision to make the Viceroy of
Moçambique independent of the Goan colonial government.

Now a museum, the **former palace** is a fascinating place to explore. The
original church, which was formally opened in 1640, is worth looking at
for its garish pulpit, a cylindrical wooden protrusion decorated with some
beautiful carvings of the apostles, below which is a chaotic assemblage of
rather less lovable but arguably more compelling creatures, evidently a
mixture of gargoyles, angels and dragons. Also notable is the copper plate
altar and the dozen or so religious paintings which decorate the otherwise
bare walls. The courtyard separating the church and the former palace also
has several large statues, for some reason painted in a loud shade of green.

The interior of the former palace is a revelation. The 20-odd rooms are
all decorated in period style, I would imagine with the furniture left behind
when the governor moved to Lourenço Marques, though it's perfectly
possible that some of it was collected from other old homes on the island.
In addition to any number of four poster beds and antique chairs and tables,
most of them Goan in origin, the rooms are liberally decorated with vases
and other porcelain artefacts from China. There is something strange and
disorientating about walking from the ostentatious riches of the palace back
out into the dusty, run-down alleys of the old town.

The most remarkable artefact in the palace is the large tableau that hangs
in the banquet hall, a depiction of one of the shipwrecks which, in the 16th
century alone, stranded or killed many thousands of Portuguese along the
coast of East Africa. The right-hand side of the tableau depicts a ship being
swirled into the clouds, while on the beach a solitary grey-bearded mariner,
the picture of thirst and exhaustion, is desperately dragging his tired limbs
towards shade. On the left half of the tableau, a group of semi-naked
Portuguese maidens sits in a circle below the trees, subjected to the secret
scrutiny of two Africans whose wide-eyed expression could easily be
interpreted as a sign of curiosity, but in my opinion is more likely to signal
recognition of an easy meal. If, as seems probable, this tableau is of some
antiquity, then it is a remarkably resonant testament to the fears, prejudices
and bravery of these first Europeans to settle in East Africa, one that is
somehow made more vivid by its touches of the fantastic: a line of wooden
crosses has already been erected on the beach below the still airborne ship,
while the maidens' breasts, dangling unnaturally from below their armpits,
are spared the immodest realism of nipples. Fascinating as the island's old
buildings are, this tableau offers the one real glimpse into the minds of

their constructors: pale, God-fearing immigrants who for all their cruelty, greed and arrogance were evidently haunted by the fear and horror of shipwrecks and the African 'savages' that surrounded them.

Situated right next to the former palace, the **Sacred Art Museum** is housed in the former Church of the Misericordia. Translating loosely as the 'House of Mercy', the Misericordia was a religious organisation, nominally charitable in its aims and blessed with a notable gift for raising revenue through bequests and later from a large prazo in Zambézia. The church which houses the Sacred Art Museum served as the island headquarters of the Misericordia from when it was built in 1700 until the organisation was disbanded in 1915, and the majority of the artefacts it contains are the former property of the church. I found it difficult to get very excited about the dozens of statues of saints displayed in the museum, especially after having spent some time in the palace next door. The most unusual artefact is a Makonde carving of Jesus. It would be interesting to know when and how this statue was acquired, since it is very different in style and subject to any other Makonde carving that I've seen.

Also of interest in the old town is the gateway and cannon on the main square near the palace, and the rather risible statue of a 15th-century Portuguese captain on the waterfront between the palace and the Pousada Hotel. Roughly where the old town merges into the reed hut part of town, the hospital is housed in a large and very grand whitewashed 18th-century building which formerly served as the administrative headquarters of the colonial government.

Around the causeway

On the southern end of the island, not far from the causeway, the **Church of Senhora Saude** is the third oldest building in Mozambique. A rather plain building, founded in 1633, Senhora Saude reportedly underwent extensive renovations in 1801, which makes it difficult to say how much of the original church is intact. The interior has a haunting atmosphere, created as much as anything by the psychedelic array of mosses that colour the wall behind the crucifix. The cemetery in which the church lies is one of the oldest on the island, with many hundreds of tombstones marking Christian, Muslim and Hindu graves.

Facing the Church of Senhora Saude, the island of **São Lourenço** consists of a tiny, mushroom-shaped coral outcrop that can be reached on foot at low tide. The small island is entirely taken up by a 17th-century fort, now rather overgrown but still in good shape with several cannons in place. If you want to walk across, check the tides in advance, since the island is accessible by foot for no longer than an hour. Despite the presence of a couple of rusty iron ladders in front of the fort, the best way to climb up to the island is through a gap in the coral overhang which can be reached by walking around the right side of the island for about 100m.

Also of interest in this part of town is the whitewashed **Catholic**

Cathedral, an 18th-century building that stands on a palm-covered peninsula about 500m northeast of São Lourenço. On the beach in front of the cathedral, shipbuilders still practise the craft for which Ilha do Mozambique was famous even before the Portuguese arrived.

On the mainland about 5km from the causeway and signposted along the main road towards Nampula is a war cemetery containing the graves of 80 soldiers killed at Lumbo fighting the Germans in 1918.

MOSSURIL

This small town on the mainland facing Ilha do Moçambique is of interest to travellers as the best place to pick up dhow transport to Angoche and other nearby coastal centres. It is also close to the only beach resort in this part of Mozambique, the Complexo Chocas Mar, which has rooms for around US$50/double, a campsite and a good restaurant. If you do head out to this area, it's worth making a visit to the nearby town of Cabaceira, where you can see the 18th-century Church of Nossa Senhora de Remedios and the remains of a fort of similar antiquity. The turn-off to Mossuril is signposted from the main road between Monapo and Ilha do Moçambique. There are a few chapas daily between the turn-off and Mossuril, where you will have to pick up another vehicle covering the 25km road to the Complexo Chocas Mar.

NACALA

The modern port of Nacala is situated on the deep and attractive Bay of Fernáo Veloso roughly 70km north of Ilha do Moçambique as the crow flies. Connected by rail to Malawi, Nacala is a port of some regional importance and it has been maintained largely through the use of Malawian and Zambian capital. The town is of little interest to travellers, though we did find the relatively bustling atmosphere in the compact, modern town centre to be somewhat refreshingly after the air of stagnation that hangs over Ilha do Moçambique.

As a rather bizarre aside, I've been told that a few hostels in Malawi have notices pinned up stating either that Nacala is paradise or else that there is a backpackers' hostel called Paradise Lodge in Nacala, perhaps both. The former assertion is decidedly fanciful and if a backpackers' lodge exists in the area then it must be doing very slow business – nobody that we spoke to in Nacala knew anything about it, and I've met a couple of travellers who visited Nacala in a vain attempt to find it. You may also read elsewhere that Doogles, the backpackers' hostel in Blantyre, has a branch in Nacala; this is presumably a remnant of the 'expansion' that has also resulted in non-existent Doogles hostels in Zomba and Mulanje being mentioned in several guide books.

Roughly 15km from Nacala, there is good snorkelling and diving off the beach at the entrance of the Bay of Fernáo Veloso. There are regular chapas to this beach, and once there you'll find a small restaurant where you should be allowed to camp. There is no formal accommodation at the beach, nor is there any snorkelling or diving equipment for hire.

Getting there and away

Nacala is connected to Nampula by a good surfaced road which branches from the main road to Pemba at Namialo, 87km from Nampula, and from the road to Ilha do Moçambique near Monapo, 38km past Namialo and 64km before Nacala.

At least two buses daily travel directly between Nampula and Nacala, leaving in either direction at around 05.00. There are also several chapas covering this route daily, though you may have to change vehicles at either Monapo or Namialo. All transport towards Nampula leaves Nacala from the main road opposite the Hotel Nacala.

Coming from Pemba, the best thing to do is catch the Transnorte bus towards Nampula and disembark at Namialo, from where there is plenty of transport through to Nacala. If you are heading from Nacala to Pemba, I would recommend you to catch a chapa to Namialo, spend the night there, and then pick up the Transnorte bus coming from Nampula when it passes through Namialo at around 08.00.

To cross between Ilha do Moçambique and Nacala, take any vehicle heading towards Monapo and ask to be dropped at the junction of the Nacala and Ilha do Moçambique roads, which lies roughly 3km east of Monapo.

Where to stay

There are only two places to stay in Nacala. The anonymous **pensão** is a real dump and very overpriced at US$10 for a squalid double with lumpy beds and no fans. The pensão isn't signposted. If you're heading there from the bus stop, walk downhill for a block past Carioca Pastelaria, turn

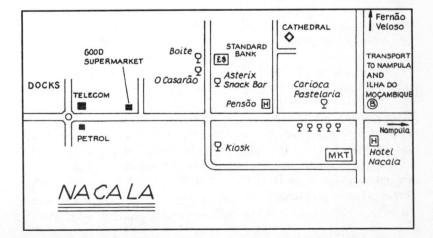

into the road to your right, enter the first doorway to your left (next to a sign for a Video Club), and walk up two floors to the reception.

In contrast to the pensão, the **Hotel Nacala** is clean, pleasant and well-maintained. It's also fair value for money: self-contained rooms cost US$15/25 single/double with fans and US$20/30 with air-conditioning. If the rooms aren't full, the management may allow two people to occupy a room at single person rates, in which case it's emphatically worth paying the extra US$5 to avoid the pensão.

Where to eat

The **Restaurante Boite** comes as a bit of a surprise: it's one of the smartest restaurants in northern Mozambique, with attractive furnishings, air-conditioning and a television. The food is superb and not too expensive – most meals are in the US$6–7 range. If you are only moderately hungry, a portion of eight tiger prawns costs around US$10 and is ample for two to share. The minimum charge of US$5 for a man or US$2 for a woman means that it's only worth coming here if you're eating or you plan to settle in for an evening's drinking.

Right next door to the Boite, the **Restaurante O Casaráo** also looks worth a try, with most dishes costing a dollar or so less than at the Boite. Cheaper still is the **Asterix Snack Bar**, which has sandwiches and other snacks for around US$1.50 and a limited range of meals for US$4-5. The **Carioca Pastelaria** serves burgers, ice-cream cones, fresh bread, imported sweets and the cheapest sodas in town.

ANGOCHE

This ancient trading town on the mouth of the Mluli River is thought to have been founded in the 15th century by an offshoot of the ruling family of Kilwa. Following the reorientation of gold mining in the interior during that century, Angoche became the terminus of a new trade route from Sena on the Zambezi. Like the Querimba Islands, Angoche became an important refuge for Muslim traders in the early years of the Portuguese occupation of the coast. The town enjoyed a boom period between 1505 and 1511, during which time the route from Sena assumed increasing importance to Muslim traders as a clandestine way of getting gold to the coast without Portuguese knowledge. It has been estimated that the town's population stood at around 10,000 during this period. In 1511, Angoche was bombarded by Portuguese ships and burned to the ground, and its sheikh was taken into captivity. The town slid into relative obscurity when ivory replaced gold as the major trading commodity along the coast, and its trade links were dealt something of a death blow after Baretto's army massacred the Muslim traders at Sena in 1572.

Angoche's revival is linked to the slave trade in the early 19th century. By 1830, it had become a thriving trade centre, and it assumed even greater importance after slavery was abolished by Portugal and the trade went underground. Because Angoche is difficult for large ships, it was easy for the Muslim traders to avoid detection by the British boats which started policing the coast in 1842. In early 1847, a Portuguese warship attempted to impose an anti-slaving treaty on Angoche, but was driven away. Later in the same year, Britain and Portugal bombarded the town from the sea, but despite causing great damage to its buildings, they were unable to occupy it. Angoche finally fell to Portugal in 1862, following a bloody battle which caused the leading trader, a Muslim called Mussa Quanto, to flee into the interior. The town has since sunk into relative obscurity, though it remains the local administrative centre.

Angoche today sees few visitors, but it would be a worthwhile diversion for travellers with enough time. Surprisingly, there is nothing in the rundown old town that dates to before the turn of the century, but it is not without atmosphere and the long, wide beach is very attractive. Basic accommodation is available at the Pensão Oceania, where it is also possible to arrange dhow trips to some of the nearby islands.

Angoche is connected to Nampula by a 170km-long unsurfaced road, for which a 4WD vehicle is strongly recommended. At least one bus daily covers this road, leaving Nampula at 05.00 sharp, as do a few trucks which also generally leave in the early morning. The bus and chapa stop for Angoche is a good 20–30-minute walk from the town centre, so I would advise you to be out of your hotel room by 04.15. To get to the bus stop, follow Avenida Paulo Kamkomba south to the large traffic circle just after the Pensão Parques. Here you must turn right for about 100m then left immediately after passing the Commercial Bank and before the Pensão Brasilia. Follow this curving road for about 500m until you hit a T-junction where you must turn left. Roughly 1km along this road, you'll notice the World Vision office to your left – the stop is shortly after this and you'll see plenty of people waiting there.

Chapter Fourteen

Cabo Delgado

Cabo Delgado (which roughly translates as Cape Thin) is Mozambique's most northeasterly province, bounded by the Rovuma River and Tanzania to the north, an Indian Ocean coastline of roughly 300km to the east, the Lúrio River to the south, and Niassa Province to the west. Pemba, the provincial capital and the largest port in the province, sees a small amount of fly-in tourism from South Africa, but otherwise this is a somewhat remote and little-visited part of Mozambique.

Pemba is a pleasant enough coastal town, and the obvious focal point of tourism in Cabo Delgado, but its attractions seem somewhat mundane when compared to those of Ibo, an ancient town and island that forms part of the Querimba Archipelago, a string of small offshore islands running parallel to the coast between Pemba and the Tanzanian border. Also of interest in Cabo Delgado is Mueda, the unofficial capital of the Makonde Plateau, and the attractive small port of Palma, which is also the main springboard for the little-used route between northern Mozambique and southern Tanzania.

The main ethnic group in Cabo Delgado is the Makua. In and around Pemba, you'll frequently see Makua women wandering around with what appear to be white masks, the result of plastering their faces with a white paste made from the bark of a particular tree. Strange as they may appear to Western eyes, the painted faces have no ritual or other non-cosmetic significance. The white paste is merely a skin softener, serving a similar purpose to the face masks put on by many Western women, the difference being that the Makua wear their face masks in public. Interestingly, this custom shows distinct similarities between these people and those of the Comoros, 200km away.

Getting around

Cabo Delgado can be approached from three directions: Tanzania to the north, Niassa Province to the west and Nampula Province to the south. The latter is the most straightforward approach, whether you're using public or private transport, since Pemba is connected to Nampula town by a reasonable surfaced road and regular public transport.

In a private 4WD, it's also possible to drive to Pemba from Niassa via Marupa and Montepuez, bearing in mind that some river crossings may become impassable after heavy rain. There is no public transport along this route, and hitching will normally be very slow.

From the north, access in a private vehicle is impossible, since there is no bridge or motor ferry across the Rovuma. Backpackers can enter the province easily enough using a dhow between Mtwara and Palma – for further details see the chapter on *Getting to Mozambique*.

Within Cabo Delgado, reasonable roads and fairly regular public transport connect Pemba to points along the main road south towards Nampula and to the north as far as Palma and Mueda. There is also a good unsurfaced road connecting Pemba to Quissanga, the departure point for dhows to Ibo and the other islands of the Querimba Archipelago.

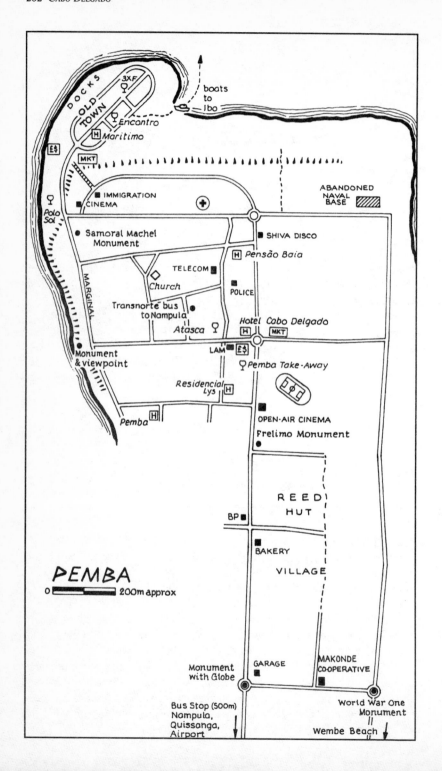

DOCKS

OLD TOWN

3XF

boats to Ibo

Encontro

Maritimo

E$

MKT

Polo Sol

IMMIGRATION
CINEMA

ABANDONED NAVAL BASE

● Samoral Machel Monument

SHIVA DISCO

Pensão Baia

MARGINAL

TELECOM

Church

POLICE

Transnorte bus to Nampula

Atasca

Hotel Cabo Delgado

MKT

LAM E$

Monument & viewpoint

Pemba Take-Away

Residencial Lys

Pemba

OPEN-AIR CINEMA

Frelimo Monument

R E E D
H U T

BP

BAKERY

V I L L A G E

PEMBA

0 ▭▭▭▭ 200m approx

GARAGE

MAKONDE CO-OPERATIVE

Monument with Globe

Bus Stop (500m)
Nampula,
Quissanga,
Airport

World War One Monument

Wembe Beach

PEMBA

Formerly known as Porto Amelia, the provincial capital of Pemba is a relatively modern town by coastal standards. Lying on the site of a failed Portuguese attempt at building a colony in Cabo Delgado in 1857, the modern town was founded in 1904 as an administrative centre for the Niassa Company. By the late 1920s the old town centre had more or less taken its present shape, and it supported a population of over 1,500. In more recent times, Pemba was largely untouched by the both the liberation and civil wars, despite lying in one of the most unsettled provinces, and it is generally less run-down in appearance than most Mozambican towns.

Pemba town is situated on the tip of a peninsula on the southern side of the Bay of Pemba, a semi-enclosed natural harbour which, depending on whom you believe, is the second or third largest in the world. There is hardly a bay to compare with Pemba on the entire Mozambican coast. The beaches are wide, sandy and clean, and lined with palm trees. A coral reef protects the beach and guarantees safe swimming as well as good snorkelling. Needless to say, Pemba has enormous potential as a tourist resort, though it is currently a rather off-the-beaten-track destination and is likely to remain so until such time as airfares from Maputo drop – South Africa is the most obvious market for fly-in tourism to Pemba, yet it is considerably cheaper for South Africans to fly to Europe than to Pemba.

Most tourists visiting Pemba stay at Wembe Beach, which lies about 6km from the modern town centre. There is a tourist complex on the beach, with rooms and space to pitch a tent, as well as a couple of restaurants, a new hotel which should be operating by the time you read this, a telecommunications centre, a curio shop, and Pemba's most popular disco. Near the disco is a diving centre run by a South African where you can arrange scuba diving excursions for around US$25 per head and hire snorkelling equipment to explore the shallow water off the beach.

Pemba's modern town centre is a rather bland place, but it's worth walking down to the old centre near the port, where a small grid of roads lined by run-down colonial buildings is fringed by a very attractive and remarkably neat reed-hut village. Also of interest is the Makonde wood-carving co-operative about 1.5km from the town centre along the road to Wembe Beach.

The best time to visit Pemba is between April and October, when the cooling trade winds blow. During the rainy season, the monsoon blows from the northeast, and this can makes the beach very unpleasant. Because Pemba is the most easterly place running on Central African Time (the same time zone as South Africa) it gets light very early in the morning (04.15 in midsummer) and the sunset occurs before 18.00 practically throughout the year.

Getting there and away

LAM flies between Maputo and Pemba three times a week in either direction, stopping at Beira and on some flights Nampula. Flights currently run on Wednesdays, Fridays and Sundays, with flights out of Maputo leaving in the morning and return flights from Pemba leaving in the afternoon. The airport lies about 3km out of Pemba along the Nampula road. There are no taxis or buses into town, but it's easy enough to hitch a lift. The Complexo Náutilus on the beach has a courtesy bus to meet all incoming flights.

The 420km road between Nampula and Pemba is surfaced for most of its length and should be passable in practically any vehicle at any time of year, though you should watch out for potholes. Bank on the drive taking six to eight hours.

A variety of chapas and pick-up trucks cover the road between Nampula and Pemba, leaving Nampula from the traffic circle in front of the railway station and Pemba from a bus stop on the Nampula road about 1.5km out of town and 500m past the turn-off to Wembe Beach. Most traffic covering the whole route leaves at around 05.00.

The most comfortable and reliable public transport between Nampula and Pemba is the Transnorte bus which runs once daily in either direction, leaving at 05.00 sharp and taking around 12 hours. Northbound buses leave Nampula from the same place as chapas. Southbound buses leave Pemba from a side road around the corner from the Pensão Baía, which is very convenient if you're staying in town. They also stop at the normal bus stop, more convenient if you are staying out at the beach. On the day we used it, the bus was only three-quarters full, so there shouldn't be a need to book. It's worth getting a seat on the east side of the bus to avoid the afternoon heat. The bus appears to have scheduled stops of 20 minutes or so at Namapa, where there's a bar with a fridge and toilet at the back, and at Namialo on the junction to Ilha do Mozambique.

To get to Wembe Beach from the town centre, follow the Nampula road out of town for about 1km, then turn left at the junction marked by a traffic circle on which there's a monument with a large globe at its base. After a few hundred metres, passing the Makonde Co-operative to your left, you'll reach the waterfront and a very large traffic circle and a monument to soldiers who died in World War I. Here you should turn right and then follow the beachfront road for another 4–5km, passing an abandoned resort to your left and a large baobab forest to your right, before arriving at Wembe. There is no public transport along this road, but it's easy to hitch a lift.

Where to stay

There is a fair choice of accommodation in the town centre. For budget travellers who don't want to camp on the beach, the best place to stay is the **Pensão Baía** on Avenida I Maia in the new town centre, which has clean and reasonably pleasant doubles with a fan for US$15. In the old town centre, the only place to stay is the **Maritimo** on the main road. This place is rather run-down and at a cost of US$6/12 single/double without a fan, it is poor value for money for couples. However it's significantly cheaper than the Baía for single travellers.

There are several mid-range hotels in the new town centre. The best of these following recent renovations is the **Hotel Pemba**, which has smart comfortable rooms with air-conditioning in the US$20–30 bracket. The **Hotel Cabo Delgado** is similar in standard and price, but it could do with a lick of paint. The **Residencial Lys** on Rua Forças Populares is also a bit shabby at the edges.

At the time of writing, the only accommodation on Wembe Beach is to be found at the **Complexo Turistico Náutilus** (tel: Maputo 42 5016 or Johannesburg 880 5534 for reservations). The complex consists of 11 sea-facing, air-conditioned, thatched bungalows, each with two bedrooms, a small kitchen, and toilet/shower and costing around US$60 per unit. The manager of the Náutilus will generally let backpackers pitch a tent in the children's playground for free, depending on how full the place is.

Also on the beach, behind the Náutilus, the **Complexo Turistico Caracol** was under construction in late 1996 and should be operational soon.

Where to eat

The **Pemba Take-Away** on the Nampula Road about 100m from the main traffic circle serves a variety of good, inexpensive meals – for instance, lobster and chips at US$3.50, excellent hamburgers for US$1.50 and ice-cream cones for US$0.50. The covered verandah is a pleasant place for a few drinks – the lack of breeze is compensated for by the cheapest beers and sodas in Pemba. It's a good idea to pay for things as you order them, or at least to check the bill with some care, since we were overcharged on all three occasions that we ate here, I would say as a result of dubious mathematical skills more than any desire to cheat us.

The **Restaurante A Tasca** is a bit more expensive but the food, a varied selection of beef, chicken and seafood dishes for around US$6, is the best in town and the portions are very generous. Ice-cream is available and it's the only place in Pemba where you can get real coffee. There are a few tables outdoors which generally pick up a good breeze.

All the other hotels in the town centre do meals. The food at **Residencial Lys** is ordinary but very reasonably priced. There are good prego rolls and petiscoes at the **Pensão Baía**. The busiest market in the new town centre is the one downhill from the main traffic circle. It's a good place to buy fresh fruit and bread, and there are few bars with relatively cheap beers. The most popular disco in the town centre is the Shiva near the Pensão Baía, decidedly dead when we looked in but reportedly *the* place to head for on Friday nights.

If you are staying in the old town, do drop into the **Restaurante Encontro**, a Portuguese run place serving cold beers, sandwiches and a limited selection of meals by advance order. The walls of this restaurant are covered in Makonde carvings and old bottles, giving it an interesting atmosphere. Further down the same road, the **3xF Snack Bar** has a rather cavernous, barren interior, but it does affordable meals such as fish and chips for US$3. The main market, built in 1941, is in the old town centre.

On the beach, the **Complexo Náutilus** does the standard fish dishes for around US$5 per plate. The **Restaurante Mar de Sol** next door does similar food at similar prices. You can also eat at the disco, which gets into full swing on Saturday nights.

IBO AND THE QUERIMBA ISLANDS

The small town of Ibo lies on the island of the same name, part of the extensive Querimba Archipelago. Ibo is one of the most ancient settlements in Mozambique, and after Mozambique Island it is arguably the most fascinating and atmospheric town in the country. Little-known to outsiders, relatively difficult of access, and lacking in tourist facilities, Ibo currently sees few visitors, but those who do make the effort to get to Ibo are likely to regard it as the highlight of their time in Mozambique.

Little is known about the Querimbas' history prior to the arrival of the Portuguese, but they were certainly occupied by Muslim traders well before the 15th century, and they are assumed to have formed an important link in the mediaeval coastal trade network between Kilwa and Sofala. The Querimbas were originally known to the Portuguese as the Maluane Islands after a type of cloth that was manufactured on the islands from pre-Portuguese times until well into the 17th century.

At the time the Portuguese first landed in the area, it would seem that the main trading centre in the archipelago was on Querimba Island immediately south of Ibo. This island became the main refuge for Muslim traders from Kilwa after that city was occupied by Portugal in 1507. Because the Muslims of Querimba refused to enter into trade with Christians, Portugal attacked the islands in 1523, killing some 60 Muslims, burning down the town, and looting large amounts of ivory and other trade goods. However, this massacre had little long-term effect in subduing the Muslim trade, for which reason Portugal attempted to gain control over the islands by more devious means of leasing them to Portuguese citizens.

By the end of the 16th century, seven of the nine largest islands in the archipelago were ruled by Portuguese traders and the other two by Muslims. The islanders were forced to pay a tribute of 5% of their produce to the island's ruler, as well as a tithe to the church. By this time, Ibo had evidently become the most important town on the islands. A description dating to 1609 reveals that Ibo was substantially fortified, and that the islands were reasonably prosperous and a major source of food supplies for Mozambique Island. By the 18th century, prazos had been established on all the main islands, and the archipelago was lorded over by two *mazungo* families, the Meneses and Morues.

Ibo came into its own in the second half of the 18th century, as the major supplier of slaves to the sugar plantation owners of France's Indian Ocean

Islands. The Portuguese Crown resented the prosperity of the islands' independent traders, and fearing that the islands might fall into Omani or French hands, they granted Ibo municipal status in 1763. By the end of the 18th century, Ibo is regarded to have been the second most important Portuguese trading centre after Mozambique Island. It was still an important trading and administrative centre when it was leased to the Niassa Company in 1897, but the shallow, narrow approach to the island wasn't suitable for modern ships, so the Niassa Company relocated their base to Porto Amelia (Pemba) in 1904 and Ibo gradually went into decline. Ibo today supports a population of less than 5,000, most of whom speak a Swahili dialect. That this small town remains the district headquarters of the Querimba area says rather less about Ibo than it does about how remote these formerly important islands have become in recent decades.

Ibo today is fantastically run-down, chronically isolated and utterly compelling: a strangely haunting backwater that in my experience of Africa compares only to Kilwa Kivinje on the south coast of Tanzania. The abandoned palaces and villas have fallen into disrepair, the clay tiles falling off the roofs and the walls slowly being strangled by layers of moss and undermined by the vast sprawling tendrils of strangler figs. The exposed rag coral walls and fading whitewash of the crumbling buildings give the town a washed-out pastel air that is strangely at odds with the deep blue tropical sky and the bright red flame trees and lush greenery that line the streets.

As with several other old Mozambican towns, it is difficult to establish the antiquity of many of Ibo's buildings. Based on dates on the tiles and a few buildings, it would appear that much of the town centre dates to the early 19th century. Many of the buildings along the semi-fortified southern waterfront are even older, for instance the moderately sized fort on the southwestern tip of the island, which was built by the Portuguese between 1752 and 1770.

Next to this fort, and facing the colourful town square, is the large whitewashed Church of Our Lady of Rosaria. According to one source, this church was built in 1580, but we couldn't find somebody to let us inside, where there might well be a plaque to confirm or refute this claim. I must confess that it struck me as unlikely that a church of this size would have been built at a time when only a few Portuguese had settled on the islands. However, since visiting Ibo I've read that Dominican missionaries were busy on the Querimbas in the late 16th century (their records claim to have made 16,000 converts by 1593), which does lend some credence to a date of 1580. All the same, on the basis of appearance alone I would guess that Ibo's church is roughly contemporaneous with the late 18th-century cathedrals at Inhambane and Quelimane, which doesn't preclude the possibility that it was built over the site of an older church. I'd be grateful for any enlightenment from more knowledgeable readers.

The most interesting building in Ibo, and one of the best-preserved, is the large, star-shaped fort to the northwest of the town centre, complete with a dozen or so cannons and ringed by a grove of tall palms. Built in 1791, this fort was used as a prison into the 1970s – it's said that the ramparts are haunted by the ghosts of Mozambicans who died there while incarcerated by the Portuguese. The fort no longer appears to have any formal use, but its entrance is occupied by some traditional silversmiths who'll happily allow you to watch them at work without expecting you to buy anything. A nominal entrance fee is charged.

Another fort, dating to 1841, lies at the back of the town near the market; there's a good view over the town from the top or (if you dare climb it) from the nearby water tower. If you walk east along the waterfront past this fort, passing a volleyball field to your left, you eventually come to an interesting old graveyard. I have also heard that some relics of pre-Portuguese times are to be found in the town, including two ancient mosques and an Arab fortress, but I saw no trace of these.

Ibo sees very few tourists, but in my opinion at least, it is the most alluring off-the-beaten-track excursion in northern Mozambique. If there is an obvious point of comparison it is Ilha do Moçambique, but oddly enough Ibo is far from being a miniature of the former capital. Ilha do Moçambique may have been the Portuguese capital for four centuries, but the cluttered alleyways of the town centre are evocative more of the Muslim world than of anything European. Paradoxically, Ibo, which frequently served as a base for clandestine Muslim trade during the Portuguese era, has an uncluttered and overwhelmingly Mediterranean character, its wide roads lined with opulent high-roofed buildings boasting classical facades and expansive balconies supported by thick pillars. Ibo is also in a more advanced state of decay than Mozambique – it's been suggested to me that Ibo's present ruinous condition dates to the Portuguese abandonment of the town in 1975, but I find it difficult to accept that its deterioration from relative prosperity could be so recent and rapid. Ibo is heading in the direction of being little more than a glorified fishing village superimposed on a once prosperous town; but before we lament its decline too deeply, it should be remembered that Ibo's former prosperity was created largely by the exportation of Africans into slavery.

The Querimbas are likely to be gazetted as a national park in the foreseeable future, and for those who have the time they are open to more extensive exploration. The archipelago consists of 27 offshore islands, which form a string running parallel to the coast north of Pemba and south of the Tanzania border. Composed of fossil coral rock, the islands are lushly vegetated and the surrounding shallows support extensive mangrove swamps and a wide range of wading birds. The islands also protect an important breeding colony of terns and a variety of turtles. For those with limited time, the best option is to organise a dhow trip out of Ibo. This should cost around US$5 for a day and you stand a good chance of seeing dolphins, turtles and other large marine creatures. With your own snorkelling equipment, you could explore the water around the lighthouse, though ask local advice about tides as the currents can be dangerous at times. Querimba Island, immediately to the south of Ibo, is the obvious target for a longer excursion from Ibo. It is reputedly a very attractive place, and there are a couple of old Portuguese houses on a former prazo estate.

Getting there and away

Getting from Pemba to Ibo is not necessarily difficult, but it would nevertheless be fair to say that getting to Ibo should be considered part of the adventure. The most straightforward and expensive way of going about this is to charter a light aircraft with STA (Sociedade de Transportes Aereos) out of Pemba. The cost for this service is about US$100 per person.

In a private vehicle, the best way to get to Ibo from Pemba is to drive to Quissanga on the mainland opposite the island, and catch a boat from there. The unsignposted turn-off to Quissanga lies about 25km along the road to Nampula, to the right as you come from Pemba. Quissanga is about two hours' drive from this turn-off. The unsurfaced road has recently undergone extensive maintenance and it should be passable in almost any vehicle as things stand. Once at Quissinga, ask directions to Taganyara, a small fishing village reached by a 5km road which might well prove testing to anything but a 4WD vehicle. At Taganyara you'll have to ask around about transport to Ibo and for somewhere safe to leave your vehicle. A motorised boat known locally as the Yellow Submarine (a reference to its colour rather than its ability to stay afloat) makes the trip across on some days. If it isn't running, then it should be perfectly straightforward to arrange for a fishing dhow to take you across – either way expect to pay around US$5 per person.

Backpackers can follow much the same route. There isn't any formal public transport between Pemba and Quissinga, but a couple of private vehicles go through most days so you should get a lift. You could wait for a lift at the bus stop on the Nampula road about 500m past the junction to Wembe Beach, though it might improve your chances if you took the first vehicle heading towards Nampula and leapt off at the junction to Quissanga. From Quissanga it's about a hour on foot to Taganyara, from where directions are the same as for motorised travellers.

The other option open to backpackers, more romantic but less comfortable, especially if the winds are against you, is to catch a dhow heading between Pemba and Moçimboa da Praia near the Tanzania border. These dhows depart to an erratic schedule dictated by a combination of tides, winds and demand – and no doubt a fair element of whimsy – which makes it almost impossible to predict how easily you'll find one or how long the trip to Ibo will take if you do. The best place to ask about boats to Ibo (*bargo para Ibo*) is the beach at Paquite Quete, the reed hut village about five minutes' walk from Pemba old town. A boat that does the trip at least once a week is the *Madanio,* owned by Senor Sadaca Incaixa. At the minimum, you'd be looking at around 12 hours by dhow from Pemba to Ibo, and the trip can take considerably longer, so carry plenty of food and water, cover up against

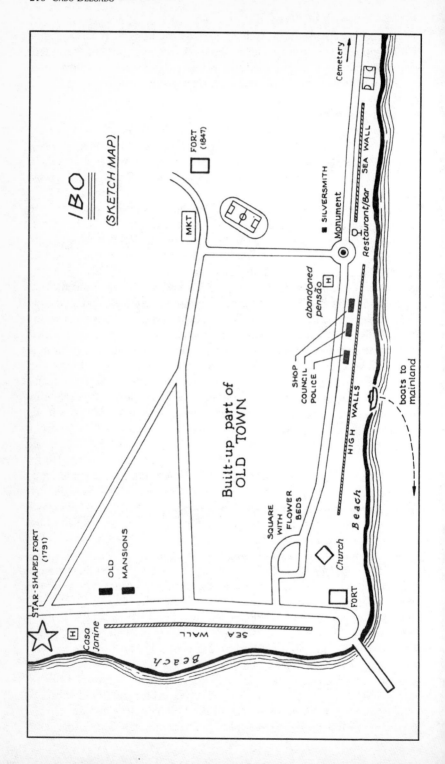

the sun, and bear in mind there'll be no toilet facilities on the boat.

Before trying any of the above, backpackers are advised to ask around at Complexo Náutilus on Wembe Beach for lifts to Quissanga or boats going to Ibo. A group of youngish expatriates, all of whom live on the beach and have travelled a fair bit themselves, are currently running a sea cucumber enterprise between Ibo and Pemba. They travel up and down about once a week and they are generally happy to give lifts to travellers for a sensible fee.

Once on Ibo, you'll have no difficulty arranging dhows to take you out for the day or on to neighbouring islands.

Where to stay and eat

There is a Pensão signposted on the main road through Ibo, but it doesn't appear to be operating any longer. A better bet is to ask for a Frenchwoman called Janine who is resident on the island, owns a few houses, and has a couple of rooms and standing tents for rent in her own garden. Anybody will be able to point you to Janine's place – *Casa Janee-nee* – it overlooks the beach very close to the star-shaped fort. Failing this, you should have no problem finding a room in a private house.

Food can be a bit of a problem on Ibo. The restaurant and bar near the Trabaldahoras Monument is often closed and the nearby market has little on offer other than a few mangoes, stale bread and biscuits, and warm tins of coke. In theory, you shouldn't have any difficulty getting hold of fresh seafood cheaply (a kilogram of prawns can cost as little as US$1 on Ibo) but in practice you may have to ask around to find out when the fishing boats are coming in that day. As with everything on Ibo, tides dictate the day's activities, so the best thing to do is start making enquiries first thing in the morning and find somebody who can locate what you want and prepare it for you. Things like potatoes and rice are probably best brought across from Pemba.

There is no formal accommodation elsewhere in the Querimbas, so would-be explorers are advised to carry a tent.

PANGANE

This attractive beach, which lies on the mainland roughly halfway between the towns of Pemba and Mocimboa da Praia, is likely to become a popular destination for travellers following the recent erection of a small backpackers' hostel by a group of English guys. In addition to the usual seaside activities – it's easy to arrange to hire a boat to explore the surrounding reefs – the Pangane area is noted for still boasting significant populations of large mammals such as buffaloes, elephants and lions.

Getting there and away

To get to Pangane from Pemba, follow the Nampula road west for 87km to the junction town of Silva Macua (marked on some maps as Sunate), then follow the main road north towards Moçimboa da Praia for 100km until you reach Macomia, where you must turn right onto the R528 to Muconjo. You'll reach Muconjo after roughly 50km, and then it's another 2km to Pangane Beach.

Even without private transport, you should be able to get from Pemba to Pangane in a day, provided that you get an early start. The best idea is probably to take the Transnorte bus towards Nampula as far as Silva Macua, and wait on the side of the road there. You shouldn't have to wait too long for a lift to Macomia, but there is less transport from there through to Muconjo. There's a basic pensão in Macomia if you have to spend the night.

Where to stay
The recently constructed Pangane Backpackers consists of several reed huts costing US$4 per person, as well as a campsite. Food is available and the sound system – originally brought in with the idea of having full-moon rave parties – is quite possibly the most powerful on the East African coast between Beira and Dar es Salaam!

MOÇIMBOA DA PRAIA
Moçimboa da Praia is the springboard for travellers heading through to Tanzania, and one of the few places in Mozambique where educated people tend to speak English as well as, or instead of, Portuguese. It's worth remembering that Moçimboa is where you'll find Mozambique's northernmost post office.

There are several chapas a day from Mueda for just over US$1, though the journey on potholed roads takes between three and four hours. Vehicles also go from Pemba for about US$6. If you want to get to Palma, walk 500m north of the Pemba/Mueda stop.

The Pensão Mahometana Magid is colourful and quite comfortable, except for cockroaches in the bathrooms. The food is good, with possibility of getting cheap lobster. Rooms start at around US$7 per person.

MUEDA
Mueda is the principal town on the Mozambican part of the Makonde Plateau, the only part of the country not to have been conquered by Portugal at the start of World War I. Even after the Makonde Plateau was quelled in 1919, the Makonde people after whom the plateau is named retained a tradition of resistance, one which was intensified after an infamous massacre which has been called Mozambique's equivalent of Sharpeville. On 16 June 1960, Portuguese soldiers fired on an officially sanctioned meeting of peasant farmers in Mueda, killing an estimated 600 people. Partly as a reaction to this massacre, though also because of their proximity to the Tanzanian border, the Makonde provided Frelimo with strong support during the war of liberation. Most of the plateau was under Frelimo control after

1964, though Mueda itself remained in Portuguese hands. After the operation known as Gordian Knot, in which 350,000 Portuguese soldiers drove Frelimo underground in Cabo Delgado, roughly 300,000 people in the Mueda area were resettled into *aldeamentos,* collective villages that were wired off to prevent contact with Frelimo. Needless to say, the fact that many of these villages were arbitrarily placed in arid areas did little to help Portugal win over the hearts of the people of Cabo Delgado.

The Makonde of northeastern Mozambique and southeastern Tanzania are among Africa's best known craftsmen, and their intricate carvings follow a tradition that dates back for several hundreds of years. Makonde society is strongly matrilineal, and the carvings in their purest form celebrate a cult of feminity. The carvers are always male and the carvings are mother figures carried for protection. Oral histories suggest that the origin of the carving tradition is linked to the Makonde's original occupation of the plateau. The progenitor of the first Makonde, so the tradition goes, was a genderless being living alone in the bush who one day carved a statue in the shape of a woman, left it outside his hut overnight, and awoke to find that it had been transformed into flesh and blood. The carver, apparently also transformed from his formerly genderless state, married the woman and they conceived a child, which died three days after it was born. They decided to move to higher ground, and again they conceived, and again the child died after three days. Finally they moved to the top of the plateau, and the woman gave birth to a child who was to become the first Makonde.

Traditional Makonde carvings characteristically depict a stylised figure of a woman, sometimes with children, but the subject matter of the carvings has diversified greatly in the last three decades. Like any dynamic art form, Makonde carvers have responded to fresh input, particularly in Tanzania. Two important new carving styles have emerged since that country achieved independence: *Ujamaa* carvings relate to the policy of social collectivism delineated by Tanzania's first president, Julius Nyerere, while *Sheteni* carvings are grotesque, distorted depictions of Makonde ancestral spirits. The ebony sculptures sell at a high price in the West, and they are widely available in Tanzania's main tourist centres, Arusha and Dar es Salaam for instance. In Mozambique, a good place to see carvings is at the co-operatives in Nampula and Pemba, and of course around Mueda itself. If you actually want to see the carvers in action, you need to get out to the villages, which is still where most of them work.

Mueda is accessible by road from Pemba via Macomia in a chapa. The journey takes four hours to Macomia, then a further six hours (including diversions) to Mueda, with each leg costing US$3. There is frequent transport to/from Moçimboa do Praia, but the journey to Moçimboa do Rovuma on the Tanzanian border may entail a wait of a few days.

There is an anonymous pensão in Mueda. Rooms are acceptable and cost around US$8 per person. Water for washing and flushing toilets comes in a bucket.

PALMA

This small but beautiful town lies on an attractive natural harbour which is thought to have formerly been a mouth of the Rovuma River. The government buildings and hospital are up on the hill, overlooking a coconut-palm-fringed lagoon and private residences by the sea. Unfortunately, as elsewhere, the beach near the houses is used as a toilet.

The journey along the unsurfaced but well maintained road from Moçimboa takes three or four hours. From Palma, it is possible to go on to Quionga and eventually on to the Tanzanian border.

The rather basic Hotel Palma is situated beside the sea. Rooms are musty and hot, and the outside *casa de banho* (bathroom) is frequented by giant land snails.

Appendix One
MOZAMBICAN PORTUGUESE
Sally Crook

Mozambicans speak Portuguese in a more sing-songy way than the Portuguese themselves, and their speech is much easier to understand than the gutteral string of consonants Europeans use. For example, they speak of *"Mozambeeky* and *"a cidady de Mapootoo"* rather than *"Mozambikuh"* and *"a cidaduh"*. Their speech is more like European Portuguese than Brazilian (not as lilting), however, and the "s" at the end of a syllable is pronounced like "sh" in English, the "z" like a French "j", and the unstressed "e" at the beginning of a word is hardly voiced. As in Spanish, there are two renderings of the verb "to be". *Ser (sou, é, somos, são)* is more or less for characteristics or permanent states, and *estar (estou, está, estamos, estão)* for temporary states. Many words can be guessed from English or Spanish and some Spanish speakers get along quite well with a mixture of *português* and *espanhol*, popularly known as *portanhol*. Examples include many words ending with -ion in English and -on in Spanish which are similar in Portuguese but end in -ão (plural usually -ões) – *televisão, razão* (reason), *verão* (summer). As in many other latin languages, "o" and "a" denote the masculine/feminine adjective.

Take care, though, for some similar Spanish and Portuguese words have completely different meanings: *Niño* (Spanish = child) versus *ninho* (Portuguese = nest); *pretender* means "intend" rather than "pretend" (*fingir*) and it is best not to describe an ordinary man as *ordinário* as this implies he is common or vulgar. Be careful also when choosing a dictionary, as many (even those published in Britain) are of Brazilian Portuguese, in which some words and many spellings differ from African and European Portuguese.

The letters "k", "w" and "y" are not found in Portuguese words. With a couple of exceptions, the only consonants which can be doubled up are "c" (the first pronounced hard and the second soft), "r" and "s".

PRONUNCIATION
ã + a vowel followed by m = nasal (similar to a vowel in English followed by "ng").
c = ss before i or e; k elsewhere
ç = ss
cc = ks
ch = sh
g = soft j before i or e; hard g elsewhere
j = soft j (as in French)
lh = ly (as in Spanish ll)
nh = ny (as Spanish ñ)

o or ô = oo when unstressed
o or ó = o when stressed (as in hot)
ou = o sound (as in both or window)
õ + a vowel followed by m = nasal (similar to a vowel in English followed by "ng").
qu = k before i or e; kw elsewhere
s = z or sh (at end of syllable)
x = sh or s
z = soft j
double vowels are pronounced separately:
   compreendo = compree-endo
   cooperação = coo-operassaoo

WORDS AND PHRASES

(* asterisks denote words derived in or specific to Mozambique or Africa)

please	*se faz favor* (or *por favor*)
thank you	*obrigado/a* (I'm obliged)
you're welcome	*de nada* (ie "it's nothing" – reply to thank you)
yes	*sim*
no	*não*
perhaps	*talvez* [talvej]
excuse me	*disculpe* (or *perdone me*)
good	*bom / boa* (m/f)
yesterday	*ontem*
today	*hoje*
tomorrow	*amanhã*
day	*dia*
night	*noite* [noyty]
morning	*manhã*
good morning	*bom dia*
good afternoon	*boa tarde*
good evening/night	*boa noite* (meeting as well as taking leave)
hello	*hola*
goodbye	*até logo* (until later)
how	*como*
how much	*quanto*
how much (cost)	*quanto custa / é isso*
what	*(o) que*
what's this (called)	*como se chama isso*
who	*quem*
when	*quando*
where	*onde*
from where	*donde* (contraction of *de onde*)

where is	*onde fica está*
do you know	*você sabe*
I don't know	*não sei*
I don't understand	*não compreendo* (also *não percebo*)
never	*nunca*
now	*agora* [agwara]
before	*antes* (*de*)
after	*depois* (*de*)
large	*grande*
small	*pequeno/a*
high	*alto/a*
low	*baixo/a* [baeesho/baeesha] (*a baixa* = downtown)
a lot (very, much)	*muito/a*
a little (not much)	*pouco/a*
nothing	*nada*
there is no	*não há* (or *falta*)
too much	*demais/damasiado/a*
enough	*bastante*
that's enough!	*basta!*
more or less	*mais ou menos*
you	*você* (polite, formal), *tu* (familiar)
what is your name	*como se chama*
my name is	*me chamou*
how are you	*como está* [komo shta]
I am well	*estou bem* [shtow be(ng)] (or a reply to *como está* might be *bom obrigado / boa obrigada* = I am good, thank you)
I would like (to)	*gostou de*
give me	*dê me*
sea	*mar*
to swim	*nadar*
on the beach	*na praia*
swamp, marsh	*pântano*
lake	*lago*
river	*rio*
valley	*vale*
hill	*colina*
mountain	*montanha*
city, town	*cidade*
small town	*vila*
village	*aldeia*
block (of buildings)	*quarteirão*
tall building	*prédio*

house	*casa*
hut	*palhota*
shop	*loja*
supermarket	*supermercado*
market	*mercado*
black market	*candonga* (in the south) *dumba nengue* (* Ronga and Shangaan) *tchunga moyo* (* Beira)
hotel	*hotel*
boarding house	*pensão*
church	*igreja*
mosque	*mesquita*
school	*escola*
cinema	*cinema*
nightclub	*boite* [booat(y)]
hospital	*hospital*
casualty department	*banco de socorros*
doctor	*médico*
ill	*doente*
to hurt (or ache)	*doer*
malaria	*malária, paludismo*
headache	*dor de cabeça*
stomach ache	*dor de estômago*
diarrhoea	*diarréia*
fever	*febre*
bank	*banco*
money	*dinheiro* (*money*)
change	*cámbio*
(hard) currency	*divisas*
travellers cheques	*cheques de viagem*
street, road	*rua, highway*
road	*estrada* [shtrada]
railway	*caminho de ferro* (noun) *ferroviario/a* (adjective)
aeroplane	*avião*
bus	*machimbombo* (*) *autocarro* (Portuguese)
car	*carro*
lorry, truck	*camião*
train	*comboio*
book	*livro*
newspaper	*jornal*
magazine	*revista*
film (roll of)	*película*
(dry) battery	*pilha*

(bed)room	*quarto*
bed	*cama*
sheet	*lençol*
pillow	*almofada*
mosquito net	*mosquiteiro*
bathroom, toilet	*casa de banho*
toilet paper	*papel higiênico*
shower	*chuveiro*
cold/hot water	*água fria/quente*
light	*luz*
candle	*vela*
matches	*fósforos*
there is no power	*não há luz* (or *a kuna magezi* [* Shangaan and Ronga])
restaurant	*restaurante*
to eat	*comer*
breakfast	*matabicho* (* lit. "kill beast")
lunch	*almoco*
dinner	*jantar*
snack	*merenda* or *lanche* (elevenses)
bon appétit	*bom apet*
eggs	*ovos*
meat	*carne*
pork	*carne de porco*
beef	*carne de vaca*
chicken	*frango* (as food)
fish	*peixe* [payshy] or *pescado* (as food)
rice	*arroz*
pasta	*massa* (NB *pasta* = file or briefcase)
potato	*batata*
sweet potato	*batata doce*
chips, french fries	*batatas fritas*
cassava, manioc	*mandioca*
bean	*feijao* (*feijoada* = a dish of rice, beans and pork)
maize, mealies	*milho*
maize porridge	*vuswa* (*) or *nsima* (* in the north [nsheema])
bread	*pão*
cake	*bolo*
coffee	*café*
tea	*chá*
milk	*leite*
water	*água*
drink (verb)	*beber*
drink (noun)	*uma bebida*

fizzy soft drink	*refresco*
juice, squash	*sumo*
beer	*cerveja*
maize beer	*byalwa* (*)
spirits	*aguardente*
(local) rum	*cachaca*

sun	*sol*
rain	*chuva*
rain shower	*chuveiro*
wind	*vento*
dry season	*estáção seca*
rainy season	*estáção das chuvas*

man	*homem*
woman	*mulher* (also = wife)
child	*criança*
mother	*mãe* (*mamá* = mummy)
father	*pai* (*papa* = daddy)
sister	*irmã*
brother	*irmão* (pl. = *irmãos*)
spouse	*esposo/a*
white person	*mulungo* (* pl. *valungo*) *muzungo* (* in the north)

dog	*cão* (pl. *cães*)
cat	*gato*
chicken	*galinha*
livestock (cattle)	*gado*
cow	*vaca*
ox	*boi*
goat	*cabr(it)a* (nanny) or *bode* (billy)
horse	*cavalo*
lizard	*lagarto* (NB *lagarta* = caterpillar)

South Africa	*Djoni* (* actually, Johannesburg)
Sunday	*domingo*
Monday	*segunda-feira* (2nd fair)
Tuesday	*terça-feira* (3rd fair)
Wednesday	*quarta-feira* (4th fair)
Thursday	*quinta-feira* (5th fair)
Friday	*sexta-feira* (6th fair) [seshta fayra]
Saturday	*sábado* (Sabbath or 7th day)

January	*janeiro*
February	*fevereiro*
March	*março*
April	*abril*

May	*maio*
June	*junho*
July	*julho*
August	*agosto*
September	*setembro*
October	*outubro*
November	*novembro*
December	*dezembro*

Numbers

Each part of a cardinal number is changed to ordinal when referring to a place in a sequence (eg: 2112th = two thousandth hundredth tenth second), so it is simpler to call the 11th floor of a building *andar numero onze* than *o decimo primeiro andar*, for instance. For days of the month only the first is an ordinal number (first of May, but two of May etc). Therefore, one can get by with only the cardinal numbers and *primeiro/a* (= first).

1	*um/uma*	30	*trinta*
2	*dois/duas*	40	*quarenta*
3	*três*	50	*cinquenta*
4	*quatro*	60	*sessenta*
5	*cinco*	70	*setenta*
6	*seis*	80	*oitenta*
7	*sete*	90	*noventa*
8	*oito*	100	*cem*
9	*nove*	101	*cento e um/uma*
10	*dez*	200	*duzentos/as*
11	*onze*	300	*trezentos/as*
12	*doze*	400	*quatrocentos/as*
13	*treze*	500	*quinhentos/as*
14	*catorze*	600	*seiscentos/as*
15	*quinze*	700	*setecentos/as*
16	*dezesseis*	800	*oitocentos/as*
17	*dezessete*	900	*novecentos/as*
18	*dezoito*	1000	*mil*
19	*dezenove*	1001	*mil e um/uma*
20	*vinte*	2000	*dois mil*
21	*vinte e um/uma*	3000	*três mil .... etc*
22	*vinte e dois/duas*	1,000,000	*milhão*

Appendix Two

FURTHER READING

History and background

Malyn Newitt's *A History of Mozambique* (Wits University Press, South Africa, 1995) is probably the best single-volume history of an African country that I've ever come across. Clocking in at roughly 600 pages, it is authoritative, up-to-date, stimulating and highly readable – I'd go so far as to say that nobody with more than a passing interest in Mozambique's colourful history should visit the country without reading it. I'm not certain how easy it will be to locate this book outside South Africa, but if you are having problems you can contact Wits University Press directly at PO Wits, Johannesburg, South Africa, tel: (011) 484 5907, fax: 484 5971, e-mail: wup@iafrica.com.

For those requiring greater detail on a particular period, books that I found to be both useful and readable included three by Eric Axelson, namely *Portuguese in East Africa 1488–1600, Portuguese in East Africa 1600–1700* and *Portugal and the Scramble for Africa 1875–1891* (all Wits University Press), as well as Allen and Barbara Isaacman's *Mozambique: From Colonialism to Revolution 1900–1982* (Westview Press, 1983). For wider coverage of the Karonga Kingdoms and Manomotapa, a recommended read is David Beach's *The Shona and Zimbabwe 900–1850* (Heinemann 1980).

Some of the better books covering more recent events in Mozambique are William Finnegan's *A Complicated War* (University of California Press 1992), Joseph Hanlon's *Mozambique: Who calls the shots?* (James Currey 1991) and Alex Vine's bang up-to-date *Renamo: From Terrorism to Democracy in Mozambique* (James Currey, revised and updated edition 1996).

Michael Main's *Zambezi: Journey of a River* (Southern Book Publishers, 1990) is an eminently readable introduction to practically every aspect of southern Africa's largest watercourse, with solidly researched material on the region's history and a wealth of obscure anecdotal detail about some of the more eccentric characters who have been associated with the Zambezi.

According to the cover blurb of Kerry Swift's *Mozambique and the Future* (Don Nelson Publishers, 1974), its author was the last journalist to conduct a comprehensive tour of Mozambique before the 1974 coup in Portugal. Notwithstanding a few reservations about assertions such as "South Africa ... appears to be sincere in her promises of sovereign independence for the Homelands", not to say the author's evident admiration for the gung-ho antics of the Portuguese officers he encounters along the way, this book does offer an interesting and plausible on-the-spot snapshot of Mozambique during the closing stages of the liberation war.

Something of a companion piece to Swift's book – though infinitely better – is Nick Middleton's *Kalashnikovs and Zombie Cucumbers: Travels in Mozambique* (Phoenix, 1994), which offers a similar snapshot of Mozambique twenty years on, during the closing stages of the civil war and shortly after the signing of the 1992 Peace Accord. Hanging out with NGO workers rather than generals, Middleton punctuates his languid and often very funny travelogue with some pithy insights into the detrimental effects of the western aid industry, a clear background to the civil war, and some fascinating stuff on the occultism that lies close to the surface of rural life in Mozambique – along with Newitt's *History* this book would top my list of recommended reading.

Other books which I consulted during the course of my research were Lawrence Green's *Harbours of Delight* (Howard Timmins, 1969), a lively and anecdotal travelogue covering most of Africa's main harbours; Genesta Hamilton's *In the Wake of Da Gama* (Skeffington & Son, 1951), which covers Portuguese exploration up to 1729; CF Spence's rather dry *Mozambique: East African Province of Portugal* (Howard Timmins 1963); the *Lourenço Marques Guide* (edited by Carlos Alberto Viera da Silva); and James Kirkman's excellent survey of the important old buildings of the Swahili coast: *Men and Monuments on the East African Coast* (Willmer Brothers 1964).

Also worth reading is Sally Crook's *Viva Mozambique* (Starling Books, 1996), which gives a personal account of the author's six years of living and working in the country.

The definitive annotated bibliography of books about Mozambique is *World Bibliographical Series no 78: Mozambique* (Clio Press 1987), edited by Colin Darch and Calisto Pacheleke.

Field guides

Any of several field guides to the mammals of southern Africa will be close to comprehensive for Mozambique. My first recomendation would be Chris & Tilde Stuart's *Field Guide to the Mammals of Southern Africa* (Struik Publishers, South Africa, 1988).

For birders, several field guides to southern African birds are available, and these include all species recorded in Mozambique south of the Zambezi. In my experience, Kenneth Newman's *Birds of Southern Africa* (Southern Book Publishers, South Africa) remains the most useful book in the field, but Ian Sinclair's *Sasol Birds of Southern Africa* (Struik Publishers, South Africa) is also very good. The renowned *Robert's Birds of Southern Africa* is a bit bulky in some circumstances, but it gives far more detailed species descriptions and it's the only guide with continental distribution, a useful feature if you're biding north of the Zambezi.

There is no readily accessible, affordable and portable guide to the birds of northern Mozambique, where you could see a few dozen species not recorded south of the Zambezi. Serious birders heading this way are urged strongly to carry Ber van Perlo's *Illustrated Checklist to the Birds of Eastern Africa* (Collins 1995), which illustrates and briefly describes every bird recorded in Tanzania, Kenya, Uganda, Ethiopia and Eritrea. The book includes distribution maps as far south as the Tanzania–Mozambique border, so it's fairly easy to establish which species are likely to extend their range into northern Mozambique.

For divers and snorkellers, it might be worth getting hold of a copy of Kenneth Bock's portable *Guide to the Common Reef Fishes of the Western Indian Ocean and Kenya Coast* (Macmillan, 1978) or JLB Smith's rather more bulky *Sea Fishes of Southern Africa* (Central News Agency, 1965).

Fiction

Mozambique has reputedly produced a fair body of African literature, though as it is all written in Portuguese it is not readily accessible to English readers. Highly recommended, and readily available in book shops in Maputo, is the collection *Short Stories from Mozambique* (Cosaw Publishers 1995), an anthology of 20-odd stories edited and for the main part translated by Richard Bartlett.

Maps

The best map of Mozambique is without doubt Ravenstein Verlag's 1:2,000,000 *Mozambique Road Map*, which is reasonably accurate so far as roads are concerned and shows most towns of importance. This map should be available in any good travel book shop, but if you have difficulty getting hold of a copy you can contact the publishers directly at Auf der Krautweide 24, 65812 Bad Soden, Germany.

The recently published *Time Out* map of Mozambique is more readily available than the Ravenstein Verlag one, at least in South Africa, but it really is a waste of money – riddled with errors and omitting many important towns.

INDEX